Don't Say Yes Until I Finish Talking

A Biography of Darryl F. Zanuck

by Mel Gussow

PUBLISHED BY POCKET BOOKS NEW YORK

PHOTO CREDITS

DON'T SAY YES UNTIL I FINISH TALKING

Doubleday edition published February, 1971

POCKET BOOK edition published March, 1972

This revised POCKET BOOK edition is printed from
brand-new plates made from newly set, clear, easy-to-read type.
POCKET BOOK editions are published by POCKET BOOKS, a division
of Simon & Schuster, Inc., 630 Fifth Avenue, New York, N.Y. 10020.
Trademarks registered in the United States and other countries.

L

ZANUCK—the boy genius of the 1920s, writing practically all the scripts at Warner Brothers under various pseudonyms...

ZANUCK—the man who wanted to remake *To the Shores of Tripoli* as *Rip Goes to War*, with a dog playing the John Payne part. But among his two hundred films he also made *The Grapes of Wrath, All About Eve, I Am a Fugitive from a Chain Gang* and *The Sound of Music*—films that have never lost their power to entertain and move an audience...

ZANUCK — he kept his "Trophy Room" right behind his office. In addition to the stuffed animals on display, many a starlet became a DFZ trophy...

ZANUCK—deposed as head of Twentieth Century-Fox, he fought back with *The Longest Day*, a box-office winner that put him back at the top. His first order as president: "Close the studio!"

DON'T SAY YES UNTIL I FINISH TALKING is the full-length portrait—from boy wonder to movie mogul, from nervous opening nights to the legendary casting couch. Here, beady-eyed, flourishing his trademark cigar, talking constantly and moving at full speed is Darryl F. Zanuck—the last tycoon.

DON'T SAY YES UNTIL I FINISH TALKING
was originally published by
Doubleday & Company, Inc.

For my wife, Ann

CONTENTS

Photographs appear between pages 142–143.

AUTHOR'S NOTE

On February 26, 1966, *New York* magazine, then a part of the New York *Herald Tribune,* published an article by me about Darryl Zanuck. I had become interested in Zanuck largely because of his phenomenal comeback at Twentieth Century-Fox, which in less than a year had transformed the company from near-bankruptcy to prosperity, and had transformed him from a washed-up producer, with a reputation as a playboy, into one of the most powerful men in Hollywood. This book began with that article. I wanted Zanuck's co-operation, but I also wanted the book to be unauthorized. In a cable from London to his New York office, Zanuck agreed, and underscored my intention by insisting, "I would not want this to be an autobiography as it should be his project from beginning to end and he has merely chosen me as the subject to write about . . . I do not want it to be a 'first person' story but it should be like his article in *The Herald Tribune* an observation of me. Of course he can quote me as he did in *The Herald Tribune.*" When I cabled my agreement to his agreement, he added, "I want to make it very clear that this is to be a book written by Gussow about me and I am not in any manner to appear as coauthor." He said he would make himself available to me for interviews during his various trips to New York.

In the three years that followed I interviewed Zanuck on innumerable occasions, spending countless Sunday mornings in his suite at the Plaza Hotel, also seeing him in his office at Twentieth Century-Fox in New York, in Hollywood, and in Cannes and Cap d'Antibes, France. The agreement was that these were to be interviews, that they were not to be tape-recorded, that I was not to be privy to business conferences and the like, but because of the sheer number of sessions, if nothing else, I occasionally found myself an accidental observer and

overhearer. Our discussions ranged broadly in subject and
spanned all of his years. Without doubt he talked to me more
than he ever has to any writer or reporter, and being something of a taciturn man in private matters, probably more
than he has to some of his friends. He has his favorite subjects (*The Longest Day,* his hunting, polo, croquet, and war
experiences), and also a tendency to ramble. During all our
talks, he smoked cigars, usually sipped Coca-Cola (his present
co-favorite drink, along with near beer). At the Plaza, he
always wore a silk dressing gown, monogrammed DFZ, and
slippers. The first time I saw him outside the Plaza, in his
office, I almost didn't recognize him. I had never seen him
dressed before.

Zanuck gave me access not only to himself but to his
family and friends. At his suggestion, his son Richard Zanuck
saw me in Hollywood and we spent many long informative
hours talking about his father (and about him). At Richard
Zanuck's suggestion, his mother, Virginia Zanuck, saw me.
To assure the interview, Darryl Zanuck also cabled her from
Paris suggesting that she see me. This was, I believe, one of
the few communications between them since they separated
in 1956. Mrs. Zanuck, who had not been interviewed since
they parted, was most cordial, talking to me at her homes
in Santa Monica, and in Palm Springs. Later I saw Zanuck's
younger daughter Susan, Mrs. Pierre Savineaux, at her home
in Cannes, and also his eldest grandchild Robin de Pineda in
New York.

Although I neither asked for, nor accepted, any favors,
financial or otherwise (and none were offered), Zanuck did
give me access to people and material at Twentieth Century-
Fox. During my stay in California, I borrowed a desk in the
Fox Story Department, and spent much time reading, and
researching the memos, story outlines and scripts in the story
files and library. Jim Fisher, Dick Huckans, and all the people
in the Story Department were my guides. Barbara McLean,
Zanuck's favorite film editor, talked about her boss, and set
up screenings of many of his movies. In New York at Fox,
story chief David Brown and promotion vice-president Jonas
Rosenfield have been very co-operative over the years, as has
Johnny Friedkin in Rosenfield's office, as well as past Fox
press agents with whom I've worked: Michael Alpert, Howard
Liebling, Arthur Rubine, and Dick Brooks. My thanks to

all Fox secretaries, but particularly to Zanuck's stalwart pair, Vinnie Argentino and Bonnie McCracken, who have been the chief intermediaries between me and their boss. The people in Fox's London office were helpful, and in Paris Edward Leggewie and his entire staff readily offered assistance.

Zanuck furnished me with a list of suggested people to interview but I was on my own in contacting them. Some were easily accessible. Others were wary. Spyros Skouras, for one, had a game of his own to play. He agreed to see me, asked me to Fox for lunch (before he was deprived of his private dining room), and brought along a surprise guest: his lawyer, Vincent Broderick, former police commissioner of New York City. He insisted that Broderick was not present in an official capacity, but it was the only time in the course of the book that I was guarded about what *I* revealed. When I pulled out my note pad, Skouras said I should put it away. "I interview you this time," he said. He gabbed on platitudinously about Zanuck, and there was no next time—in spite of the fact that I later besieged his office with calls.

I will not list everyone I talked to, but in addition to those named above, those who were especially helpful—some even more than they realized—were Bella Darvi, Juliette Greco, Irina Demick, Genevieve Gilles, Irving Hoffman, Charles Feldman, Michael Romanoff, Jack Warner, Nunnally Johnson, Phoebe and Henry Ephron, John Huston, Peter Viertel, Sy Bartlett, Richard Burton, Rex Harrison, Elia Kazan, Joseph Mankiewicz, Otto Preminger, Budd Schulberg, Art Buchwald, Olivia de Havilland, Françoise Sagan, Marc Doelnitz, Romain Gary, Cornelius Ryan, Sam Silver, Nick Janios, André Hakim, Judy Mullen, Harry Brand, Irwin Shaw, Helen Gurley Brown, Anatole Litvak, Jean Renoir, Kitty Carlisle, Reginald Gardiner, Dan Dailey, Zero Mostel, Ring Lardner, Jr., Millen Brand, Arnold Grant, Georges Cravenne, Gene Tierney, Philip Dunne, Lord Louis Mountbatten, Earl of Burma, Irving Lazar, Claude Terail, and Robert Gordon Edwards. I would like to thank James Jones and Cornelius Ryan for permission to quote from letters; Kitty Carlisle, to quote from a poem; UPI, to quote from an INS dispatch by Emily Belser. I am indebted to John L. Taylor of the Omaha *World Herald* for material on Wahoo and Oakdale, Nebraska, and for supplying me with the names of people there I talked to, and to Keith Torpin, Jesse and Irvin Wagner, among others, for talking to me. My particular thanks to Karen Lerner, who tracked down some of the more important, and older, personages in California (including John Ford and Henry King), and to those people for being interviewed by her. My thanks to the people in the Film Library at the Museum of Modern Art for giving me access to their files and for letting me screen all the Fox movies in the Film Library's collection. I spent many long hours watching old Zanuck movies, at the Modern, at Fox in New York and in Hollywood, whenever they turned up at one of New York's art houses, and particularly on television. I have watched more late shows, late late shows, early early million dollar movies in the last three years than ever before in my life—a special award to my wife Ann (who is also my best editor) for staying awake, and keeping me awake, during the worst of them. Zanuck made some very poor movies, along with some very good ones.

One day, while I was sitting in his office in New York, Zanuck suddenly pulled out a piece of paper and read, "My philosophy of life: all my life I believed in action—even if wrong—as action can sometimes be better than no action at all." Then he took the paper and reached over to a machine on the floor, and fed the paper into it. It was not, as I thought, a copying machine, but an electric wastebasket, which disintegrated his philosophy of life. Then he changed the subject back to movies.

PROLOGUE

A junk man from Minsk, a furrier from Ricse, a glove sales-man from Warsaw, a song plugger from the Lower East Side of New York, delivery boys, errand boys, shoe repairmen, druggists, carnival concessionaries—those were the men who founded and built the American movie industry. Almost all of them were Jewish. Most of them were refugees from Middle Europe (or at least their parents were). Most of them were refugees from the lower-middle class. A combination of their own ambition and Hollywood's receptivity drew them there in a bond that was both curiously fraternal (they were *landsmen* and co-pioneers and like European royalty they mixed their families in marriage) and bitterly competitive. In the land of Zukor, Mayer, Cohn, and Warner, there was also Darryl F. Zanuck, and although many people assumed Zanuck was Jewish—how could he be in the business and not be?—he clearly wasn't. He was born in Nebraska, on the plains, a second-generation middle-class American, a Westerner. He was white, Episcopalian/Methodist and imbued with American traditions about fresh air, the frontier, freedom, patriotism, opportunity, and adventure. In this most American of indus-tries, Zanuck, the American, was the outsider (he didn't even have a relative in the business). But soon he was the insider. There were other native-born Americans in the industry, for instance Walt Disney, but Zanuck was the only one who won the titles of mogul, and tycoon, those two words, of Oriental origin, used to describe the potentates of Hollywood. These bosses (and in each of their kingdoms they were omnipotent) learned the business while they invented it—and for many years they defined it, even more than the stars they crowned, the movies they created.

In mogul-comparison tests, four are usually singled out of the mainstream on the basis of creativity: Irving Thalberg,

David Selznick, Samuel Goldwyn, and Darryl Zanuck. There were distinct differences. Selznick was a custom manufacturer, nurturing individual projects into existence, Goldwyn was something of a grand host, inviting all-star casts to make all-star pictures about all-star subjects. Thalberg was the tragic poet, in a symbolic, not in an actual, sense (he was not at all a writer). He is the tycoon Zanuck most admires—he made good movies, many of them, and cared about them, and he, of all of these, had a kind of class to him. Where does that leave Zanuck? For twenty-eight years, at Warner Brothers and at Twentieth Century-Fox, he was a studio boss, which in his case meant that while supervising the entire studio's product, he personally produced much of it. He supervised and produced more pictures than any of his rivals. Unlike them, he was involved in every foot of film that came out of his studio, not just in the conceiving and casting, but in the day-to-day construction. The movies that came out of the studios he ran clearly represented his taste. As studio boss, Zanuck was both authoritarian publisher and demanding editor-in-chief. With his staff of producers, directors, and writers, he slaved over the copy, editing, rewriting, polishing, and then when shooting was finished, cutting, and recutting. He himself began as a writer, a writer of pulp fiction off and on the screen, but his contribution to the movies has not been as a writer (even his best friends and closest associates score him low as a writer) but as an editor, as a recognizer of writing that works, as a catalyst for rewriting that works better. Bursting with enthusiasm and ideas, he could turn writers on, tap some unseen supply of adrenalin and imagination that would inspire them to exceed their own best efforts. On the other hand, sometimes he demanded so much that he succeeded in turning writers off. Zanuck is more a student of plot and character than substance and style. He prefers to read synopses than treatments, treatments than scripts, scripts than books. Certain materials grow best in his hands. For one thing he is a master at manipulating melodrama, for another at humanizing a situation of social concern. His talent is not in complication but in simplification. The who, what, how, where is more important than the why to him. His best movies, such as *The Public Enemy, I Am a Fugitive from a Chain Gang, The Grapes of Wrath, Gentleman's*

Agreement, How Green Was My Valley, The Snake Pit, Twelve O'Clock High, All About Eve, are instructive and in some cases, ameliorative, but they fall short of profundity. For one thing, Zanuck is a popularizer, an entertainer. He is also an editor, not an editorial writer. He does not have a consistent viewpoint in a philosophical or political sense—or if he does, he has not let it influence his judgment, which is why he could vote for Landon, become an intimate friend of Franklin Roosevelt's, and still dine with him at the White House while campaigning for Wendell Willkie, and why he could be bereaved at the death of Robert Kennedy, impressed by Eugene McCarthy, and support Richard Nixon.

But then his life is studded with seeming paradoxes and enigmas. He has been hated and loved, and sometimes by the same people. He is a gross exhibitionist and sensualist, yet he can worry about impressions and appearances. He is a cut-throat when it comes to disloyalty, but with those he considers loyal, he can be sentimental to the point of self-injury. He is a compulsive worker and a consuming hedonist, a rustic and an international cosmopolite. He thrives on his position and prestige, yet is a very private person. The ambiguities abound, depending on whom you talk to and what aspect of Zanuck's life you're talking about, and there is some truth in all of them. Probably not one person truly knows him, although several know several of his faces. The real Zanuck lurks somewhere behind the big cigar and the dark glasses. And maybe he's just a small boy from Nebraska.

Some qualities are clear and consistent. He loves the movies, and he loves making movies, especially when people go to see them. He is a doer, an activist, who allows no passivity to intrude in his life. He is a little man, Napoleonesque in his outsize appetites, enthusiasms, and ambitions. He is a man of great physical (and occasional moral) courage. "Zanuck would spot a tiger the first two bites," a friend once said. He has suffered both physical and psychic wounds and survived. At least twice in his career, he was counted out, the last time, in 1963, for good. But he fooled them. At a time when both he and the movie company he had helped create (some thirty years before) were on the verge of extinction, he assumed command of the company and brought both it and himself back to life. Today, he is a relic, an artifact of Hollywood-past, but a living artifact, a young old man, not only active but still enormously powerful. He is indomitable. From the early silents to next week's releases, from Rin Tin Tin to *Tora! Tora! Tora!* from *The Jazz Singer* to *Hello, Dolly!* Zanuck is the movies, a self-made man and a self-made myth.

"We had a great preview up to the last ten minutes. Then the bottom dropped out. It ended on a laugh and it was no comedy. The preview cards were average, mostly marked fair, but gave us no clues to the ending. (God, how I hate audiences.) Suddenly that non-existent, invisible bug whispered in my ear, as he has done all my life. I had the *answer*. I started to talk. Before I was half through the first sentence, the director Michael Curtiz yelled 'Wonderful! Darryl! Yes! Yes!'

"I glared at him and said 'For Christ's sake don't say *yes* until I finish talking!' "

Darryl F. Zanuck

I | *The Boy Wonder*
1902-35

1.

The Wahoo Kid

Slap him down and he'd bounce right back.
　　　　　　　—Jesse Wagner on Darryl Zanuck as a boy

In an otherwise unsettled childhood, Nebraska satisfied both Darryl Zanuck's need for security and his desire for adventure. Neglected by his alcoholic, Bible-thumping stepfather and his tubercular mother, and ignored by his roguish, gambling father, he was shunted between them in California, and found his only home with his mother's parents in Nebraska. Every summer he went back from Glendale, California to Oakdale, Nebraska, where his grandfather, Henry Torpin, regaled him with stories of the Old West. To his awed grandson, Henry Torpin became a mythical figure, "a giant of a man," as he recalls, taller than an oak and twice as sturdy. A pioneer! As a railroad construction engineer, he helped build the Canadian Pacific Railway. To his eager grandson, it sounded as if he had singlehandedly hewed the railway out of stone with his ax. He had survived an Indian massacre and had twenty-one arrow scars on his back to show for it. To the insecure little boy with rabbity teeth and a stutter, he was A Hero.

On one of his solitary train trips from California to Nebraska, Darryl was stirred by the anticipation of a wonderful summer—the hunting, fishing, swimming, the wilds of Nebraska and the wilder yarns of his grandfather. He could see himself in his grandfather's day, opening the West. Cowboys and Indians. Cattle and buffalo. The whistle of arrows. In his imagination, the idols of his youth whipped past the train window: Billy the Kid, Jesse James, Buffalo Bill. And who is that? Henry Torpin!

3

A month later, in the dullness, if not necessarily tranquility, of his Glendale home, he recalled the marvelous train trip, transcribing the memory as a letter to his grandfather. Henry Torpin passed the letter on to the editor of the Oakdale *Sentinel.* July 17, 1914, the newspaper printed it under the jawbreaking title: "Observations of Darryl Zanuck, age 11, on his trip from Los Angeles, Calif. to Oakdale, Nebr., to spend his summer vacation with his grandparents, Mr. and Mrs. Henry Torpin." It was the first public work of Darryl Zanuck, written, edited, cut, previewed, and released by him, and cast with himself in the lead.

Wahoo, Nebraska, is a tiny farming town, thirty miles west of Omaha. It gets its name from the Otoe Indian word "wahoo," meaning burning brush. The population is 3610. On the outskirts of town there is a sign, erected by the Chamber of Commerce, which reads:

Nebraska is proud of:

WAHOO

Home
of

Darryl Zanuck
Sam Crawford
Howard Hanson

That Zanuck gets top billing is probably an accident, but undoubtedly he is the only one of the three who would know how to demand it. Wahoo Sam Crawford, the former slugging outfielder of the Detroit Tigers, is the most popular local hero, and Hanson, the composer of *Merry Mount,* probably the most admired. In other words, Zanuck is not the only pride of Wahoo. Zanuck himself has a curiously ambivalent attitude toward his home town and home state. He has no ties there, no friends, family, and his memories about Nebraska are old and short. But he does like to say he is from Wahoo, and cherishes the notion that he is The Wahoo Kid. Probably it's that Indian word that gets him. It sounds not so much like the name of a burning bush as a war cry. Wahoooo! The fact is that Zanuck did not spend much of his life there. His childhood lasted barely fourteen years, and most of it was spent in Glendale, California (with his mother), and in Oakdale, Nebraska (with his maternal grandparents). For all Zanuck's latter-day negligence of his home state, he is definably Nebraskan. To this day he speaks with a Nebraska twang, a sort of high nasality that seems much more appropriate to the campfire and the cracker barrel than to high-level board meetings and jet-set dress parties.

Wahoo at the turn of the century was not very different from Wahoo today, except that the roads were unpaved, and horses-and-buggies filled the parking spaces now held by cars. On the corner of Fifth Street and Broadway stood—and stands—the only hotel in town, the Le Grande Hotel. Today, inexplicably, it is called La Grand Hotel. Le Grande, or La Grand, the adjective is an overstatement. It had only three stories and twenty-five rooms. The manager of the hotel was a young Iowan named Frank Zanuck. On September 5, 1902, in a corner room on the second floor Darryl Francis Zanuck was born. He was the second child of Frank and Louise Zanuck. The first, Donald Torpin Zanuck, was kicked in the chest by a horse three months after his younger brother was born, and died—at nine. No other children followed. Darryl was named after a book his mother was reading during her pregnancy, *Darrell of the Blessed Isles,* by Irving Batcheler. "Darrell sounded like a girl, so they named me Darryl," he says. Then he adds with characteristic objectivity, "I read the book many years later. It was a lousy story."

Darryl Zanuck doesn't have much to say about his parents. Frank Zanuck was short, about the same height his son grew to be—5 foot 6, but he was stocky, muscular, very strong, a powerful swimmer, and a bit of a show-off. Friends remember that he swam across the Missouri River to win a bet. He was a hotel man who traveled throughout the west working as a night clerk. He preferred working nights because it gave him access to poker games. He was an inveterate gambler. "He would have been a very good executive if it wasn't for the gambling," swears his son. "He would rather sit around with five bums in a poker game than anything else." Darryl does not remember him as a big drinker, but others do. "He had a fiery temper," admits the son.

He remembers his mother as "very attractive. She had prematurely white, absolutely, white hair." She was taller than her husband and slim. Very early in their married life, there was trouble—about Frank's gambling. "All the fights I remember," says Darryl, "fights I would come in on between them, were over money." The root of the problem, besides Frank's profligacy, was the fact that Louise was a Torpin. Her father, Henry Torpin, owned Le Grande Hotel, and Frank married the boss's daughter. "My grandfather supported us completely," says Darryl.

The name Zanuck is Swiss. Frank's father emigrated from a town Darryl remembers as Zweibach Falls. "I've never been able to locate it," he says. "It must be a whistle-stop," and with that he slams shut the genealogical book on his father's family. On his mother's side he is much more knowledgeable and concerned. The family was English. Torpin was originally Turpin, until Dick Turpin, who was not a relative, became notorious as a highwayman. (Years later Zanuck considered making a movie about Dick Turpin, but rejected a screen treatment because it was "a very weak and feeble version of *Mark of Zorro* with a British background"—two other movies have been made about him). The other Turpins began calling themselves Torpin, and the name stuck. The ancestral home was Bolton Abbey, and later, on three separate occasions, Darryl Zanuck drove out from London, and with guides tried to find it. He found nothing, not a ruin or relic. "One of my ancestors became exchequer to the king," says Zanuck. "His head appeared on a British coin. They sided with the wrong side and fled with Charles to France." And from there, they —Zanuck's great-grandparents—came to America, settling in Pennsylvania and Illinois. Zanuck was most impressed by his grandfather, Henry Torpin, and his great-uncle, Richard, a rich, flamboyant gentleman: he would visit his relatives in Nebraska riding in his own railroad car, sporting his own hunting dogs, and go birdshooting in style. Henry Torpin left Philadelphia permanently and headed west to work on the railroad. After recovering from that Indian massacre, he became a surveyor for the Union Pacific and worked his way through Nebraska, from Omaha to Fremont. His section of the railroad was finished in Laramie, Wyoming, and he settled down there and became the town's first vigilante judge. Finally he moved to Nebraska, to Oakdale, a small but prosperous railroad center with a population of about 1000. In the 1930s, when the railroad left, the town dried up, but in Torpin's day there was opportunity—and he took advantage of it. He formed the Torpin Land and Livestock company, and owned farms, grain elevators, the bank, telephone company, two homes, and as his grandson remembers, "practically every store on the main street. He owned damn near everything in town. He was the rich man of the town. The Torpins! It was like saying The Rockefellers." Once he briefly considered entering politics. Williams Jennings Bryan wanted him to run for Congress on the slate with him, and came to Oakdale to court him. He visited the Torpin home. "The whole town turned out on my grandfather's lawn," says Zanuck, "and Bryan made a speech." Torpin declined to run because of his lack of education. His partner ran instead, and won. The point is that not just economically, but politically, and (what passed for) socially, Henry Torpin was the pinnacle of Oakdale, and an influence in Wahoo.

When Darryl was six, his mother contracted tuberculosis, went to Arizona for three or four months, and then moved to Los Angeles. At first her son stayed behind with her parents in Nebraska, but then went to live with her in California. Her life with Frank had been disintegrating and soon after she settled on the coast, she got a divorce, and then remarried, an accountant named Norton, the son of a minister. He was an alcoholic and to hear his stepson talk, close to being a deadbeat, someone who makes Frank Zanuck look like the pillar of rectitude. About Norton, "We never hit it off from the very beginning. I hated him. He had a disregard for me. He was drunk 80 per cent of the time, and always carrying a Bible under his arm. He would slap my mother down and I'd jump into the middle of it and he'd hit me. I can remember the neighbors rushing in when they heard the screaming one night. The neighbors, to my astonishment, didn't take my mother's side or mine. They just broke it up. I remember lying in my cot. My mother in her bed. Waiting for him to come home. I would be shivering almost . . . as I heard footsteps coming up to the door. Reeling drunk! Falling down! If I had a gun," he says softly, "I would have killed him a couple of times. And with the Bible, always with the Bible. A big black Bible under his arm."

Around this time, at the age of seven, Darryl Zanuck entered the movies. The movies were still in their peep-show infancy in Hollywood, but through some kind of mystical magnetism, little Darryl gravitated toward what there was of it. There were no studios yet. Movies were made outdoors, many of them around Glendale because of the generally fortuitous weather. The Kalem company was filming in Edendale, near Darryl's home, and he stood and watched—instead of going to school. As he remembers the historic occasion, "one guy came up and said, 'Would you like to work for us? Here, put on these clothes.' They were Indian kids clothes. Another man put Indian make-up on my face. I had a long black wig. Just as they were about to shoot, Bessie Barriscale, the star, decided she didn't like the color of her hair, so they took my wig away from me. They gave me a girl's wig." And so Darryl entered pictures as an Indian maiden. He was given a silver dollar for his day's efforts, worked for four or five days, long enough to feel at home in the movies. He began asking questions. "I remember once I asked the Kalem cameraman how the camera worked. I was curious how it got so big on screen. I guess the seed was planted along about that time." He might never have left the movies except that his mother discovered the employment and horsecollared him back to school. "Christ, I got hell," he recalls.

At the age of eight he was placed in Page Military Academy in Los Angeles. "They didn't want me around," he says about his mother and stepfather. Oddly enough, at first he liked Page, at least the military side of it, especially the drilling and the hiking. "Being with a lot of boys, in a way, was a refuge. I was goddamn glad to get away from my mother and Norton." But Page soon paled, particularly when his mother left him there during the summer—as the only summer student. He ran away—many times. "I would just wander, look in windows. I ran away out of just pure boredom. One of the many times I ran away, my father found me. I said I can't stand it there." Frank Zanuck was working then in a Los Angeles hotel as a night clerk, and with a sudden feeling of compassion for his son, he began seeing him regularly, taking him out of Page twice a week. Usually they would go to the movies together, Darryl making him sit through some of them three times.

When he was thirteen, because of his problems with his mother and stepfather, he moved to Oakdale to live with his grandparents. He registered in the eighth grade and, as usual, paid scant attention to his education. He liked to draw, mostly pictures of animals, and as his cousin Keith Torpin recalls, "He liked to make up stories—tall stories." The taller the better. His attitude did not exactly ingratiate him with his teachers. "I was always in trouble in school," he remembers. "School was very easy for me. I could bluff my way through." If the teacher called on him and he didn't know the answer—and he often didn't—he would jump out of his seat and start talking. He would improvise, and then elaborate on his improvisation, and soon be swept up in his monologue (and often the other kids were too).

Mostly he liked to be out in the fields and woods. "I loved to hunt," he says. Sometimes he went with another boy, or his grandfather took him, but often he went by himself, trapping muskrats, weasels, coyotes, beaver, mink, and badger. Mostly he hunted for the sport of it, but even as a youngster Zanuck had business instincts. With money given him by his grandfather, he leased trapping ground in Oakdale. Occasionally he would buy animals caught by other kids. He was so successful professionally that he pratically filled the basement of his grandfather's house with hides. The Torpin place soon smelled like a tannery, to the dismay of his neighbors—and of the Torpins. Shrewd, clever that he was, only occasionally did Darryl allow something to be put over on him. He wanted to buy trapping rights from his friends, the Wagner boys, Irvin and Jesse, and they leased him the land in back of their farm for five dollars, paid of course by Henry Torpin. But the land was the cemetery, and as Jesse remembers with a chuckle, all you could trap there was skunks. Darryl wasn't mad, he says, because he was a practical joker, "and if you got one on him, he took it."

"I had a very happy childhood," says Darryl, "especially when I was hunting—out in the open—and being *free*. Being penned up was something I've never gotten over. I remember, one time at lunch, I talked 80 per cent of the class into playing hooky and going swimming." On one of his swimming expeditions, to Clarks Slough, a bayou in the Elkhorn River, he almost drowned. One of the other boys, a rough, rugged kid named Johnny Griffith, jumped in and saved him. According to his friends, Darryl was undeterred by the close brush with death. As soon as he caught his breath, he was ready to go in again. "Just like getting bucked by a horse," says Jesse. "He got right back on." Many years later, when Zanuck had taken over the Fox film company, Johnny Griffith made his way out to California and looked him up.

"Remember me?" he said. "You ought to know me. I saved your life." Zanuck always pays his debts. He got Griffith a job as Shirley Temple's bodyguard.

At thirteen Darryl staged his first show in the loft of the Torpin barn, a schoolboy version of the railroad melodrama *The Black Diamond Express*. He charged a penny a head, and sold out the loft. Later—in 1927—he filmed it for Warner Brothers, with a different cast.

He was very much a boy's boy, felt ill-at-ease with girls. "I was awkward . . . awkward and shy with girls. I don't know why." As he tells it, his first sexual experience was "at thirteen" and an unsettling one. The occasion was a school outing at night and "this older girl practically raped me. She was a minister's daughter," and he worried about it. Later to his relief, "I found out half the guys in the school had her."

The young Zanuck was in a desperate hurry to be a man. America was about to enter World War I, and wherever he turned he saw posters encouraging him to join the fight. He remembers, vividly, one in particular, of "Germans cutting off the breasts of women." To defend those debreasted women, and to fulfill his own desire for adventure, he decided to enlist, undaunted by the fact that he was in the ninth grade and still only thirteen.

On one of his periodic visits to Omaha with his grandfather, Darryl dropped in on the local recruiting office, announced his intention, went through a brief physical and was turned down. He had made the height limit—barely—but at 106 pounds he was four pounds underweight. "How old are you?" he was asked. "I'll be seventeen on my birthday," he answered, not saying which birthday. They told him to come back then. For the next several months he stuffed himself with milk shakes, potatoes, and cake, frantically trying to put on the extra weight, finally making it up to 109 pounds. On September 4, one day before his fourteenth birthday, he returned to Omaha with his grandfather and sneaked off to the recruiting board. Even though he was one day early (actually three years and one day early), they gave him another physical. To take care of that extra pound, he had arrived a half hour early and began filling himself with water from a water cooler in the toilet in order to bloat his way up to the minimum. An officer said, "You're not going to get by in the Army with braces on your teeth." Zanuck grabbed a buttonhook and ripped his braces off. Bloody, bloated with water, and stark naked, he took his place in the inspection line. Immediately, he realized he had an erection, the result of the overabundance of water. "Is it always like that?" asked one of the astonished doctors. "Yes, sir," said the young recruit. "You're very lucky," said the officer. Whatever the reason, his compulsive desire to be a soldier, a bellyful of water, or the accidental display of his manhood, he passed the test.

Meeting his grandfather, he told him what he had done and how much he wanted to go into the Army. Remembering his own adventurous youth, the old man was sympathetic and said, "You'll just have to go. I'll take care of your mother." As Darryl recalls, "He had a helluva time with her. She was going to write the authorities, but he told her I might be liable for arrest." Two days later he reported for induction. His first night in the Army, in Omaha, ended in a whorehouse (legal in Omaha) with three of his roommates. "They invited me. I was afraid to say no. I wanted to be accepted as 'one of the boys.' When it came my turn, I couldn't make it. The whore shrugged. 'Don't worry, kid, it happens to half of them.' "

2.

A Soldier's Life

If you look at him when there is military music playing, he is like a child.

—Genevieve Gilles

So much of the problem in describing the life of Darryl Zanuck is in differentiating between fact and legend. Zanuck has done little to encourage the legend, but then he has done even less to discourage it. From the press clippings of the day, it is clear that Zanuck at fourteen singlehandedly chased Pancho Villa back to Mexico, and then went off, like a pint-size John Wayne, to win World War I. The very least of the legend is that Zanuck was a *Stars and Stripes* correspondent, reporting on battles and even his own boxing matches—which of course he always won by a knockout. It hurts the script, but Zanuck was none of the above.

He was not sent to Mexico to battle Villa, but to Deming, *New* Mexico, to sit around and wait. "All we did was cut sagebrush and live in the open while building the camp." It was just like Boy Scouts, except he was getting paid for it. He was transferred to a remount company which meant that he got to ride horseback—something he was very proficient at. One day, for no reason he can remember—probably it was out of boredom—he rode his horse into town. For being absent without leave with horse, he was dismounted and put on kitchen police. "Thirty days in the officers' mess!" he remembers in agony. "I had no experience in this kind of thing." Only once in New Mexico did he see any sort of action. One day he was on border patrol. It is fifty years later but slowly Zanuck begins re-enacting the scene. "It was late afternoon. I was in twelve-foot-high mesquite. A bullet whipped by me. I yelled out, 'Hey, what are you doing? Stop that.' Another bullet! It scared the piss out of me. I thought it was some soldier quail-shooting." He thought fast. "I got down on the ground with my horse." Zanuck crouches close to the floor to demonstrate. "I hid in a gully." Cowardice paid off. He waited a while, then rode back to camp, bearing no scratch but a good barracks-room tale to tell.

While Zanuck was in Deming, his unit was made a part of the 34th U. S. National Guard Division, and after six months of training, he was shipped to Fort Dix, New Jersey, "a six-day ghastly trip in boxcars." After two months' training, he was shipped out cf Hoboken on the S.S. *Baltic,* sailed north to avoid enemy submarines, and landed at Liverpool, and then was sent to southeastern England where "we went into intensive training," for two weeks. "Every night we heard distant firing on the western front. Then one night we were put on a train to Southampton and went across the English Channel at night by boat. We were packed in like sardines. Body against body. Awful!" They landed at Brest. "Our first welcome to France: we were marching up a hill, in full packs, carrying every God damn thing. Sweating! Kids were running alongside selling champagne." He bought some, and to his fury, "It was piss." His second welcome: waiting for a troop train to carry them to their assignment, they were suddenly confronted with a hospital train full of American casualties. "Jesus Christ, three hundred guys, with arms gone, holes in their chests. They were staring at us. My first real shock. This was war where they were killing people. The guys were pushed out of the train and we were pushed on." To Alençon for training, then to Le Mans. The 34th Division was dissolved and its members transferred to the 37th U. S. (Buckeye) Division from Ohio, which was taking "terrific losses" at the front. The troops joined their new unit near the Belgian border. "In the middle of our first engagement," recalls Zanuck, "the false armistice occurred, and the fighting stopped, only to start up again a few days later." By this time he and his comrades (all of whom were older) had already waged several off-duty on-duty campaigns, going AWOL to visit bordellos. "I went AWOL four times. I always escaped." The fear was less of the MPs than of gonorrhea. For being absent without leave with a whore, you "got a case of clap," and for the case, "you got six months in the stockade. A barbed wire stockade!" Ominously, the stockade stood right on the road to the bordellos.

By the time he got to Belgium, Zanuck was a private first class, an orderly, and a company runner carrying messages to advance positions. One day he had to cross the Scheldt River seven times—during the Lys-Scheldt campaign. He escaped unscathed, except for one bad experience with a rock. "I fell on it." He needed seventeen stitches in his forehead. And on another occasion, "I had one shoe blown all the way off and one blown half off."

Like all soldiers, he wrote letters home, except that his were mostly to his grandfather, and were at least half directed toward posterity. He showed one of the letters about "a soldier's life" to his commanding officer who liked it and passed it on to *Stars and Stripes,* which printed it. Meanwhile Henry Torpin had the letter printed in the Oakdale *Sentinel,* giving Darryl's literary career a second, and double, exposure. Several more letters to his grandfather were printed in *Stars and Stripes* and the *Sentinel* (one of the letters described a delousing process). Contrary to some reports, he was never a full- or part-time correspondent on *Stars and Stripes.* However, he did box—as a flyweight in regimental tournaments, while the war was still going on. "The trouble was I was always fighting bantamweights. But I was light on my feet. I had fifteen or twenty matches. I won most of them." His only other war wound occurred during target practice when a rifle split open, injuring his right eye slightly. With Zanuck still under sixteen, the war ended, and soon thereafter his first military career. Although his two years in uniform had been at least partially under fire, it had not really been an ordeal. It was much more than that; it was an adventure, one that he would remember fondly, almost wistfully, his entire life.

As a private first class, he was shipped back to the U.S., and sent from Mineola, New York, to Omaha to be discharged. Ex-soldier, combat veteran, he returned to Oakdale. No parade greeted him. His friends were still in high school, hunting, trapping, playing pranks, and dreaming about growing up. Briefly, he moped around town, and considered alternatives if he stayed in Oakdale. He could go into Torpin Land and Livestock, and if he could edge past all his cousins he might be the richest man in Oakdale. One day an older cousin, Dr. Richard Torpin, asked him what he was planning to do. On the spot, he made up his mind. "I want to go into some form of the arts," said Zanuck. "You're crazy," said Dr. Torpin. "What training do you have? You'll starve." Without a second thought, Zanuck packed his bags, turned his back on Nebraska and moved to California to become a writer. His exit from Oakdale was as unmarked as his homecoming from the war. His school chums almost didn't know he had been there, and they didn't know where he was going. "He stayed only three or four days," says Jesse Wagner, "and then disappeared."

3.

Mad Desire

"It's a horrible story," she wearily replied, "full of complications and disappointments. I'll give you the facts."
  —Loma in "Mad Desire" by Darryl Zanuck

Soon after his arrival in California, Zanuck was walking down a street and was stopped by a stranger who said, "You know, you ought to be in pictures." At least he *almost* said that. The stranger was the director Frank Lloyd, who was casting a silent-film version of *Oliver Twist*, and needed an Oliver. Something about Zanuck struck him, perhaps his youthful appearance—he was sixteen but looked younger—or his leanness, or his postwar pallor. He asked the boy if he would like to test for Oliver. Although he had not acted since that fleeting appearance with Bessie Barriscale, Zanuck thought he would give it a try. As instructed, Zanuck went to the United Artists studios, roamed around a bit (catching a glimpse of Douglas Fairbanks, Sr.), then reported for his screen test. He was given a ragamuffin costume to put on, and with Lloyd directing, he made his first sustained appearance before a movie camera. "Obviously," says Zanuck, "I didn't get the role." Zanuck didn't hold the slight against Lloyd. Years later, when he was head of Twentieth Century-Fox he hired Lloyd as a director. Zanuck's acting career ended, and his writing career began in earnest.

His literary model was O. Henry, but his market was the pulps. His *real* literary influences were dime novels and tabloid journalism. He was a teen-age sensationalist, and for a long time a decidedly unsuccessful one. He ground out tales of romance, violence, and degradation (all tales had to have romance, violence, *and* degradation), sent them in, unsolicited, to the pulp magazines and had them all turned down. "I had 50 rejections," he recalls. The number varies, but not the effect. Once rejected, Zanuck pulped again, and again, and again.

To support his subliterary career, he undertook a series of odd and ill-fated jobs. In the Wilmington, California, shipbuilding yards, he was a rivet-catcher, a boring but dangerous occupation, something like a sizzling game of jai alai. He lived in "a lousy rooming house in Los Angeles." Commuting from Los Angeles to Wilmington was a long, tiring occupation in itself. He would get up at four in the morning, take a streetcar to the shipyards, make his sixty-five cents an hour (about forty-five dollars a week), and then take the long ride back. The combination of the hot hull and the long ride finally got the better of him. After three weeks he caught cold. It turned into flu, a bad case, and he took to his bed. He never returned to rivets. Although according to the legend Zanuck was fired for dropping a hot rivet, the truth is he just stopped showing up for work. He got a job with a shirt company "as the only male employee." Then he created the Darryl Poster Company, which specialized in advertising, took advantage of his adolescent talent for drawing, and failed. He boxed for a while. In a period of about a year, he tried eighteen occupations and was fired and/or flopped in every one of them.

His only successful (at least, ultimately successful) business venture was working for A. F. Foster, inventor and manufacturer of Yuccatone Hair Restorer. Zanuck's job was to assist in advertising, promotion, and sales. When Foster and Zanuck met, Foster had just discovered the desert Yucca plant and the magic properties of its juices. Zanuck's first contribution was to create a sales slogan. Since the Yucca was a desert plant he assumed if anyone used it the Indians did. He further reasoned: "You've Never Seen a Bald-Headed Indian." The slogan stuck and Yuccatone sold. What Foster wasn't saying was that Yuccatone's magic properties were not only restorative, but potable. Yuccatone's second major ingredient after Yucca juice was alcohol. This was Prohibition, and Foster, as a drug manufacturer, had an unlimited liquor license. Zanuck took cases of the stuff with him to the state fair in Sacramento, demonstrated it, and sold every bottle. Zanuck soon terminated his professional relationship with Foster—they remained friends—but in a short time Foster was to play a role of utmost importance in Zanuck's literary career.

Almost from the beginning Zanuck was interested in Hollywood and Hollywood wasn't interested in him. He decided it would help if he knew some important people, so he decided to join the Los Angeles Athletic Club. At the time it was the center of social activity for most of the top men of the movies—actors, directors, writers. Charles Chaplin, Mack Sennett, Fatty Arbuckle, Lloyd Hamilton, Raymond Griffith, Raoul Walsh, Tom and Matt Moore, William Russell, Frank Lloyd, Oliver Hardy, Winfield Sheehan, were all members. Zanuck was turned down. Dejected, he asked his grandfather in Nebraska if he could help him get in. Torpin contacted the club and asked why it had rejected his grandson. "Because he's a Jew," came the answer. "Like hell he is!" said Torpin. "And I won't let him join." Nevertheless, Zanuck insisted. "Everybody has some kind of prejudice," he explained, "and this is the way I can further my career." Torpin reluctantly paid for his membership. As the newest, youngest, most unsuccessful member, he became the butt of everyone's jokes. But he persisted. He got to know the others, particularly William Russell, a cowboy star and former heavyweight boxing champion.

Zanuck continued writing for the pulps, and one day to his astonishment he sold a story, "Mad Desire," to Bernarr Macfadden's *Physical Culture* magazine. Payment of $500 came soon, but publication was not until 1923. Zanuck's first fiction appeared among the ads for trusses, barbells, and organic foods and the self-help articles ("A Rum-Ridden Ruin Rebuilt by Physical Culture" by Ira J. Abernathy). "Mad Desire" seemed very much in context. In juicy verbiage, and acrobatic imagery Zanuck described the downfall through drugs and degeneracy of Malcolm Dale and his resurrection through physical exercise and the love of a good woman. All horrors are "unimaginable" (and described in glowing detail), all problems "immense" (and always solved), all perditions "everlasting" (until the end of the story). Zanuck knew the market he was writing for: Macfadden, where body conquers all. "Yes, Loma dear," says the hero at the end, "it was happiness and you—or grief and the dope. I chose the first."

Zanuck sold several more stories, and the Fox Film Company became interested in purchasing one of them as a vehicle for William Russell, their top star. Zanuck was ecstatic until the story was rejected. Undiscouraged, Zanuck improvised on the spot another story for him. Russell liked it and asked Zanuck to tell the story to Sol Wurtzel, who at the time ran Fox productions. Wurtzel heard it, then said, "The story stinks." "I like it," insisted Russell. "It's my next production, or the one I'm making now is my *last*." The story was purchased for $525 and made into a movie. When the movie was finished, and with great anticipation, Zanuck attended the first "sneak" preview. As the credit, "Story by Darryl Francis Zanuck" came on screen, there was a loud laugh from the audience. "It was such a funny name," says Zanuck. He thereupon dropped the Francis and became Darryl F. Zanuck.

4.

Habit

. . . here, at the end of a forgotten trail, he had experienced in one hour more original action than the previous events of his twenty-three years combined.
— "The Forgotten City" by Darryl Zanuck

Zanuck soon realized that pulp fiction was a very low-paying profession, even if the stories were sold to the movies. However, the screenwriter such as the one who adapted his story to the screen made money. The play *Storm* was a big hit in New York, and on a trip there Zanuck saw it, contacted its author's agent and convinced him to give him a sixty-day free option. "I wrote my own version in rough scenario form and took it to Lucien Hubbard who was editor at Universal Pictures. He was looking for something for House Peters who was then a big star. He recommended it to Irving Thalberg [who was then acting studio head at Universal]. Since I would have to pay the author's agent $10,000 for the property I said the price was $15,000." Universal bought *Storm*, but to assure a sale Zanuck had also offered the play simultaneously to Paramount, and now that studio called him. He tried to alibi his way out of a delicate situation, but Paramount was so incensed at the nerve of the young writer, he was thrown out, with "Get off this lot and never come here again."

Soon Zanuck found that his career faced a new obstacle. Led by Famous Players-Lasky Company, Hollywood discovered "authors" and began importing them in droves. With Joseph Conrad, Somerset Maugham, James Barrie, Rupert Hughes, Elinor Glyn, Rex Beach, and Arnold Bennett all writing screenplays, who needed a Zanuck? As his wife,

Virginia, recalls, "He peddled his stories all around," and was generally ignored. "As I remember he tried to see Jack Warner once and Jack wouldn't let him in the gate." One day at the athletic club, Zanuck was complaining about his failures, when Raymond Griffith, the silent-picture star (and years later one of Zanuck's producers), gave him a casual bit of advice: "Write a book."

Was there time? Zanuck as usual was in a hurry. Sifting through his rejected manuscripts, he decided he would not have to write a book—he could patch some of the pieces together and make a book out of them. There were two rejected scenarios and one rejected short story he had written that past year in San Francisco while running around with a part-time call girl. (Many years later, Zanuck reports, "A friend of mine went to an exclusive call house in New York, and he said in the whore's room was a photograph, autographed, 'with love, from Darryl.' Jesus Christ. I asked him, 'How can we get it back?' ") But in San Francisco, inspired by the affair, Zanuck wrote the three breathtaking melodramas. But how could he publish them? He decided to sell out his artistic integrity—a little. He cornered his old boss, A. F. Foster, and made him a proposition. He would write a short story in praise of Yuccatone if Foster would pay for the publication of the book (which would include the Yuccatone story). Foster agreed. Zanuck wrote a fictionalized testimonial and took the four pieces and financed by Foster, the book was published by the Los Angeles *Times Mirror*. It was 1923, and at twenty-one Zanuck was an author.

The book was called *Habit*, and subtitled, A *Thrilling Yarn That Starts Where Fiction Ends and Life Begins,* a considerable misstatement of fact. In these stories life ends and fiction begins. All are concerned with the moral regeneration of people corrupted by "liquor, hop, and women." Actually the degradation is far more exciting and even appealing than the regeneration, which must say something about Zanuck's divided allegiances in matters of morality. The stories are loaded with plot—enough for forty movies—and in a general way they are the progenitors of the movies that Zanuck was to make in the twenties and thirties.

The title story uses a big American city as the background for a personal adventure (*In Old Chicago? The Bowery?*). It's about Ling Foo Gow (George Arliss? Paul Muni?), "the mute peddler of lichee nuts" in San Francisco's Chinatown, who "rivets his jet orbs" and sees more than he seems to see—murder.

The second story, "The Scarlet Ladder," is a romantic melodrama in an exotic setting (*The Rains Came? Suez?*). Its hero, Ralph Weston (Tyrone Power?), is the "Lowest, the filthiest morsel of young manhood on the Pacific," who is shanghaied by the mysterious Captain William Nelson, falls in love with the captain's daughter (Gene Tierney?), Loma (another Loma?).

"Say It With Dreams" reads like a non-musical *Alexander's Ragtime Band:* a dance-hall girl named Irene Dare, "The Kid from Madrid" (Alice Faye?), works in a Barbary Coast saloon, rebuffs the attentions of Rufus Gunning (Brian Donlevy?) "Political Boss of the underworld," whose "vulgar after-show orgies were common talk." She is rescued from this den of iniquity by her two admirers, the deaf and dumb Loko (who has sparkling jet eyes, just like Ling Foo Gow, and is a pantomimist to boot), and the fast-talking but basically honest salesman Ralph Fenton (not Tyrone Power again?).

The hair-tonic testimonial "The Forgotten City" is a western (*The Mark of Zorro?*). On the book jacket it is described as "the story of the forgotten city on the desert, where the man with three names rolled the dice of destiny and won." In fifteen pages of raw melodrama, the U. S. Calvary rides to the rescue, Yucca Tonic and Shampoo become household words, the hero and his father are reunited, the hero marries the heroine, and dandruff is banished from the land.

His first "novel" published, Zanuck sent announcements to all the movie studios followed by autographed copies. He made sure that book stores displayed it in their windows. He made a trip to New York, soliciting publicity. On Sunday, April 15, 1923, it was reviewed in the New York *Times Book Review* favorably, by an unsigned critic with considerable perspicacity about the future of the young author.

"The four short stories that compose this volume," began the review, "are all marked by ingenuity of plot and great fertility and variety in the invention of incident. Apparently when Mr. Zanuck sits down to write he takes all the harness off his imagination and gets off at a gallop without bridle, halter or bit . . . If he were as skilled in the writing of fiction as he is ingenious in the imagining of it, and as versed in the use of the English language as he is resourceful in fancy, the author could probably look forward to a successful career as a novelist. But, even though they lack some of the essential qualities of good writing, his stories afford much entertainment."

Apparently Hollywood agreed. All four stories were sold to the movies for a total of $11,000. Three of them, even including the hair-tonic yarn, were made into pictures. As an author, Zanuck was suddenly in demand in Hollywood. At twenty-one, he had discovered a valuable product—his own vivid imagination—and, more importantly, he had learned how to market it. His enterprising partner, A. F. Foster, was, however, not as successful. "Habit" probably would have helped sales of Yuccatone were it not for an unfortunate occurrence. One day Foster called Zanuck. "God Almighty!" he exclaimed, like a character in a Zanuck story. "We're in terrible trouble. We've blown up twenty-five drugstores!" It seems that the alcohol in Yuccatone had fermented and exploded Foster completely out of business. And now . . . Yuccatone, "one of the greatest natural products of the century," lives on only in hard covers, long out of print.

5.

Breaking Back into Pictures

"When treated right, I ain't bad—but cross me and I'm poison."

—Hurricane Sherlock in "Sherlock's Home"
by Darryl Zanuck

Zanuck was now an author, and with that title came a turning point in his Hollywood career. He was incredibly young-looking and had no relatives at the studios, but he suddenly was able to open doors for himself. His first sustained employment in Hollywood was as a gag writer for—in quick succession—Mack Sennett, Carter DeHaven, Harold Lloyd, and briefly for Charles Chaplin. Of them all, Sennett in later years became the closest friend (and years later worked for him at Twentieth Century-Fox), and Chaplin became one of his few bitter enemies, but at the time the relationships were all strictly professional. He wrote gags at their order. Zanuck reflects on his time with Sennett: "Five of us would sit around in a room and somebody would start off, 'A guy wakes up in the morning and can't find his paper . . .' and then someone else would take it up," and like a baton the gag was passed from writer to writer, each adding his own embellishment. "The humor was all physical, completely physical. We would never show anything written to Sennett. He'd come and hear it." But Sennett kept close guard over his lackeys. "Sennett worked in a tower on top of the building, behind glass. He could look down and say, 'There's a carpenter on Stage Six and he's asleep on stage. Tell him to get the hell to work.' He would tiptoe up to our room to see if we were working or playing cards." More often than not, they were playing cards. To safeguard their privacy, "We loosened one of the steps, so it would squeak when he stepped on it. He'd fling the door open"—and find his gagmen hard at work. As soon as he left, out came the cards again. "He was a tyrant," recalls Zanuck, "a son of a bitch to work for . . . but he somehow liked me." Perhaps the most lasting result of his writing for Sennett was a friendship he struck up with another up and coming writer and director, Mal St. Clair. Later with St. Clair as director and Zanuck as writer, the two were to form one of the hottest movie teams in town. After about three months at Sennett's, Zanuck switched to Chaplin. Chuck Reisner, Chaplin's chief gagwriter, had heard about Zanuck and hired him. From the beginning he was Reisner's boy, and not Chaplin's. "Chaplin took an instant dislike to me, I think, because of my youth more than anything else." The dislike, or at least disrespect, was reciprocal. As Zanuck describes writing gags for Chaplin: "We would sit around working up gags among ourselves. Reisner's job was to invent gags but not reveal them to Chaplin. He would place all the props and then let Chaplin 'discover' the gag. We'd sit in the background, holding our breath waiting for him to fall on it. If you made a suggestion—you're dead! He would always finally find the gag and damn near on every occasion he would bawl the hell out of us for not discovering it." As Zanuck describes the work situation, Chaplin was very much the master. "He would love to use words he looked up in the dictionary —to crush us. Words like *outré*. He would say something was 'uttra,' and then say, 'You understand what I mean?' Very superior, you know. But if Reisner deliberately used a word Chaplin didn't know, Charlie went immediately to the toilet. He kept a dictionary there. Sometimes he would sit in the toilet for an hour at a time." Pictures were made very much according to Chaplin's schedule. "He would appear at the studio only when he wanted to. Sometimes his pictures would take a year to make." Later, in their relationship at United Artists, the conflict was to be personal as well as professional.

But Zanuck is equally quick to praise Chaplin's talent: "He was a great great comedian." At the time Chaplin scarcely knew Zanuck was around. Zanuck was just one of his many gagwriters, and after a very short tenure—only about two weeks—he quit Charlie Chaplin to join Harold Lloyd and Carter DeHaven in a new company they were forming.

Soon Zanuck was able to switch from gags to scripts. With St. Clair he moved to FBO (the Federal Booking Office, the predecessor of RKO), then under the management of Joseph P. Kennedy, which was "grinding pictures out . . . a short a week," and needed more grinders. At the time H. C. Witwer was one of the *Saturday Evening Post*'s most popular short story writers. For FBO he created two series of two-reelers, *The Telephone Girl* and *The Leatherpushers*. Witwer wrote the original stories, Zanuck wrote the screenplays, and St. Clair directed. Before Zanuck could adapt, he had to play nursemaid to the author. As Zanuck remembers it, Witwer was an alcoholic, and very casual about his writing. He would make notes for his stories on little scraps of paper and stuff them in various pockets, or in his hat. Then when a story was due, or simply had formed in his mind, he spread the scraps around him and began writing, skipping from scrap to scrap. The story completed, Zanuck turned it into a screenplay. But Witwer was erratic in his production, and Zanuck on occasion found he had to pilfer the papers out of Witwer's pockets and put together the story himself.

In less than a year Zanuck wrote twenty-four *Telephone Girl* and twenty-four *Leatherpusher* episodes. If his writing had not improved to an enormous degree, it had changed, and he was getting experience in plot manipulation and movie technique at $150 per week. Then he met "this swell dish . . ."

6.

Buster Keaton's Leading Lady

Darryl was a very restless sleeper. I pinned his side and mine—with great big safety pins to keep him from falling out of bed.

—Virginia Zanuck

Virginia Fox was short, slender, pretty, and something of a movie star when Darryl Zanuck met her. The daughter of a wealthy import-export dealer from Wheeling, West Virginia, she came to California every summer with her parents and her brother Freddie to enjoy the sunshine. One summer, fresh from boarding school in St. Petersburg, Florida, she was visiting a girl friend in Hollywood. On the merest whim, the friend suggested they visit someone she knew at Mack Sennett's sudio. Almost immediately upon entering Sennett's preserve, they ran into the boss himself. Always on the lookout for bathing-suit talent, Sennett eyed Virginia up and down and demanded, "Who are you? What's your name?" And before she could say a word, he ordered, "Come back tomorrow and bring along a bathing suit." When she told her parents, they were outraged. Our daughter in the movies? Like a heroine in a silent melodrama, she pleaded with them. No, said the father. Yes, said the daughter. The next day she returned to the studio. Sennett kept her waiting several hours, then sent for her, and told her to put on her bathing suit. When she came out of the dressing room, he said, "You start Monday." And she did. She liked being in movies. After a brief stint as a bathing beauty, she joined Buster Keaton, playing opposite him in a number of pictures. What she did, she did well, but she does not consider it acting. She simply followed direction, or rather instruction, faithfully and ex-

27

plicitly. "If I was hanging from an elk's head and they said, 'Hold it,' I held it—even if they went to lunch. I did whatever I was told."

When she was with Keaton, one of her directors was Mal St. Clair, Zanuck's old and future collaborator, and one day he came to her with an undirectorial request. He wanted her to go on a blind date with a friend of his. "What's his name?" she asked. "Darryl Zanuck," said St. Clair. She had never heard of him. St. Clair and his date (his wife-to-be) picked up the two of them in St. Clair's car, and offered them the rumble seat. "I remember I wore a little white organdy dress," Virginia recalls, "and a new hat with lilies of the valley on it. By the time we got to the Coconut Grove, my hair was all blown apart." By her measure, the evening was a disaster. The next day Zanuck sent her roses and a copy of *Habit*. She was still unimpressed.

Undiscouraged, Zanuck began waging courtship, assaulting her with flowers and phone calls. "He was always on the phone, or at the door, or underfoot, or overhead. He would always hire cars. On his salary! There was never a boring moment." She and her parents sneaked away to Murietta Hot Springs, a southern California resort, and the next morning Zanuck arrived by taxicab—a ride that cost $150 from Los Angeles. He proposed. She put him off. He persisted. She resisted. After about six months, she gave in. On January 24, 1924, at eight o'clock in the morning, they were married. The ceremony took place in the office of a Justice of Peace. Virginia's father and brother were to be the only witnesses, but as the ceremony began the Negro janitor walked in, and the minister said he should be a witness too. Mop in hand, he witnessed. "It's a lucky omen," said Zanuck.

For their honeymoon, Zanuck had planned a quiet escape by train to Coronado Beach, near San Diego. He had not figured on his wife's friends. When they got to the train, her whole club, "Our Club," was there—Mary Pickford, Gertrude Olmstead, Billie Dove, Carmel Myers, Mildred Lloyd, Colleen Moore—bearing and throwing rice and American Beauty roses. Finally aboard the train, the newlyweds picked rice out of their hair, and tried to be casual about the enormous bouquet of roses the groom was carrying. They sat back and relaxed. Suddenly the calm was shattered by a crash of cymbals and a blast of a trombone. John Philip Sousa and his band just happened to be on the train. They marched into the Zanucks' car and played the wedding march, more march than wedding. The band was going to San Diego to perform, Virginia's club had found out about it, and asked them to salute the Zanucks. They played all the way to Coronado. "Darryl made me give the roses to the first little girl he could find on the train," says Virginia, "but he couldn't get rid of Sousa's band so easily." But he has always liked Sousa and years later made a movie of his life called *Stars and Stripes Forever.*

When the Zanucks returned to Los Angeles a week later they moved into a house in the bungalow court owned by Darryl's mother in Beverly Hills. His mother gave them six months' free rent as a wedding gift and her father gave them a Hudson sedan. Darryl gave Virginia a platinum band with three diamonds on it. "He always acted like a millionaire," says Virginia. She kept, and treasured, the ring until their eldest daughter, at the age of one and a half, threw it down the toilet. Virginia made one more picture, and retired. Darryl continued working in earnest, and very much as he had before he had been married. Through the night, he wrote scripts. "Our first year of marriage," says Virginia, "I was always going back to mother. I didn't understand him. He used to pull tantrums. One day I said to mother, 'I can't stand this.' She said, 'He's a genius.' I said, 'A genius, heck!' "

As she soon discovered, being married to Darryl Zanuck was like being married to a typhoon. Adjustment was necessary for survival. His word was law. One day early in their marriage when they were still living in his mother's bungalow court, he came home and announced that they were moving. He had bought a house, an entire house, fully furnished down to pots, pans, and china—without consulting her. She of course blew her top. He of course wondered why. They argued, and then they moved. In home as in the office, Darryl made the decisions, determined what were necessities, what were the superfluities. And where they lived and what they ate was something he easily attended to.

He liked creamed chipped beef on toast (an obvious hangover from his military days) and, of course, she made it for him. He got so sick that she had to take him to the hospital. From then on, most of their meals were at the Los Angeles Athletic Club. Only on rare occasions did they eat at home, even though they soon had a maid, named Myrtle, working for them. One day he called to announce, "I'm bringing Prince Michael Romanoff home to dinner." (Within several years he was calling her and saying, "I'm bringing twenty people home to dinner!") Quickly Virginia and Myrtle drafted up a lamb roast for dinner. For the occasion Myrtle, who was bald, wore a boudoir cap. She did not lose her cap (which was a possibility) but she did drop the lamb right in Romanoff's lap. Nevertheless Romanoff became a close friend. The Zanucks went back to the Athletic Club to eat.

Occasionally Virginia stood up to him. Two years after they were married, they went to Europe with three other couples. In Vienna one night they all went to a club to see a show called the Hollywood Redheads. Then, leaving their wives back at the hotel, the men declared that they were going to a gambling club they had heard about. It turned out that they went back to the Hollywood Redheads. Some time later, Virginia heard noises outside, stepped out on her hotel balcony and saw the troupe of men coming down the street each with a redhead on his arm, Darryl still spiffily dressed in a derby and a fur-lined coat with a great fur collar. There were geranium pots on the balcony and, taking careful aim, she heaved one down on Darryl. Clunk! There went his composure, to say nothing about his hat. Virginia threw her coat —a mink—on over her nightgown, strode downstairs and dragged him back. "I thought you were going to the club," she said. "We went back to the Hollywood Redheads," he revealed. "We were just walking them home." But to salve his conscience, the next day he bought Virginia a watch, which became her favorite bit of jewelry. Says she about the incident, "I never did like that hat anyway. It made him look like a butter and egg man."

During the early years of their marriage, Virginia was the perfect helpmate for Zanuck. She was in love with him, and very much involved with his work and his ambition. "Darryl and I married very young," she says, "and we grew in the business together."

She went to previews with him. "I would cry at movies," she says. "I'm a sob sister and if I didn't cry he would say, 'You didn't cry at that. Virginia didn't like that scene.' I've seen every picture he worked on." She loved and admired him, even for his ambition. "One thing I admired about

Darryl: he never thought he had reached the top rung. He would always keep going for a higher rung . . . I always had such pride in Darryl. I knew he'd be a success. I knew he was a man of terrific ability. Whatever he did he did on his own. He was a self-made little boy who didn't have relatives in the business."

7.

Rin Tin Tin

. . . with a superhuman effort, Rinty shakes the bull [dog] off of him, clamps his own fangs on the dog's neck and throws him upwards out of scene.
— Darryl Zanuck in "Lighthouse by the Sea"

During the closing months of World War I, an American sergeant named Leland Duncan discovered a German shepherd and her new litter of five puppies in the wreckage of an airfield in France. He saved the dogs' lives and, after the war, brought one of the puppies back to California with him. Duncan, and a succession of other people, most of them less dedicated to dogs, were rewarded amply for his good deed. As Rin Tin Tin, the dog became a movie star, earned Duncan some five million dollars, saved the Warner Brothers from one of their periodic descents into bankruptcy, and made a name for a young screenwriter named Darryl Zanuck.

At the time of their first meeting, Rin Tin Tin was only slightly better known than Zanuck. Rinty, as he was called, had played in one feature, *Where the North Begins,* opposite Pat Hartigan. Jack Warner decided to make a star out of the dog. He wanted to hire Mal St. Clair as director. St. Clair suggested that his friend Zanuck write the screenplay. The two of them were granted a combined audience with Jack and Harry Warner and on the spot improvised and acted out a Rin Tin Tin story. As Jack Warner remembers it, Zanuck played the dog (presumably in a crouch) and St. Clair the two-legged hero. More likely Zanuck played all the parts with St. Clair coaching from the sidelines. Recalls Zanuck, "Mal was a great director, and eventually became the darling of the New York critics, but he was inarticulate." Zanuck, on

32

the other hand, had the ability even then to take the most banal story, inject it with his own sometimes violent enthusiasm, and make it seem like the most exciting idea in the history of motion pictures. In any case the Warners caught enough of Zanuck's enthusiasm to sign the team to a contract.

Zanuck's first Rin Tin Tin picture, a wild yarn full of desperate perils and incredible undog-like feats of daring, was about a dog's slavish devotion to his master—which is what could be said about all Rin Tin Tin features. About all that changed were Rinty's stunts and the setting.

Find Your Man, starring Rin Tin Tin, was made on location in Klamath Falls, Oregon, in order to lend authenticity to the lumber sequences. Zanuck himself was immediately caught up in the rugged atmosphere of the lumbering camp. Every day after shooting was over, he would go to the camp, and like a lumberman, he would walk on logs—which is not quite walking on water, more like falling in water. But Zanuck persisted in trying to master the art. The last day of shooting, while everyone else returned to their rooms in a festive mood preparing to change for a party St. Clair was throwing for the cast and crew, Zanuck went out for his nightly log roll. Hours later he returned to his hotel to find his wife dressed for the party which was already in progress downstairs. Cold and wet, Zanuck stripped off all his clothes. His wife made it clear that they were expected, and late, for the party. Zanuck would hear none of it. She argued. He argued, and tempers flared higher and higher. She decided that she would go by herself, turned, and walked out the door and down the hall. He followed, completely naked, screaming at her that she could not go alone. Outraged, she went anyway. When she returned after the party, she discovered that he had taken all her clothes—dresses, lingerie, everything—and systematically destroyed them, tearing every article into strips. Virginia slept in the bathtub that night, vowing to go home to mother in the morning. In the morning, Darryl apologized, Virginia forgave, and immediately bought some new clothes.

Zanuck had genuine admiration for the dog. "Rin Tin Tin could do anything," he says, or rather Rin Tin Tins could do anything. "Actually there were about five or six Rin Tin Tins at one time," he explains, "one for long shots, one for close-ups, one to play the gentle parts, one to fight. Another could jump and do terrific stunts. Another had marvelous eyes." For Zanuck, a man of multitudinous talents, a dog-star with severely limited ability would seem hard to accept. But Zanuck bore no grudge (in fact for many years he owned a son of Rin Tin Tin given to him by Duncan), and apparently neither did the star. Once early in their relationship, recalls Zanuck, "in a boat, I stepped on Rin Tin Tin's foot." Since the Rin Tin Tin he stepped on did not step on him in return (or bite, claw, or throw him upward out of scene), presumably it was not the fighter Rin Tin Tin, but the one with marvelous jet orbs.

8.

Three Charming Fellows

*Once I changed an entire silent film just by changing the
titles. The only ones who could tell were the lip-readers.*
—Darryl Zanuck

By 1924 Charlie Chaplin was the biggest star in the world,
Irving Thalberg was running production at the expanding
Metro-Goldwyn-Mayer, the industry was in the throes of
self-censorship, and Darryl Zanuck was writing dog pictures.

He was fascinated by film editing, spent most of his spare
time watching editors cut film—which later became one of
his own, and least disputed, talents. "I practically lived in the
cutting room," he says. "I could see the errors and how to
get out of things. It's a great education for a writer." He was
fascinated too by the title writers, a profession that today
seems about as important as that of caption writer, but in
those days was decidedly consequential. The best titlers in
the business were Robert "Hoppy" Hopkins and Archie Mayo
who could tell a story in a few well-chosen (though often
corny) words, a lesson Zanuck remembered when he began
making talkies.

Zanuck thrived at Warner Brothers, which is more than
can be said for Warner Brothers. While other companies
merged and expanded, Warners was still a small, struggling
family business, with all of the problems and none of the
advantages of being a family business. Perhaps there were just
too many brothers in the business: Albert, Sam, Harry, and
Jack. Jack tried to run the Hollywood production and Harry
tried to run Jack, although supposedly Harry was occupied
with money matters in the East. Basically it was the traditional movie conflict between the East Coast and the West

Coast, and between brother and brother. As Zanuck recalls, "Harry, being president, was prone to jump on Jack for any film that did not come out well. There was a time I think when they did not see each other. Sam was the bridge between them. Harry hated Jack. Jack played a role like Louis B. Mayer to a certain extent. It was a gentleman's role. He could captivate you. Harry was just the opposite. Anyone who got over $2000 a week he hated instantly even if he never met him. In Harry's mind, everybody was a thief, including Jack for condoning extravagances." The slogan around the studio was: When Not in Use, Turn Off the Juice. The brothers competed with one another as penny-pinchers, turning off lights, saving used nails. It was generally agreed that Harry Warner pinched better than any of them. "What a boring guy Harry was," concludes Zanuck. "Jack was unreliable, but never boring."

Understaffed, overworked, and in desperate need of stars, stories, and money (and without the last they couldn't have the first two), Warner Brothers was a perfect setup for a young ambitious work horse like Zanuck. "He could write ten times faster than any ordinary man," recalls Jack Warner. "He worked Saturdays, Sundays, and nights in those days. He was a very professional writer. He could leave on Friday and come back on Monday with a script," and since "it never took long to make a movie in those days—about four weeks," Zanuck was always at that typewriter. He could write anything. "Each year we made about fifty to seventy pictures," recalls Warner. "At our annual conventions the sales department wanted to know what we were making. Darryl would write synopses and at the convention it was my job to tell the salesmen. Some of the ideas were legitimate, from plays or books, but others we would make up. I would find out they wanted stories about prizefighters. Boom! Darryl would make up *The Prizefighter and the Lady*. He could do all sorts of things ad lib. He would jump up and scream, 'I've got it!' and do it. Then we'd fake up some title. Many of the stories were revamped after the film was finished." Zanuck very quickly became Warner's protégé and close friend (their wives were also close), Warner affectionately referring to Darryl Francis Zanuck as Three Charming Fellows.

One year he wrote nineteen features for Warner Brothers and at the next convention an angry exhibitor demanded of

Jack Warner, "Why the hell do you spend so much money? You've got only one writer." Actually as Zanuck remembers it, "They had two or three writers, but I practically wrote one half of the pictures." Jack didn't want to lose any of Zanuck's half, but insisted, "You've got to keep your name off the screen." Zanuck responded, "Look. I'll use a phony name." They decided on three phony names—Melville Crossman, Mark Canfield, and Gregory Rogers—and Zanuck copyrighted them. Rogers wrote comedies (*Hogan's Alley, Midnight Taxi*), Canfield, melodramas (*Black Diamond Express, The Desired Woman*), Crossman, class pictures (*Tenderloin*), with occasional overlapping. Zanuck was saved for special occasions, such as Sydney Chaplin pictures and spectaculars like *Noah's Ark*. It was not Darryl Zanuck but Melville Crossman who proved the most successful. "He became a star," says Zanuck. "Every time his name was on a picture, it became a hit." And he became a hot property. Zanuck recalls with perverse pride that M-G-M tried to hire not him but Crossman away from Warners.

Most of Zanuck's early films have disappeared into nitrate dust. They exist largely in yellowing reviews, which may be just as well. As a writer, Zanuck made no pretense of art. In 1926, a typically prolific year, among his credits Darryl Zanuck wrote a gangster comedy for Dolores Costello, *The Little Irish Girl;* a double role for Montague Love in *The Social Highwayman* ("passes muster," said *Variety,* "despite the hokum"); *Footloose Widows,* a comedy about two gold-digging fashion models, featuring subtitles the New York *Tribune* called, "probably . . . the oldest wheezes extant; in fact we had fancied them extinct." He adapted *Across the Pacific,* a melodrama about the Spanish-American war, which the *Tribune* called "dramatically sound and genuinely convincing," with a young girl named Myrna Loy "achiev[ing] distinction in the part of the native girl." In 1927 Crossman wrote *Irish Hearts,* a silly farce starring May McAvoy. Zanuck concocted *Old San Francisco,* which climaxed in The Earthquake—how could you write a movie about San Francisco and leave out The Earthquake? "A very lurid piece of work," said the New York *Times.* Zanuck fared better critically with *The First Auto,* billed as a "romance of the last horse and the first horseless carriage." Said the *Times:* "A vastly imaginative piece of work." Then Zanuck rode in on

his childhood favorite *The Black Diamond Express,* and Mark
Canfield turned to *The Desired Woman.*

The best of Zanuck's pictures were the ones he wrote for
Charlie Chaplin's brother, Sydney, comedies such as *The
Better 'Ole, Oh! What a Nurse!* and *The Missing Link. The
Better 'Ole,* which Zanuck based on the Bruce Bairnsfather
World War I doughboy cartoons, was Warner's hit of 1926
and on many ten-best lists. "My hat's off to Warner Broth-
ers . . . a comedy classic," burbled the unsigned critic in the
New York *Tribune.*

Sydney Chaplin was Zanuck's favorite Chaplin. He admired
him for many reasons, most particularly as a comic actor, but
he also had a sneaking regard for him as a ladies' man.
Perhaps, it takes one to respect one. "Sydney Chaplin was the
greatest cocksman that ever lived," announces Zanuck.
"Including Errol Flynn," he adds. "I never saw anyone as
ruthless and successful and bold as Sydney Chaplin. He used
to stand across the street from Hollywood High School and
watch the kids come out and he'd approach them—using his
real name. Ruthless! At Yosemite once I saw this guy get a
married woman on her honeymoon!"

By 1927 Zanuck was Warner's most valuable property.
Although according to legend, Zanuck was boosted overnight
from lowly writer to head of production, the truth is the
promotion was more gradual, although still accomplished in
a comparatively short time. Unofficially, for some time
Zanuck was producing—there were no producers as such in
those early days, at least none with screen credits, but there
were uncredited "supervisors." In some ways, almost from the
first, Zanuck operated as a talent scout finding not only
stories, but also actors and directors. Ernst Lubitsch, for one,
was in a sense his discovery. As Zanuck tells it, he brought
him to Hollywood from Germany, which is somewhat of a
simplification. Zanuck met him before he came to America,
but Lubitsch's initial reason for coming was to direct Mary
Pickford in *Rosita.* After completing that film, he came to
Warner Brothers, where he made some of his greatest
comedies such as *The Lady Windermere's Fan* and *So This
Is Paris* under Zanuck's supervision. Zanuck gets no "credit"
for Lubitsch, except for allowing him to function creatively
—which as it turned out in later years was one of Zanuck's

most deserved credits. Similarly Zanuck gave a home to William Dieterle, Michael Curtiz, William Wellman.

As Zanuck's value increased so did his salary from $250 a week to $1000 and finally—in just four years' time—to $5000. One day in the middle of these increases, Jack Warner called him in and said, "You know [Raymond] Shrock is out," and then added, "Well, you're *in* as head of production." His only advice to his young-looking clean-shaven protégé: "Even if you don't need glasses, get some window panes and grow a mustache. It'll give you a little age." Looking back on the historic moment, Zanuck says, "I was so excited I almost wet my pants."

9.

A Tumult of Sound

Who the hell wants to hear actors talk?

—Harry Warner

The Jazz Singer was not the first talking picture, but without question it was the most significant in terms of turning Hollywood on to sound. Before it, sound was considered a gimmick, which would kill, not save, the "industry." Later Hollywood was to respond similarly to such diverse revolutions as television, the widescreen, neo-realism, and the New Wave. Although there was some dissension among the Warner Brothers as to the importance of sound, led by Sam Warner they became pioneers in the medium. Says Zanuck emphatically, "Sam Warner was responsible for sound coming into pictures against the violent protests of Harry Warner." Actually it was not aesthetics or adventurousness but economics that propelled them forward. Facing bankruptcy, the brothers decided to risk everything, even their prestige—what little they had of it. They invested in a new method of combining sounds with images on screen called Vitaphone. Their first attempt at a commercial use of the new system was John Barrymore's *Don Juan,* which had a musical soundtrack, but no words. At its auspicious premiere the film was introduced with a Vitaphone prologue by Will Hays, and a series of Vitaphone vaudeville shorts. It was the shorts that were to have the greatest immediate impact. At last one could see such artists as Mischa Elman and Weber and Fields almost in person. In subsequent months many of Warners' features went out on a bill with Vitaphone shorts: George Jessel in *A Theatrical Booking Office,* Leo Carillo in *At the Ball Game, The Evolution of Dixie* played by Herman Heller's orchestra.

Sound remained a gimmick even at Warners until the studio bought the movie rights to George Jessel's latest Broadway hit about the son of a cantor who wanted to be a jazz singer.

When Jessel made too high demands, Warners signed Al Jolson, and, with Zanuck supervising the production, filming began under the direction of Alan Crosland. It was Sam Warner's idea that the movie should have singing, and Zanuck's that it should have talking. As Zanuck remembers it, "I was on the set when they were rehearsing the parts where Jolson sings to his mother. We were all standing around waiting for the music to be played. Suddenly it dawned on me, why don't they have a conversation? The mike was on! I said, 'Why doesn't Jolson turn to his mother and say, "Mama, I wanna sing a song for you." ' Then the guy turned the sound machine on early. When they played it back, there was Jolson's voice as clear as a bell. That was when the talking thing started."

The effect was sensational, and a talking scene was written and added to the picture. In the end there were four talking sequences. The picture was a critical failure and a fantastic financial success.

Inspired by *The Jazz Singer* and impelled by radio, all the studios rushed into sound production. Warners, suddenly the hot studio, led the rush, beginning talking pictures from scratch and injecting sound into otherwise silent pictures. Melville Crossman had written and produced a silent Dolores Costello melodrama called *Tenderloin*. Zanuck added talk and music, and, from the reviews, the movie was Vitaphone at its worst. Like an unintegrated musical score, some words were spoken, some slapped into titles. Generally the spoken words were the most exclamatory. "My God," said Miss Costello. "Oh God." "Good God." Moviemakers, actors, and writers were having difficulty adjusting to the new medium—and Zanuck was no exception.

The first all-talkie was *The Lights of New York,* supervised by Zanuck and produced by Bryan Foy (who was in charge of B pictures for Warners). It began as a two-reeler, but it grew and grew in size and in price, particularly when Jack Warner went to Europe. One problem, both economic and artistic, was microphones: where to put them. Recalls Zanuck, "Microphones had to be hidden. Every telephone had a microphone in it. We hid them in the chandeliers. We would

hang microphones on the wall, the same color as the wall."
Behind every flower pot, there was a microphone. "The
cameramen went out of their minds trying to keep the microphones out of the picture." When Warner came back from
Europe, he asked Foy and Zanuck what they had to show
him. "We've overshot a two-reeler," said Foy. "Let's look at
it," said Warner. "If it's too long we can cut it." Apparently
he liked it, because *The Lights of New York* was released
that summer, in July 1928. Disregarding its historical value—
which is impossible—*The Lights of New York* is probably
one of the worst pictures ever made. There still are titles, but
more hysterical than ever, as if the titlewriter, with the advent
of sound, had decided to speak louder himself. "In the sym-
phony of jazz," goes a typical title, "there are many blue-
notes." Worst of all is the self-conscious use of sound. The
picture is a veritable cacophony of cars screeching, whistles,
doors slamming—as if a sound man had run amuck. But
everyone went to see it—and to hear it—anyway. Even going
way over its budget it cost only $21,000. It was an instan-
taneous and continuing hit. It earned $75,000 in one week at
the Strand in New York and by 1937 it had grossed more
than $3 million. "It became a sensation" says Zanuck. *"The
Jazz Singer* turned them to sound, *The Lights of New York*
to talk. It turned the whole goddamn tide."

From then on, everything had to be a first something, and
Zanuck always had another first up his sleeve. *My Man,*
written by Mark Canfield, was Fannie Brice's first film, silent
or talkie. *Noah's Ark,* by Darryl Zanuck, was the first sound
spectacular—crashing waves, smashing cement, and noises
and screams projected throughout the theater. An arkload of
7500 extras, 15,000 tons of water, and hundreds of animals
including okapi from the Congo, sacred oxen from India,
single-striped zebras, and dikdik, couldn't prevent it from
being one of Zanuck's all-time worsts. "A tumult of sound,"
said Richard Watts. ". . . the playgoers were completely surrounded by the din of a world of destruction." *Midnight Taxi*
by Gregory Rogers had the lesser distinction of being the first
sound picture with a character that stuttered.

Hollywood was so busy fooling around with its new toy,
it scarcely noticed a small matter that occurred October 24,
1929. While Wall Street crashed, Hollywood boomed. Warners in fact netted $17 million in 1929, a record up to that

time. Studios competed to sign up Broadway musical stars—Ted Lewis, Sophie Tucker, Vivienne Segal—and cranked out one loud musical after another. "There were so many musicals you wanted to vomit," says Zanuck. Finally the studios were forced to search for new subject matter. And, once again, they looked to the Warner Brothers.

10.

Cycles

When Zanuck announced that the people were bored with lust and massacre in films, it meant that he personally was bored with them.

—Alva Johnston

In Hollywood imitation is *the* way of life. A big new star is immediately followed by a myriad of starlings with some of the manner, and usually none of the character of the original. What usually happens—whether it's a person or a picture—is a demeaning and an ultimate denaturing of the original. It can not be said that Zanuck invented the gangster movie or the musical or the costume romance. What he did was to know when it was time to reinvent them, and to his extra credit, he imitated himself well—and in most cases knew when to stop and to switch to some more fertile path. It was, as Alva Johnston pointed out in a New Yorker profile of Zanuck, at that precise moment when he became bored with something—usually several steps before the public got bored with it. "Only the first picture of a cycle really succeeds," said Zanuck at the time. "All the imitators dwindle."

First came the gangsters. Gangster movies have been around since *The Great Train Robbery,* and certainly silent pictures grew up on them, but *Little Caesar* was the first in the modern genre—cold, hard, uncompromising, with earthy (for those days) dialogue and relatively desentimentalized heroes. *Little Caesar* was, Zanuck insists, Mervyn LeRoy's picture. He was the director and Zanuck only the supervisor, which means that the picture was, Zanuck says, 90 per cent LeRoy, 10 per cent Zanuck. The split of a later Zanuck-LeRoy picture, *I Am a Fugitive from a Chain Gang,* he makes

44

clear, was also 90–10, but in favor of Zanuck. Even though
Zanuck's contribution to *Caesar* was minimal, except to let
LeRoy make it as he wanted to make it, he knew when he
had something good, a genre, a style that was worth inves-
tigating. After *Caesar,* he began what was called the gangster
cycle, the modern gangster cycle, a series of tough, hard-
bitten naturalistic films including *Doorway to Hell* (with
Lew Ayres about a gangster with a Napoleonic complex),
The Mouthpiece, Smart Money, and especially *The Public
Enemy*.

The Public Enemy, directed by William Wellman, took the
gangster cycle one step further than *Little Caesar*. For some
critics it was too merciless, homicidal, and real. What is
amazing is to see *Public Enemy* today, post *Bonnie and Clyde*
and realize how tepid its violence is, and how superimposed
is its supposed significance. The epilogue informs us that
"The end of Tom Powers is the end of every hoodlum, a
problem we must face." No such thing. Except for the early,
brief scenes depicting preadolescent Tom (James Cagney)
and his side-kick, Matt (Edward Woods), hanging out in
bars, stealing dollar watches, and drinking beer, there is not
much attempt at making any Social Statement. Tom is not
every hoodlum, just one punk and even though he is not
sentimentalized, he is sympathetic, certainly in comparison to
the gross gangsters around him and his stuffy, moralistic older
brother. What makes the movie a classic is Cagney and the
character of Tom, and they are inseparable. It is little running
things, and vignettes that capture the essence of *The Public
Enemy*. Cagney curling his hand into a fist and affectionately
pressing his mother's shoulder with a knuckle as if she were
a member of the gang. When his boss, Nails Nathan, dies
after being thrown by a horse, he goes to Nails's funeral, then
directly to the stable and says sharply to the stable boy, "You
got the horse that killed Nails Nathan?," asks how much the
horse is worth, pays the boy $1000 and walks to the horse.
An off-camera blast of a pistol! The last scene: the song
"I'm Forever Blowing Bubbles," which began the movie, is
now playing again on the phonograph. The doorbell rings.
The door is opened, and there is Cagney, encased in a sack
up to his neck, gray and stiff like the walking dead. The sack
falls face forward to the floor, and the music continues, and
the picture ends. *Public Enemy* of course made a star out of

Cagney and a weapon out of a grapefruit. In the most re-membered scene, as Cagney's mistress, played by Mae Clark, gabs away, boring him to death at breakfast, he picks up her grapefruit, escalloped around the edges, and squashes it in her face—a shocking bit of movie misogyny, at least for those days. "It was my idea, the grapefruit," says Zanuck. "I think I thought of it in a script conference. When I made *Public Enemy,* I was way ahead in thinking. No love story, but loaded with sex and violence." The praise for it that Zanuck valued most of all came from Irving Thalberg, who told him, "That's not a motion picture. It's beyond a motion picture."

Not only the grapefruit, but Cagney, too, was a Zanuck discovery. "My complete discovery," he says. "I got him off the stage. He was in a play with Joan Blondell. We bought the play. We couldn't make it gell on screen, but we signed the two people in it. The next day we signed Bette Davis. George Arliss [the British stage star under contract to Warners] needed someone to play with him in a picture. We sent him a newcomer named Bette Davis—I didn't think she was very beautiful—and he called back and said, 'I've just heard one of the greatest actresses.' That was a helluva week: Cagney, Joan Blondell, and Bette Davis." Bette Davis was signed for the Arliss picture, *The Man Who Played God,* and so was Cagney. He played a bit part, his first appearance in the movies. His next picture was *Public Enemy.*

While other studios, including Thalberg's M-G-M, were still trying to manufacture the gangster formula, Zanuck began a biographical cycle. He cast George Arliss in a talk-ing *Disraeli,* Arliss having previously toured America in a stage version. In a sense, Arliss himself became the cycle, playing, among other things, Baron Nathan de Rothschild and Cardinal Richelieu. While other studios were searching through history books, Zanuck turned to the newspapers making movies out of headlined stories: *Illicit,* about pre-marital sex, *Five Star Final,* about yellow journalism, and, most important of all, *I Am a Fugitive from a Chain Gang,* which, although based on a book, Robert Burns's exposé of Georgia chain gangs, was as timely as the day's news. Zanuck gave the story to Mervyn LeRoy to direct and entrusted the lead role, as he had with *Public Enemy,* to a stage actor, in this case Paul Muni, and made a movie star of him. A brutal, harrowing view of the chain gang system and its dehumanization of prisoners, *I Am a Fugitive* survives, even scares, today. In the final scene of *Fugitive,* which Zanuck wrote and added after the first preview, Muni visits his old girl friend and indicates his fear of apprehension. "How do you live?" she asks. His eyes dancing like a madman's, he says, "I steal . . ." and runs into the darkness. An uncompromising end to an uncompromising picture. *I Am a Fugitive* was an outspoken, courageous movie, especially in timid Hollywood in 1932, and it eventually became a classic.

11.

An Introduction to Games

On one safari I shot an elephant. His feet are in my office at the studio. Ashtrays.

—Darryl Zanuck

Darryl Zanuck's play has always paralleled his work. Whatever he does, he does with a passion, and when he loses his passion he quits cold. In spite of his height and slight stature he has always been something of an athlete. As if to prove that he is bigger and better than you think he is, he enjoys the physical challenge. In the Army he had been chosen to run messages on the front lines, because he was fast on his feet. He had boxed in the Army, and continued briefly as a civilian, giving it up when he realized his limitations. Later in life he was to take up skiing and waterskiing. His prime athletic passion was polo. He was not a great polo player by any means, but from all reports, he was a good one. "I used to plow into him on the polo field," recalls producer Sy Bartlett. "He would come back at you—hard! He was a tiger, a scrappy bulldog."

He had ridden horses since he was a child, in saddle and bareback. As he says, "A horse was second nature to me." But his riding had always been for fun, and not for competition, until one day in 1932 when he met Juan Reynal, the great Argentine polo player, at the Midwick Country Club in Pasadena. In looking for a place to practice with Reynal, Zanuck remembered the Warners' ranch, which was used for locations. Soon they were joined by Sam Engel, a druggist who Zanuck later made a producer; Raymond Griffith, comedian turned producer; Aiden Rourke, an English polo player, now a scenario writer in Hollywood; Will Rogers, then a big tar at Fox. Both Rourke and Reynal rated nine goals. "Two nine goal captains with us bums around. Rogers was no better than I was. The game was carried by the 'professionals.' I was rated one goal and so was Will Rogers. The highest rating I ever attained for one season was in Europe—three goals. I had longed to play in Europe. I timed my vacation period so that we could go together with Laddie Sanford. Aiden, Laddie, myself, Charlie Wrightsman, Eric Terrell-Martin. We set sail with forty or forty-five ponies, six grooms. We won the open high goal championship of England. *Polo* magazine wrote that I played way beyond my three goal rating." But the London *Times* was not as magnanimous. As Zanuck remembers, the *Times* polo reporter wrote, "Three polo players and a Hollywood producer today won the open championship of Great Britain."

At Warners, Zanuck also renewed his boyhood interest in hunting. Usually in large groups—a covey of producers and writers, often including Jack Warner—he would take off for long weekends. There was a great sort of conviviality about these all-male ventures. To hear the stories recounted, it often sounds like a bunch of school kids playing hooky from the studio with Zanuck, as he was in grammar school, the instigator. On one occasion, the plan was to hunt geese at Willows, California. The group—about fifteen—was traveling in three private railroad cars, which was not exactly roughing it. In Willows, as Zanuck tells it, "On the edge of a rice field, there was a tremendous flight of geese—very, very low. We all let loose. Fifteen guns. Boom! The whole swarm went down. Suddenly a police car and a sheriff's car arrived. They counted the geese. We were about seven geese over the law. They confiscated our guns. They confiscated our geese. And they cooked our geese, to the tune of $500."

Zanuck had worked his way up from coyotes in Nebraska to bear in Canada and Alaska, but more than anything he wanted to go on safari in Africa. He talked about it for many years, then in 1933 began planning for a trip the following year. In 1934 he and Virginia went on safari.

Leaving their daughter Darrylin in Capri, they flew to Cairo. From there they followed the Nile down to Nairobi, where they outfitted themselves, then on a chartered plane flew to the Serengetti Plain to meet their white hunter, George

Runton. After a lunch of buffalo tail soup and eland tongue, they began their safari education.

Zanuck soon found himself, like in a Darryl Zanuck movie, hunting The Famous Ghost Elephant of Manvara. He didn't catch him, but he did find some real elephants. He described the scene in an article in *Esquire,* with some of the pace-heightening flair he uses to spin plots:

"Suddenly, to the left of us, we heard a crashing and breaking of trees and the trumpeting of a bull . . . Then, on our right, we heard more crashing and trumpeting. We had stumbled into a herd which, accidentally but unpleasantly, had formed a half-circle around us and seemed to be closing the ring . . . We hugged the ground for minutes, not daring to breathe. A big female elephant moved closer and, through the thin screen of the trees, was a perfect photographic target.

"I could not resist the temptation. Carefully raising my camera, I pressed the button. A slight sound behind me made me turn. Our gunbearers were removing their sandals. In a whisper, I asked Runton why.

" 'They climb trees barefooted better,' he replied laconically.

"It was then that the female either sensed or heard us, as elephants are next to blind. Her ears swept forward like two huge fans and her trunk came up, sucking in the air as she strained to fix the scent. In a moment my gunbearer had snatched the camera out of my hands and shoved the big 500–465 double-barreled elephant gun at me. My hands closed over it automatically and I fired. I was dimly aware of two black blurs before my eyes: our gunbearers had taken it on the run.

"The woods were suddenly alive with the horrible, strident trumpeting of angry elephants . . . I don't believe I ever ran so fast in my life . . . It was a quarter of a mile to the edge of the forest. I think I could have made it had it been five miles. The elephants, luckily for us, did not follow us into the clearing."

The next day he killed a leopard and a lion, and Virginia killed a lion. In the Zanucks' home movie of the safari they seem like two happy kids out for a lark; a pack of natives lifting him to their shoulders after he killed a lion and bobbing him around in front of the camera; Zanuck crouching, holding his lion by its saggy head, wagging the head, and grinning; Virginia with her wildebeest; Zanuck holding up the ears of his elephant to show their great size, touching the tusk, and then leaping on its back as if it were the peak of Mount Everest.

In the absence of wild life, Zanuck took up tamer pursuits in Hollywood. Besides polo, his favorite nonprofessional occupation was playing practical jokes. Hollywood in those days was far removed from the serious concerns of the world. On screen and off the fun and fantasy continued. One day during lunch time Zanuck bought twenty-five padlocks and sneaked into the executive cloakroom, and put locks in the buttonholes of all the executives' jackets. Zanuck casually strolled to the screening room, leaving the men scrambling on the floor trying to wrench and smash the locks from their jackets. Jack Warner carried his to the screening room with him, and sat with it in his lap. In the dark, Zanuck sneaked another lock on. As Zanuck's power increased, his practical jokes became more intricate. One thing was clear. He played the jokes on other people, even on the boss. No longer did *they* play jokes on him.

12.

A Free Hand

Darryl was a kind of roughrider. You have to be. You can be soft. Or they'll eat you alive.

—Jack Warner

"When I took over at Warner Brothers," says Darryl Zanuck, "Jack *practically* gave me a free hand." But of course Jack and Harry Warner had the power to call him out of order. Since there seemed no reason to risk a confrontation—and besides Jack was a good friend of his; the same cannot be said about Harry—Zanuck would look for ways to circumvent them.

In 1932 with the country feeling the full effect of the Depression, Zanuck had the hunch that it might be time already to bring the musical back. He knew he would have to do it over the objections of the Brothers Warner. "I fel around Jack, and I think Harry and said, 'Don't you believe we're ready to go into a musical cycle again?' They said, 'O Christ no, we can't give 'em away.' " Zanuck had a property, " backstage story about a producer of Broadway stage musicals I wrote—had written—worked on—two scripts. One had ne musical numbers in it. The other was with musical numbers but had the same plot line. Lloyd Bacon, the son of a grea actor, was a director for me then. We had two lots. I decided to shoot the musical numbers without Jack knowing it at the Vitagraph studio at night. I shot about six weeks. We re hearsed the musical numbers during the day. Then the time came when we had to screen the picture. Jack went out o his mind. He never knew until it was screened that it was a musical. Only one thing, he loved it! He said, 'What am going to tell Harry?' But he sent the musical version to Harry

52

n New York and Harry wired back 'This is the greatest picture you've sent me in five years.'" The picture of course was *Forty-second Street*. It was a huge hit and began a whole new musical cycle. Every lot mobilized back into musicals. Twenty-seven were scheduled for the next season's release: eight from Fox, seven from Paramount, six from MGM, five from RKO; but only one from Warners.

With people like Lubitsch and LeRoy directing for him and actors like Muni, Robinson, Cagney, Ruth Chatterton, Leslie Howard, Adolph Menjou, Barbara Stanwyck, William Powell, Bette Davis, Kay Francis, Ann Dvorak, Ruby Keeler, Joe E. Brown, Warren Williams, Richard Barthelmess, Zanuck was riding high. He was constantly being courted by other studios, including MGM and Columbia. He remembers one such meeting with Harry Cohn, boss of Columbia. "We had pre-viewed a Warner Brothers picture one night late at Grauman's Chinese Theater. Jack had invited Harry Cohn, his great personal friend. Afterwards we were standing in the parking lot. I was alone with Harry. He said, 'How long has your deal with Warners got to run?' His friend Jack! I was taken aback. Then Harry said, 'They're the Warner *Brothers*. You never can go too far there. I'm different.' I said, 'What's the difference with the Cohn Brothers?'" Harry's brother Jack, like Jack Warner's brother Harry, ran the New York end of his studio. "He said, 'We operate differently.'"

Actually Cohn's courting was prophetic. Zanuck was not to remain long with the Warners. In 1933 Hollywood itself was finally struck by the Depression, in particular by President Roosevelt's bank holiday. In order to cut its costs, Warners, along with all the other studios, agreed to a 50 per cent reduction in salaries for all personnel. Zanuck agreed to the cut for himself and for his people. The Academy of Motion Picture Arts and Sciences and Price Waterhouse were to decide when to end the cut at each individual studio. When Warners had its cuts restored one week later than MGM, Harry Warner refused to accept the ruling. Zanuck insisted, reluctantly went before the Academy and asked them to reconsider, finally felt himself to be in an impossible situation. He had promised his people restoration of their cuts on the date specified by the Academy and Price and Waterhouse, and now he had to renege. Zanuck resisted, agreed to talk the matter over with Harry Warner; their discussion ended in a violent argument. Jack Warner and Will Hays tried to mediate, but Harry Warner ignored them. The next morning, April 15, 1933, "as a matter of principle," Zanuck resigned, walking out cold on his $5000-a-week job.

13.

The Making of a Mogul

Write your own ticket.
—Joseph Schenck to Darryl Zanuck

Zanuck's resignation was not exactly a risk. When he quit Warners, he was—with Irving Thalberg on the decline—the hottest young man in Hollywood. Everyone wanted him, including Thalberg's boss Louis B. Mayer. The first to approach him was Joseph Schenck and not just because he was first, but because he was Joe Schenck, he landed him.

"He was one of the ugliest men that ever lived," says Arnold Grant about Schenck, "but after you met him if anybody asked you to describe him you would say he was one of the most attractive, charming people." He was also smart and shrewd. "He was the best poker player," says Charles Feldman. "You could play Joe for pennies and lose ten million dollars."

Joe Schenck emigrated from Russia in 1893 at the age of fourteen, and he and his younger brother Nicholas soon began boosting themselves and each other to success. They struck up a friendship with Marcus Loew, founder of Loew's theaters, who backed them in opening an amusement area called Paradise Park, at Fort George. After the death of Marcus Loew in 1927, Nick became president of Loew's Inc. and Metro-Goldwyn-Mayer. Joe quit the company to go into independent production, made movies with Fatty Arbuckle, Norma and Constance Talmadge (he later married Norma Talmadge), and Buster Keaton. In 1924 he was elected chairman of the board of United Artists, a releasing company for UA founders Mary Pickford, Douglas Fairbanks, Charles Chaplin, and Sam Goldwyn and in 1927, the year that his brother became president of MGM, Joe became president of United Artists. But by 1933 Schenck was becoming restless. So, obviously, was Zanuck.

Schenck called Zanuck on April 18 and met him for breakfast at the Brown Derby. "Have you got a lot of confidence in yourself?" asked Schenck. "Yeah," said Zanuck. "All right," said Schenck, "you and I will start a producing company." By lunch time, terms had been agreed to. They would form a company and United Artists would act as distributor. Schenck gave Zanuck a check for $100,000 to seal the contract. The check was signed by Louis B. Mayer.

Some time later he was playing polo. On the field he collided with his friend Sam Engel. Engel, it had been decided, would join him in the new company. Both of them fell down and Zanuck cursed him out: "For God's sake, you play like the game was played in the nineteenth century." Engel replied, "Let's call the new company Twentieth Century." Mulling over the name and still wondering about the significance of the signature of L. B. Mayer on the check, Zanuck took off for Alaska to hunt for bear—and think.

On his return the mystery was solved: in a strange case of financial incest the head of one studio (Mayer, vice-president in charge of production for MGM) was partially financing the creation of a rival studio (Twentieth Century). Why? He wanted to set up his favorite son-in-law, William Goetz, an assistant director at RKO, in private business. To thicken the plot, Mayer's other son-in-law, David O. Selznick, until recently the head of production at RKO, had just joined Mayer at MGM, which meant that Selznick and Goetz would be competing against one another with Mayer seemingly in the middle. In any case, Goetz was to be a major stockholder in Twentieth and Zanuck's executive assistant. Zanuck had no objection to the odd arrangement. Probably he half expected some sort of alliance with MGM since the president of MGM, and Mayer's boss, was of course, Joe Schenck's brother Nick. To make the best of the deal, he realized, "the answer was to watch what players we got on loan from Metro." With him he had brought George Arliss, Constance Bennett, Loretta Young, Raymond Griffith (whom he made production supervisor) and very few others. He hoped that MGM might supply the acting talent he needed, and it did, immediately: Wallace Beery, George Raft, Jackie Cooper, Clark Gable (whom Zanuck had fired at Warners "because his ears were too big," a mistake Zanuck has cherished all his life as proof of his own fallibility). The first three he starred in his first Twentieth Century production, *The Bowery*, a melo-dramatic comedy (or a comedic melodrama) based very loosely on the adventures of bridge-jumper Steve Brodie (played by Raft). The catch-all script, not by Zanuck, brought in Carry Nation, John L. Sullivan, and World War I, turned Brodie from a newsboy into a saloonkeeper, and set up a friendly feud between him and a rival saloonkeeper played by Wallace Beery. The reviews were not good, but the receipts were. Zanuck's first post-Warners' effort became a smash hit, and Twentieth Century was off and running.

In his first year with Twentieth at UA, Zanuck produced twelve pictures—as specified in his contract—and in the first half of the second year, six more, all but one of them financial successes. The exception was *Born to Be Bad*, a Loretta Young-Cary Grant movie that was disapproved by the Hays Office and partially refilmed. The others were *Blood Money*, *Broadway Through a Keyhole* (created by Walter Winchell), *Advice to the Lovelorn* ("suggested" by *Miss Lonelyhearts*), *Moulin Rouge*, *Looking for Trouble*, *Gallant Lady*, *House of Rothschild*, *Affairs of Cellini*, *Bulldog Drummond Strikes Back*, *Last Gentleman*, *The Mighty Barnum*, *Clive of India*, *Folies Bergere*, *Call of the Wild* (with Gable and Loretta Young), *Cardinal Richelieu*, and *Les Miserables*. The balance—a little melodrama, a big musical, a lot of spectacle, and a preponderance of fictionalized history—was representative of the Zanuck movies to come in the thirties. The biggest hit was *The House of Rothschild*, which starred George Arliss as Mayer and Nathan Rothschild. In the early thirties Arliss became Zanuck's house impersonator. In the late thirties, Zanuck's historical figures became younger, handsomer, less credible, more callow—Tyrone Power! The difference between Arliss and Power is one difference between Zanuck's pictures in the early thirties and late thirties. *The House of Rothschild* is not a romance, as, for instance, *Lloyds of London* and *Suez* were, although there is a romance in it, between a pretty Loretta Young (as Nathan Rothschild's daughter) and an even prettier Robert Young. Today it is outrageously corny, cliché, and anachronistic. Zanuck's Roth-schild is something of a monetary Moses, leading his people out of bondage and his family into stocks and bonds. Like many of Zanuck's other favorite cinematic heroes (even Tom Powers in *Public Enemy* and James Allen in *I Am a Fugitive*), Nathan Rothschild loves his mother. But with all its simplicity, *The House of Rothschild* is a rousingly good entertainment, partially because of Arliss' quirky performance, but also because of the carefully paced and plotted structure. Against one's will, one is caught up by the machinations of the screen Rothschilds so that their quest to float the world's biggest loan finally seems as important as the greatest naval battle. Never has fiscal responsibility been more dramatically portrayed on screen.

For Zanuck, *Rothschild* was an all-star production. It was "presented" by Joseph Schenck; William Goetz and Raymond Griffith were the associate producers and the screenplay was by Nunnally Johnson. And it was personally produced by Zanuck as were all of his movies at United Artists—one a month. In contrast, his associates at UA made very few: Chaplin just one a year, or none. Only Goldwyn was actively producing. "The pictures I was working on," complains Zanuck, "had to carry the entire United Artists distributing organization. I had to carry the whole goddamn load." For his first picture, he borrowed one of Sam Goldwyn's assistant editors, a young girl named Barbara McLean, made her an editor on *Gallant Lady*. Eventually she became his favorite editor, chief cutter, and keeper of the film repository, and stayed with him until her retirement in 1969.

Under Zanuck's original contract he was to receive $5000 a week, and, he understood, 10 per cent of the gross. Months after he signed the contract, he discovered that he would receive 10 per cent of the net, which meant that his partners would get back all of the original investment before he participated. Schenck was willing to change the contract. Fairbanks, by that time a great friend of Zanuck's (part of their affection was their love of practical jokes), was on his side but as Zanuck remembers it, Chaplin was "violently opposed. He and Fairbanks almost came to blows over this issue." Chaplin was outvoted, but it did not help relations between him and Zanuck. In fact their association over the years has been one of enmity—political and personal. Zanuck traces part of the bad feeling to a seemingly minor incident when they were both at United Artists. "Douglas Fairbanks,

Chaplin and I were sitting around the studio steam room. We were talking about comedians. I assumed that Chaplin realized I was excepting him when I said, "The greatest comedian that ever lived was Lloyd Hamilton.' He didn't say anything. He went absolutely blue."

A minor and more friendly feud (something on the order of the Raft-Beery conflict in *The Bowery*) was developing between Zanuck and Mayer. "My first split with Mayer was more or less a personal thing." The cause: Goetz. When Zanuck went to Europe for two months, he decided to turn the studio temporarily over to Harry Joe Brown, his most experienced producer. "I figured I would put the best, the most dependable person in charge. Brown had far more experience than Goetz. When I came back from Europe, Goetz was as friendly as he could be, but there was a message from Mayer saying, drop in and have breakfast. He lived ten doors away from me." He dropped in. "He was in a semidelirious rage. 'How could you humiliate my son-in-law?' Such a ridiculous thing. Finally he cooled down." But that was not the last disharmony between Zanuck and Goetz. Concludes Zanuck about Goetz, "He was a very good assistant. He had a banker's kind of mind, which was far away from me. When he went into independent production [after a falling out with Zanuck in the early forties], he had a pretty dismal record. I never thought of him as a creative producer."

Goetz and Mayer were the least of Zanuck's problems at United Artists. Mostly it was a case of working too hard for too little. Both he and Schenck began looking around. As it turned out, their investigation was simultaneous with one being made by Sidney R. Kent, the latest in a quick-flowing series of presidents at the Fox Film Corporation. Once a studio giant, Fox was falling apart, largely because of the financial double-dealings of its founder, William Fox, and the resultant law suits and battles with the federal government. Long before his imprisonment, back in 1929, Fox sold out his interest in his company, and it doddered along through a succession of unsuccessful managements. Now Kent was president and he decided that young Zanuck was the man to rescue Fox. Zanuck (and Schenck) agreed. He was attracted to Kent ("a brilliant man, a wonderful man, a great great man," he says with characteristic enthusiasm, "an absolutely

honest man") and curiously enough he was attracted to
Kent's company. "Fox had the best distributing organization
in the world and the worst films." As head of the small
Twentieth, Zanuck could use Fox's distribution, and as a one-
man producing company, he had no doubt he could create
the product.

The net worth of Fox was $36 million, the net worth of
Twentieth only $4 million, but the earning power of the
respective companies was $1.8 million and $1.7 million.
Twentieth received only 130,000 shares of preferred stock,
which would earn about $200,000 a year, but half of the
common stock. Fox had not really swallowed Twentieth. As it
developed, it was really the other way around. Significantly
enough, when it came time to discuss the name of the new
combined organization, the Fox forces wanted Fox-Twentieth
Century, and recalls Zanuck, "I insisted on Twentieth Century-
Fox."

The first order before business could begin was to do something about Winfield Sheehan, the last remnant at Fox of the
old William Fox days. Sheehan, an ex-newspaperman, for
many years had been in charge of Fox's production—in the
good as well as in the recent bad days. Years later when
Sheehan became an independent producer Zanuck hired him,
and in fact, at Sheehan's funeral, Zanuck was an honorary
pallbearer (as were Joe Schenck and Louis B. Mayer—all
rivalries are reconciled in Hollywood at funerals). But for
now the feeling was bad. "Sheehan started as a whirlwind,"
says Zanuck, "as a good discoverer of talent, especially
foreign talent. But when new films came along, the kind I
had made at Twentieth Century, he was still making *The
Farmer Takes a Wife*." Kent's plan was that Sheehan and
Zanuck would split production in the new company, although
as Sheehan knew he would in effect become the number two
man. To avoid collision (and save his face), Sheehan resigned,
and retired with a fat settlement of $360,000. Now Zanuck
had the title, the power, the room—the ninety-six acres that
made up Fox Movietone City—and the budget: $20 million.
As *Fortune* said, Darryl Zanuck, "just thirty-three last September and quivering with energy" merely had to "read, re-
vise, cast, film, cut, assemble, and release one picture every
twelve days."

II | *The Twentieth Century-Fox*

1935-56

1.

Sixteenth Century-Fox

*The producer of motion pictures like every other person
engaged in large-scale creative enterprise should have, above
all, the faculty of foretelling public taste . . . Box-office
returns tell the world at once whether he has touched the
public with a success or missed it with a failure. Critics,
good or bad, have insignificant influence on the box office.*
— Darryl Zanuck

At Warner Brothers, there were always the brothers to contend with. Zanuck was, at best, the number two man. At
Twentieth Century, there was only Joe Schenck, and he had
the utmost faith in Zanuck's ability. As vice-president in charge
of production for the company he helped found, Zanuck, at
thirty-three, was no longer a boy wonder. Now he was a
full-fledged movie mogul, and he acted accordingly. Instead
of taking the easy (and probably disastrous) approach of
settling down as the king of a pre-arranged, prescribed kingdom, Zanuck took a cold, hard look at the state of Fox—
and then shook it up. Like an inspector general, he immediately pitched temporary headquarters at the studio, and
began surveying the property and the properties. He called
in all scripts, read them, rejected twelve out-of-hand, and
canceled six movies that had already begun production. On
a Saturday, he canceled a picture that was supposed to begin
on Monday. He fired people left and right—from producers
to policemen to prop boys—savagely slashing the company
payroll. Cries of liquidator went up. He began moving his
own people in, writers like Nunnally Johnson and Bess Meredyth, directors like Roy del Ruth, producers like Raymond
Griffith and Kenneth MacGowan, stars like Fredric March

and Loretta Young. One person he retained was Sol Wurtzel, who had been the executive producer at Fox since the twenties and, as Zanuck remembered, was the one who didn't want to buy his story for William Russell.

His major inherited assets at Fox were Shirley Temple and Will Rogers, and he had big plans for both. But soon after Zanuck assumed power and before he could use him in a picture, Rogers was killed in a plane crash, which left Zanuck with only half of Fox's assets—and Shirley Temple unfortunately had to grow up. Fox's legacy to Zanuck, then, was an aging Shirley, Janet Gaynor, Warner Oland, who played Charlie Chan, and Warner Baxter, who played practically everything else. The rest was up to Zanuck. Stubbornly fighting the type-casters, as his first movie under the banner of Twentieth Century-Fox, Zanuck made *Metropolitan*. A backstage story of a baritone's coming of age, it revived the faded career of Lawrence Tibbett. It opened at the Radio City Music Hall to rave reviews. *Metropolitan* would have gotten Twenieth Century-Fox off to a smashing start, except that—no matter what the critics said—hardly anyone wanted to see it. Commercially it was, as Zanuck describes it, "a big bust," and convinced him as he was to be convinced many times that critics have a very limited effect on the box office.

Much was riding on Zanuck's second picture: his own reputation and probably his entire company. This time he chose a subject he knew well, and from the very beginning he was closely involved in every detail of production. Zanuck dreamed up the plot himself and let his ace alias Melville Crossman write it. It was the story of a crooner who accidentally runs for governor. Until it reached the screen as *Thanks a Million,* the story went through several revisions. Nunnally Johnson's final script, however, was very close to Zanuck's original. The star role was originally conceived for Bing Crosby but was eventually played by Dick Powell. It was something of an all-star cast: Ann Dvorak, Raymond Walburn, Paul Whiteman, Patsy Kelly, Fred Allen; and an all-star production with songs by Gus Kahn, Arthur Johnson, Bert Kolmar, and Harry Ruby, direction by Roy del Ruth. When it was finished, Zanuck confidently previewed the picture in Santa Monica, and it was a disaster. "My God, I must have been so close to it," he says, "I lost all viewpoint. Jesus, it was a bomb!"

He discussed it with Joe Schenck, who said, "Well, it's a shame." Zanuck took the film back to the studio. "I was just sick that night. Before I ran it again, I remember going into the toilet and thinking, how could I make this? How could I do it? Then I went back to the projection room and worked on it. I ran it reel by reel, stopping after each reel, making notes. Suddenly I found the weakness. I cut twelve minutes, that's all, and rearranged the rest. I previewed it in Santa Barbara to an absolute ovation. The preview cards were tremendous." The movie opened to good reviews. Powell was greeted by the critics with cynicism, but Fred Allen, rasping Nunnally Johnson throwaways, was delightful. The picture was a resounding success, "an enormous hit," says Zanuck. "More than anything else, it made Twentieth Century-Fox."

For most of Hollywood, the late thirties were a coming of age. Free from the hysteria of the advent of sound, each studio began developing its own image. Warners, in the absence of Zanuck, synthesized what he had started: the fast, rough James Cagney and Edward G. Robinson melodramas, and had discovered a dashing newcomer, Errol Flynn, to play opposite its resident ladies. RKO had Fred Astaire and Ginger Rogers. Even disadvantaged Columbia managed to produce charming, sophisticated comedies, many of them directed by Frank Capra. The top studio was of course MGM. With its undiminishing star factory, it was producing Great Romance, Great Drama, and Great Profits. But, by any measure—stars, pictures, profits—the late thirties were not Zanuck's golden years. "I was learning—struggling and learning," he says about the period. With justification, partially because of Zanuck's costumed romantic epics, in the late thirties his studio was referred to as "Sixteenth Century-Fox."

It was during this period that Zanuck came to believe wholeheartedly in the theory that stars didn't make pictures, but pictures made stars. For him, they had to, because he didn't have any stars—except, of course, Shirley Temple. As late as 1938 he was protesting, "I think Shirley Temple is endless. There's no one in the world to compare with that child. I've made eight pictures with her, and each time I'm knocked dead. It's just beyond the case of being a freak. This child has rhythm. I always thought when we dropped the curls—this is the end. This mint, the gold mine has gone dry. But now she's good for years." This child had rhythm,

but she was getting older by the day, and to insure her end
lessness Zanuck began fooling with her formula. He increased
her budgets. He had John Ford direct her in *Wee Willie
Winkie,* a feminization of the old Rudyard Kipling hero. To
use Ford for such purposes seems in retrospect like a flagrant
waste of talent, but Ford accepted it good-naturedly. As he
remembers, "One day Darryl said, 'I'm going to give you
something to scream about. I'm going to put you together
with Shirley Temple.' He thought that combination would
make me and everybody howl. I said, 'Great,' and we just
went out and made the picture. I remembered the story from
Kipling, and it was just great. She and I are still friends, and
everybody thought it was the most odd combination. We had
only one discussion on *Wee Willie Winkie.* D.Z. said, 'Victor
McLaglen is so good in this, and we kill him off halfway
through,' and I said, 'I'd like to keep him.' We had all those
bagpipes, and D.Z. said, 'Can you give him an impressive
military funeral?' The picture made a lot of money—and
she adored me. I'm the godfather of her child." Shirley
was the number one box-office attraction in the U.S. in 1935,
1936, 1937, and 1938, but in 1939 she fell to five, and by
1940 she was out of the top twenty and out of Fox. Even
while Shirley was number one, Zanuck went hunting for new
faces.

It didn't take much imagination to discover the most famous
children of the day, the Dionne Quintuplets. To direct their
debut, he named Henry King, whom he had inherited when
he took over Fox. Zanuck assigned Nunnally Johnson and
Sonya Levien as screenwriters, and with King, turned them
loose on the material, which was mostly a batch of Hearst
clippings about the Quints that Fox had purchased. The idea
was conceived to do the picture about the doctor who delivered
the Quints. King wanted the Danish actor Jean Hersholt for
the part. "But he has an accent," said Zanuck. "So does every
one in Canada," said King. They borrowed him from MGM
and went on location to Canada—the Quints were only two
years old and no amount of blandishments could lure them to
Hollywood. The public devoured news about the filming: the
Quints' screen tests were placed in steel-lined vaults and in
sured for two million dollars against everything from theft
to hurricane; the Quints cut new teeth and "film executives
groaned." They had already shot some toothless scenes out

of sequence. In the end the Quints appeared only in the last ten minutes of *The Country Doctor*, but it was a phenomenal success, even with the critics. It began a medical career for Hersholt, who went on to play Dr. Christian on radio for what seemed like centuries, and it really did begin a career for the Quints. By the end of the year, Zanuck brought them back for a *Reunion*, for bad notices, but good grosses, and then for a re-reunion in *Five of a Kind*. But the Quints were not endless, and they had no rhythm.

In search of performers, Zanuck turned his attentions away from the cradle, toward radio, vaudeville, and other studios. He discovered Tony Martin and Borrah Minnevitch (and all his Harmonica Rascals). MGM had the Marx Brothers, so he discovered the Ritz Brothers—and they only *seemed* to be in every Zanuck musical. And every movie the Ritzes weren't in, Elsa Maxwell was (was she really a Ritz Brother?). None of these was exactly movie star material, which is what some people said about Zanuck's real stars: Tyrone Power, Alice Faye, Sonja Henie, and Don Ameche.

Power, the heir apparent to the talents of a great acting family, was making sixty dollars a week as a novice actor on Broadway in Katharine Cornell's *Saint Joan*, when Fox talent scout Joe Pincus tested him. The test was shipped to the coast, and by chance the day that Zanuck looked at it, his wife Virginia was in the projection room. One look at Power and Zanuck ordered, "Take it off. He looks like a monkey!" Power had a hairline that grew low on his forehead and long hairy eyebrows that almost grew together over his nose. "Shave his eyebrows!" suggested Virginia. And they did. An astounding transformation—from monkey to matinee idol. Zanuck put him in his first picture, *Girls' Dormitory*, which also marked the American debut of Simone Simone. Power had an even shorter part than the Dionnes did in their debut. He walked on in the last scene, and asked, "Could I have this dance?" but when the preview cards said what they liked best was "that guy in the last scene," Zanuck decided Power was a hot property. For his most important production of 1936, *Lloyds of London*, he had originally wanted Don Ameche, but decided to take a chance on Power, and overnight *Lloyds* made Power, at twenty-three, into a big star. In the absence of other stars, Zanuck put him in everything—historical romances, Westerns, contemporary comedies, musi-

cals. Very soon he was one of the top moneymakers in mo
tion pictures.

Power played opposite most of the studio's leading ladies
particularly its two biggest female stars of the day, Alic
Faye and Sonja Henie. A former band singer, Miss Fay
had a brief career with the pre-Twentieth Fox company. Sh
was at that time something of a carbon copy of Jean Harlow
Then in 1936 Zanuck cast her in *King of Burlesque,* like
what he saw, and decided to remake her in her own image
Off came the Harlowesque hair, and, dechromed, she becam
Little Miss Alice Faye. Her big break came in *In Old Chicag*
Taking his cue from MGM's *San Francisco,* Zanuck wante
to make a romantic spectacle about a big city, starring Clar
Gable. He wanted to one-up MGM by starring Harlow op
posite him. But when Gable proved unavailable, he name
Power, and when Harlow got sick he named Alice Faye. A
was customary, Don Ameche filled out the cast. *In Ol*
Chicago became the archetypal Zanuck movie of the lat
thirties. A massive melodrama about the supposed birth c
modern Chicago, it had only the flimsiest basis in fact. Bu
it was a lively show with colorful performances (Alice Brad
won an Academy Award for playing Mrs. O'Leary) and on
spectacular episode: the burning of Old Chicago.

In *In Old Chicago,* Power and Ameche played brother
and in Irving Berlin's *Alexander's Ragtime Band,* Power an
Ameche were best friends, co-bandsmen, and of course riva
in everything including love, i.e., Miss Faye. The relationshi
was as unvarying as Sonja Henie's dimples or Don Ameche
mustache. Just once, one wondered, why didn't Ameche pla
the heel and Power the hero?

Eventually Ameche worked his way into solo starrin
parts, but there was something in his nature that made hir
second best. Perhaps it was that silly mustache (why woul
Alice Faye have taken him even on the rebound, except fo
his strong heart and her strong stomach?). In comparison t
Miss Faye, Sonja Henie was as pure as driven snow, and i
all her movies she was surrounded by it. A ten-time worl
champion ice skater, she was probably the world's bigges
non-movie star in 1938 when Zanuck discovered her. As h
remembers, "I was told to watch the boy she was dancin
with." Instead he could watch only her, and signed her to
contract without a screen test—in purely commercial term

one of Zanuck's best decisions. After *One in a Million,* she went into *Thin Ice,* opposite Power fresh from *Lloyds of London.* The result, a creaky vehicle about a skating instructor who is wooed by a prince disguised as a commoner, was the highest grossing Fox movie of the year. In 1937 she was the highest-paid actress in Hollywood, making $210,729 (compared to Zanuck's $260,000).

Henry Fonda's position at Fox during these years was an unusual one. He had worked at the company since before Zanuck, in *Way Down East* and *The Farmer Takes a Wife,* and he continued to work there during Zanuck's regime, but until *The Grapes of Wrath* he was not under contract for a series of pictures. He never made the box-office impact that Power did, but in the thirties he was by far the better actor, which was never so apparent as in *Jesse James,* which was also directed by Henry King. He played Frank James to Power's Jesse, parts which in outline sound like Classic Power and Ameche: Jesse, daring, roguish, singleminded; Frank, the temperate, judicious voice of conscience. With his cool, understated presence, Fonda stole the picture. Under Zanuck, Fonda also had a prolific collaboration with John Ford, with *Drums Along the Mohawk, Young Mr. Lincoln,* and culminating in *The Grapes of Wrath.*

Zanuck fought to build up his stock company, so that like a mass-audience Medici, he could dub whom he wanted. Casting was a relatively simple process. Barring a loan-out to another studio (and Zanuck's stars were not in demand as much as MGM's were) or a star willing to risk suspension and the wrath of the boss, everyone was available. But as their characters came to be clarified, it was often obvious whom he would cast in what parts. Zanuck did not have, and probably did not want, anyone with too strong a personality.

In the end, as Zanuck intended, the story of Fox in the late thirties is not of stars but of pictures. Unfortunately not many are remembered—or worth remembering. There was Howard Hawks's *The Road to Glory,* starring Fredric March, Warner Baxter, and Lionel Barrymore, and written at least partly by William Faulkner. Zanuck hired Faulkner at Hawks's suggestion, set him up in a bungalow on the studio's writers' row. About five days later he walked into Zanuck's office, and announced, "I can't work in my office. It's driving me crazy. Would you mind if I worked at home?" Zanuck agreed. Faulkner left, and to Zanuck's amazement went home to Oxford, Mississippi. "I thought home meant where he was living in Beverly Hills!" recalls Zanuck. Eventually Zanuck called in Joel Sayre to finish the screenplay with Hawks. There were the John Ford pictures, two of which concerned Lincoln, *Young Mr. Lincoln,* and *The Prisoner of Shark Island,* which was about Dr. Samuel Mudd, the man who treated Booth after he shot Lincoln. The picture was one of the rare instances of an argument between Zanuck and Ford. Zanuck watched the rushes and decided that Warner Baxter, playing Mudd, had a terrible southern accent. He visited the set and told Ford. "If you don't like it, get someone else,' snapped Ford. "God damn it to hell," shouted Zanuck. "Don't threaten me! People don't threaten *me. I* threaten them!" Baxter changed his accent.

The good ones and the bad ones—and in the late thirties Zanuck's bad ones outweighed his good ones—had much in common. The characteristic Zanuck picture of that period was a romanticized look at American history: the building of a city, the founding of a religion, the finding of a musical sound, the making of a president, the invention of a telephone. As Zanuck saw America's past, it was the same movie over and over again, one huge brawling sprawling Quirt-and-Flaggian epic, where in the end, usually with the help of mother love, all conflicts were resolved.

Considering Zanuck's devotion to Americana, it is amazing that he let the greatest American historical romance of all, *Gone With the Wind,* get away, but at least he, unlike Irving Thalberg, tried. "I loved the book and made an offer of $40,000 for it. Zukor offered $45,000. I offered $55,000. Selznick offered more. To end the bidding, at the suggestion of L. B. Mayer, we met in Thalberg's bungalow, the head of the studios, about five. Mayer was for it. The lawyer for the producers presided. Someone suggested, let's put our names on slips of paper and put them in a hat and draw one slip out and whosoever's name is on the slip will purchase it —whatever the price. The lawyer churned the slips around. 'All right, draw one.' The first paper he touched had Selznick's signature on it. That's how he got *Gone With the Wind.* I remember Thalberg smiling like hell because Metro didn't get it."

One of the best measures of Zanuck in the late thirties was

Frank Nugent, the movie critic of the New York *Times,* probably the first and last critic Zanuck paid serious attention to. When they first met in 1935, they were both thirty-two, Zanuck, head of production for Twentieth Century Pictures, Nugent, a reporter on the New York *Times.* When he became a movie critic, Nugent did not pick on Zanuck; it just sometimes seemed that way. Either Zanuck made more bad movies than others did, or his movies were more easily derided. Whatever the case, Fox films of the late thirties were often devastated by Nugent's wit. *Champagne Charlie* he called "graveyard exploration," and thoroughly deplored the "exhuming of a story skeleton that De Maupassant, and others, buried with full literary honors many years ago." He began his review of *A Message to Garcia:* "Gene Fowler, who once proudly confessed that he left his conscience behind whenever he went to Hollywood, proves it beyond a doubt in the ridiculous screenplay." He saved his best invective for Shirley Temple movies. To take just one year, 1936, in April there was *Captain January.* "As a footnote to the operatic cycle," wrote Nugent, "it must be recorded that Shirley Temple sings the sextet from 'Lucia' in her latest picture 'Captain January,' which was trundled into the Capitol yesterday," with a "moss-covered script." In June there was *Poor Little Rich Girl,* "an exercise in Templana," also starring Alice Faye. "Short of becoming a defeated candidate for vice president," said Nugent, "we can think of no better method of guaranteeing one's anonymity than appearing in one of the moppet's films . . ." And in October there was *Dimples.* "The Shirley Temple for President Club reconvened yesterday," wrote Nugent, "and displayed flattering attention to their candidate's latest assault upon the nation's maternal instinct. 'Dimples' is its apt title, apt because it is just another word for Little Miss Precocity and does not pretend to describe the story material it employs. Why they bother with titles, or with plots either . . . is beyond us."

Occasionally Nugent unbended in admiration for Zanuck pictures. *The Country Doctor* was "an irresistibly appealing blend of sentiment and comedy." *Alexander's Ragtime Band* he found the best musical show of 1938; *Wife, Husband, and Friend* "quite the pleasantest show of the week" of February 25, 1939; *Sing, Baby, Sing,* "one of the most amusing picture shows at the Roxy this year," in which Alice Faye "sings . . .

well," passing praise for another passing nemesis. But Nugent kept count of the few Zanuck movies he liked and March 20, 1938, wrote about Zanuck being given the first Irving Thalberg Award, "How can anyone keep a straight face at the antics of the infant industry?" asked Nugent. The jury's selection of Zanuck, he said, "impresses me as being a flat abnegation of the principles for which Mr. Thalberg is supposed to have stood . . . We hate to rub it in, but where was Mr. Zanuck when the 10 best lists went out?" One Zanuck movie Nugent liked was *The Story of Alexander Graham Bell,* which to his amazement starred not Tyrone Power but Don Ameche. He decided to bring that fact to the attention of his public and began his review of the picture "If only because it had omitted Tyrone Power, the Twentieth Century-Fox production of 'The Story of Alexander Graham Bell,' at the Roxy, must be considered one of that company's more sober and meritorious contributions to the historical drama." Incensed at a slam of an actor who wasn't even in the picture, both Fox and the Roxy Theater canceled all advertising in the *Times* for almost a year, a loss of revenue to the *Times* of about $50,000.

About a year later, Zanuck released *The Grapes of Wrath,* and Nugent loved it. "In the vast library where the celluloid literature of the screen is stored, there is one small, uncrowded shelf devoted to the cinema's masterpieces. To that shelf of screen classics, 20th Century-Fox yesterday added 'The Grapes of Wrath.' " Two months later, Zanuck hired Nugent, for $750 a week. As legend had it, Zanuck hired him not for love of his *Grapes of Wrath* review but to stop him from panning lesser efforts. For most of his four years indenture there his duties were undefined. While Bosley Crowther wrote movie reviews for the *Times,* Nugent supposedly wrote them for Fox. He was a sort of resident critic and script doctor. "Zanuck told me he didn't want me to write," he later recalled, "that he just thought the studio would save money if I criticized the pictures before they were made." Occasionally he tried his hand at script writing, but his words never, as he said, "reached the screening except indirectly." On June 7, 1944, he graduated from Fox, but having tasted three-times-salaries, did not go back to criticism. He became a full-time scriptwriter and formed an alliance with John Ford, whose work he had praised so highly in

The Grapes of Wrath. It was, for both, a very creative experience. Nugent wrote, among other pictures, *Fort Apache, She Wore a Yellow Ribbon, The Quiet Man, The Last Hurrah, Cheyenne Autumn.* When Nugent died, the obituaries emphasized the legend: not Nugent the critic, or Nugent the scriptwriter, but Nugent the critic who was bought by Zanuck.

2.

Zanuck in Motion

They don't call them moving *pictures because they* stand
still—*they* move!

—Darryl Zanuck

For most of his Hollywood life, Zanuck lived in Santa Monica
in a beachhouse he had built to order on a stretch of the
Pacific shore. Apparently, in the early years in Santa Monica,
Darryl and Virginia Zanuck were very happy. Looking back
on those days, Virginia says, "We were married in January,
1924. We had thirty-three wonderful happy years. There was
so much love, so much harmony." It was something at least
she worked hard at. One friend remembers Virginia "as a
trim, little, self-disciplined person—like a drum major. She
was a real pro at being Darryl Zanuck's wife."

The children came two years apart, Darrylin in 1931,
Susan in 1933, and Richard Darryl in 1935. When each of
them was born, their father was right there in the delivery
room, up close, on top of the action. "I wanted to be there,"
he explains, "rather than outside waiting for an answer.
Especially I wanted to be there when the boy came." Years
later when his grandchildren were born, Zanuck wanted to
witness those events too, but to his astonishment, the doctors
wouldn't let him. He was disappointed but not as outraged as
he would have been if he couldn't see his son enter the world.
Joyously he greeted his heir and successor, and then went
back to work.

On more normal days, six days a week, Zanuck woke up
at 10 or 10:30. His French tutor of the moment (at first
Edward Leggewie and later Jacques Surmain) would drive
down for a much interrupted daily French lesson, beginning

over breakfast, continuing while Zanuck drove to the studio in his Cadillac. The car was painted Zanuck's private shade of green, called Zanuck Green, the color being prepared especially for Zanuck at the studio. It was used to paint every car owned by every member of the Zanuck family. Even after Darryl Zanuck left Hollywood, Richard Zanuck continued having a green car, and even after Darryl Zanuck left his wife, she continued having a green car. Why green? Susan Zanuck once speculated that it might have something to do with Darryl's mother, who Susan remembered had long, long nails on which she put green lacquered nail polish. Similarly, the license plate on his car was always number 13—his lucky number (his son was born on December 13, "Darryl F. Zanuck" has thirteen letters; later he changed the name of one of his best movies from *32 Rue Madeleine* to *13 Rue Madeleine*). Chatting in French with his tutor, Zanuck drove fast, so fast even on the Fox lot that he was picked up twice by studio policemen for speeding. By 11 he arrived at the studio. Operations had already been humming for several hours, but the pitch intensified as the boss approached. He would enter his office on the first floor of the main administration building. Actually there were four rooms in his office, an outer room (for secretaries and waiting); a long inner office climaxing in Zanuck's desk, a duplicate of George Washington's (a leftover prop from a long-forgotten movie), a back room for trophies and assorted memorabilia; and a narrow bedroom adjacent to the trophy room. The walls of all the rooms were painted Zanuck Green, and so were the telephones.

Pacing the floor of his main office, he would dictate to a battery of secretaries a barrage of memos to producers, directors, and writers, with copies going to all parties concerned—and sometimes to parties not directly concerned. An office boy would stand by for immediate delivery. Sometimes the memos were the briefest notes, which would be typed in red on the original questioning letter: "Go ahead," "Make the best deal you can," "Not interested," "Take me off the hook," "Investigate this." Usually they ran at least a page or two, sometimes twenty, and covered the entire area of moviemaking.

There were criticisms of synopses, story treatments, and scripts:

"The new treatment on *The Great American Broadcast* is, in my opinion, an almost deliberate attempt to sabotage an excellent story idea. All character, punch and vitality has been eliminated.'

Sometimes he was terse in his criticism:

"I read first the synopsis of *Low Tide* by John Truesdell. It made me vomit."

He analyzed audiences:

"Somehow or other audiences are always suspicious and unsympathetic to the idea of a mother surrendering her child . . ."

"I know the audiences today want popular crap, but I cannot believe that we are so lacking that we cannot dish it up to them with some traces of originality."

And the box office:

"The enormous box-office success of *Samson and Delilah* does not indicate that the public wants biblical pictures. It indicates that they will accept a biblical picture providing it is loaded with box-office ingredients and showmanship. *Samson and Delilah* is basically a sex story and when you can get one in biblical garb apparently you can open your own mint."

He contemplated his own pictures:

"In *Public Enemy* I gave Cagney one redeeming trait. He was a no-good bastard but he loved his mother and somehow or other you felt a certain affection and rooting interest for him even though he was despicable."

"The woman in *Leave Her to Heaven* deliberately kills her own unborn child, drowns the crippled brother of her husband, and endeavors to send her adopted sister to the electric chair. And yet, despite all this, there are certain things about her that you rather like."

And those of his rivals:

"*The Treasure of Sierra Madre* was a box-office failure in spite of receiving high critical acclaim and the reason it failed was because it turned out to be one long, detailed character study. It lacked pace, excitement, and the *sweep* of action. I think the same story told in hard-hitting, realistic terms with accent on honest and legitimate melodrama would have found a different reception from the public. Let us not fall into this pit.'

He discussed casting:

"Fonda should never play [George Washington], in my

opinion because he has already played Young Mr. Lincoln. If he does play it, then by all means we must eventually let him play Young Benjamin Franklin."

He worried about length of treatments and scripts:

"A treatment should not exceed 20 or 25 pages . . . Many times after reading a 70-page treatment, I have gone back and written in six or seven pages, my own sequence-by-sequence skeleton synopsis of the story. I have done this so that I could properly judge the story line itself stripped of all embellishments."

He announced assignments, assigned credits, including his own (whether a picture should be "produced by DFZ" or "DFZ's production of"), suggested old movies to be rerun as guides for new movies, rewrote dialogue, canceled projects, moaned about the state of Hollywood and the state of the world, welcomed new employees (to Charles Brackett: "the steam room downstairs is at your disposal, and also Sam, the barber"), distributed praise as well as scorn, changed titles, and changed his mind (depending on the grosses, a picture could go from great to terrible in a swirl of memos). Except to his top personnel and specific producers, directors and writers he was working with, he was accessible largely through memos. He hardly ever met an agent, and actors only when he had to. Strangers seldom invaded his lair, although on one occasion a man named Carl Erickson did. He hid in Zanuck's office, and when the boss entered, he appeared holding a revolver. He demanded a job in the story department. Zanuck convinced him to put his gun away and hired him. Erickson subsequently worked several years for Zanuck— until he shot himself.

At one-thirty Zanuck would have lunch in his private dining room in the company commissary, the Cafe de Paris, with all his producers and directors, and sometimes important outsiders (such as Joseph P. Kennedy). To his right was the position of honor, and usually it was occupied by the pet director of the moment. His favorite food, remembers Nick Janios, his trusted commissary keeper, "was bread and gravy. He would push the meat aside. He never ate his vegetables. He liked cream gravies—and steak and potatoes." He smoked all morning, during lunch, and the rest of the day. In fact then as now he was never without a cigar in his mouth, in the center of his mouth, usually tipping his head towards the floor. (The cigars came from a plantation in Cuba he bought with Douglas Fairbanks, Sr., Cecil B. de Mille, and Alexander Korda.)

After lunch, he held his story conferences, usually with the producer, director, and writer, on each picture. One hard-backed chair was placed dead center in front of Zanuck's desk. The rest of the chairs were lined along the wall. The hard chair was the hot chair, and everyone was afraid to sit there. One had to be prepared not only to defend one's contribution to a picture but one's existence. Usually no one had anything to say about it. Zanuck sat whom he wanted in the hot chair, and usually it was the Writer, or as he was more often known, to distinguish him from those who replaced him, "The Present Writer." The producers and directors were allowed the safety of the arena. During the conference, Zanuck would sit at his desk, stand up, pace the room, swinging his practice polo mallet and puffing on his cigar. The assembly listened. Molly Mandaville, his script coordinator, transcribed. And while he talked and walked, he straightened photographs and statues. If a janitor had moved an object so much as a millimeter he knew it, and replaced it in its proper spot. He never lost track of the conversation. Mostly he analyzed scripts, often ripping one to shreds and improvising another. He threw out ideas with machine-gun rapidity. He would act out all the parts, and narrate as well. Demonstrating what he wanted Jimmy Stewart to do in *Jackpot,* he suddenly dropped to the floor, and under his desk, and never stopped talking. He could always smell a weakness and never seemed at a loss for a solution. A writer would come up with a solution that was better than his, and he would say, "That's it." But if he thought his solution was better, he held to it with an iron fist. As one writer says, "He couldn't stand stubbornness in anybody but himself." Conferences would go on for hours—with no food or drink allowed. Then Molly Mandaville would write up the notes, smoothing out some of the prose but otherwise leaving it untouched. Sometimes an unsure director and writer would put something verbatim from Molly's notes into the script (usually something made up by Zanuck) and run it off on the mimeo. Zanuck would read the new material and blow up. "Who the shit wrote this dialogue?" he would say. Smart writers knew that Zanuck's dialogue was only meant as an outline, or an

approach. Just to accentuate the point, Molly would sometimes add a note to the transcript, instructing the writer, "For
God's sake, don't take it word for word."

At 6 P.M. business stopped at Twentieth Century-Fox, and
Zanuck briefly rested. He went down to the basement steam
room (painted Zanuck Green), barber shop, swimming pool,
massage table, card room, and social club run by his old
friend Sam Silver. Zanuck had discovered Sam in 1933,
barbering at the Hillcrest Country Club (and made him into
a star of the steam room). For thirty-seven years Sam the
Barber had been, along with Nick Janios (Nick the Greek),
one of his most trusted employees. The steam room was the
scene of many of Zanuck's most famous practical jokes, and
Sam was a party to most of them, either as collaborator or
victim. Once after some heavy horseback riding, Tyrone
Power, one of the few actors ever granted steam room priv-
ileges, came in for a steam, then jumped in the pool, which
he liked at exactly 52 degrees. This particular day, the pool
was more like 2 degrees; Zanuck had put four tons of ice
in it. Seldom did the gag backfire on Zanuck. Twice a week
he and Sam, who looks like a huge, bald Cossack, went
horseback riding, Sam riding first to blaze a trail for the boss
(each time a new trail). Once producer William Perlberg
joined them, and Zanuck said, "Let's take him somewhere
there's poison ivy." Perlberg didn't get poison ivy, but Zanuck
did. On occasion Zanuck called employees, fully clothed,
into the steam room for a conference. After he steamed,
Zanuck would have a massage, then he would sleep, lying on
his side with his finger to his mouth (which in fact, says
Sam, is the way Richard Zanuck sleeps too). At 7:30 he
would be awakened, usually by a studio policeman, and he
would have dinner, either in the commissary, or at Romanoff's. Then he would go back to the job, and beginning at
8:30 he would work on pictures into the night, sometimes as
late as 3 or 4 A.M. These were long, hard work sessions and
few outsiders were allowed to break his regimen. One who
did, on frequent occasions, was another night person, Howard
Hughes, "a man I admired and still do," says Zanuck. The
only regular intrusions on this six-day-and-night studio week
were his yearly excursions to Sun Valley. He traveled abroad
frequently of course, and as always carried his business with
him, but Sun Valley was the only trip that was ritual. Every

year he would ski there and take along a portable studio—secretaries, producers, directors, writers—whomever he was working with at the moment—set up an office and a projection room, and *après* ski he would relax with rushes and rough cuts. He even carried his film-compulsion into the skiing itself. At Sun Valley he discovered his ski instructor, Otto Lang, and liked him so much that he made him a producer. He produced many pictures for Zanuck including Joe Mankiewicz's *Five Fingers*.

Back at the studio, Zanuck had his private projection room with his private projectionist, Irving Holden. Every evening sitting in the same leather chair with his hand on the volume control and chainsmoking cigars—he would never light a match—he immersed himself in the world of film. He would watch the rushes of every movie shot by Fox, and he would screen rough, and then final, cuts of all of his pictures, and when there was time would show film from rival studios. His closest associates would attend these screenings; producers, directors, and writers involved in the film (although on occasion those most directly would be excluded), top personnel not involved in that picture (other producers and directors, Lew Schreiber, Henry Lehrman), his favorite film editor, Barbara McLean, Molly Mandaville, Edward Leggewie, and his trio of house critics: Sam Silver, Nick Janios, and Harry Wardell, a jury of peers that he trusted probably above all others. "I valued Nick's opinion," says Zanuck. "I knew he was the total audience. I knew that Sam the Barber was a reflection of the noncreative people, audiences not interested in bloody dissolves, who laugh when the joke was good—or bad." One thing he liked about the three of them was that they were never afraid to speak their minds. "Wardell didn't know what end of the camera to look through, but he would be violent for or against a picture. He would say, 'How can that sonofabitch director draw a salary?'" Actually Wardell's position was more court jester than court critic. He was the prime butt of Zanuck's practical jokes. "The worst trick I ever did on him," remembers Zanuck. "He had a complete upper plate. No teeth at all. I found out who his dentist was and got another set of plates, with a little difference so that they didn't fit. Wardell took his plate out at a screening, as he always did, and I switched plates. After the screening was over, he couldn't talk!"

Under Zanuck's orders, all was quiet while a movie was on, and when it ended, the silence continued. The lights came on, and everyone waited for Zanuck to speak, trying to read his reaction from the back of his neck. Then Zanuck would rise, begin to pace, and dissect the movie, inch by inch. He could be ecstatic in his enthusiasm or brutal in his assault. When he finished talking—and only when he finished talking —the yes-men joined in. "I knew I was surrounded by yes-men," says Zanuck. "Sometimes I encouraged them, purely for the sake of amusement: if I said green and knew damn well it's red, just to see what they would say. They were not really yes-men, they were want-to-please men." But he also had no-men like Lamar Trotti and Nunnally Johnson. "Nunnally was brutally frank, a Rock of Gibraltar. If he thought something stank, it stank." But, wisely, the no-men kept their opinions to themselves until he asked for them. "If I didn't say anything for a long while they knew I hated it. They would hope maybe I would lift the iffiness from them, or maybe I could cure the picture, or explain to them why it wasn't good." The atmosphere was tense, the audience nervous— almost beyond belief. Only Zanuck relaxed, and he working the hardest of all.

One producer-director was so panicked by an approaching rough cut that he asked writer Dick Murphy what he should do. "For one thing," said Murphy, "don't open your trap until he says his piece." The night of the rough cut, Zanuck sat in his chair at the controls with, as usual, Molly on one side of him and Barbara on the other. Whenever something in the picture bothered him, Zanuck would nudge Barbara with his elbow and she would remember the point. "Sit behind Bobby," Murphy advised the producer, "and every time he nudges, you'll know what's bothering him." The producer followed instructions. He couldn't keep his eyes on the screen. He was too busy watching for the nudging. The first few minutes, Zanuck kept nudging every second, and then he didn't nudge her again for the rest of the picture. The lights went on. Silence. Twenty minutes went by. Still no sound. Everyone waited. The producer began to sweat. Finally Zanuck spoke: "Let's run it tomorrow night. I fell asleep after five minutes."

After watching the rough cut of *Three Coins in the Fountain*, Zanuck got up, left the projection room without saying a word to anybody. Everyone sat in stunned silence. Then the movie's director, Jean Negulesco, went out and threw up on the sidewalk. The picture was a total disaster, and in a classic case of Zanuck's editing ability, he reworked the entire script on film, redubbing new dialogue into actors' mouths, having other new dialogue come from actors' backs. The result was an enormous commercial success.

As Zanuck explains his talent, "I work hard on scripts. I'm a good script editor. But I think if I have any talent at all, it's in editing in the cutting room, more so even than editing a script. All pictures are invariably long. I found out that sometimes it's good to start with them too long. Then when you see it in the cutting room you realize what the hell, you've already expressed the same thought. I run a picture three times, stop after every reel, ask what does that tell us. That's why cutting sessions run so long at night."

When Zanuck was satisfied with a cut, he would take the movie off to be previewed, and would tote his staff with him —including Sam, Nick, and Harry. Immediately after the picture they would all gather for a conference, which producer Sy Bartlett remembers as "curbstone autopsies." Sometimes they became violent. On one occasion, Zanuck got so angry at something director Michael Curtiz—a huge, hulking Hungarian—said, he flattened him cold outside the theater. On another occasion, after a preview, he and his staff huddled in the doorway of a candy store. A bystander who had seen the picture wandered into the huddle and gave his opinion. Everyone figured he was from the studio and listened intently. Zanuck thought he made a great deal of sense. Then the man walked away and got on a bus. Zanuck asked what department he was in and when he discovered the man did not work for him at all, he sent someone to follow him and hire him. Another time, after a preview he shouted to an assistant director to get him some item, and when he brought the wrong thing, Zanuck said, "The next time I want to send a dumb son of a bitch for something, I'll go myself." Gregory Ratoff previews were often disasters, and were not mitigated by the fact that when Zanuck attacked a picture, Ratoff broke down in tears. One was an absolute fiasco. Solemnly they drove back to the studio for the burial, with Ratoff crying all the way. "How could I have done this to you, Derril? What a tragedy." As the car approached the gate of the lot,

Ratoff, weeping wildly, opened the door and said, "I'm going to kill myself," climbed out, and began running. "For Christ's sake, stop him," said Zanuck, and he shouted after him, "Don't worry. I'll cut it. I'll fix it. Come out to the house." Ratoff got back in the car and, sobbing uncontrollably, he was driven to the Zanuck home in Santa Monica and put into bed in a spare room. Zanuck went downstairs, and when a long time had passed and he hadn't heard anything, he decided to tiptoe back upstairs. He peeked in. Ratoff was sleeping soundly, like a baby. Zanuck shook him awake violently and shouted, "You son of a bitch! How the fuck can you sleep?"

Actually Zanuck had little faith in previews and finally abolished them entirely. "I'm not going to take a picture out to San Bernardino or some jerk town and let a lot of yokels tell me what I think. Give even an intelligent moviegoer a preview card and ask him or her to fill it out, and they automatically become Vince Canby or Judith Crist." In the final analysis, there was one person whose opinion mattered most.

3.

"Family Pictures"

*Listen, I'm apolitical and so is Darryl. Darryl just said ".
think there's a good story in it."*

—John For

In May 1939 Zanuck addressed himself to Nunnally Johnso
whom he had assigned to write the screenplay of his lates
purchase, John Steinbeck's current and controversial best
seller *The Grapes of Wrath*. "I think you should start to worl
immediately on a skeleton outline . . . so that we can defin
where we are going and what is the time and what is th
climax objective . . ." In July, he added, "I want complet
secrecy in reference to *The Grapes of Wrath* script. Instea
of having the first script mimeographed, as is our usua
custom, I want you to make only three copies—one for your
self and two for me. A number of more or less unfriendl
newspapermen are waiting to grab our first script to actuall
find out what we have done with this great book."

Very early he decided to talk with John Steinbeck. Havin
sold the book outright to Zanuck, for $100,000, Steinbeck
had no power over the screenplay, but Zanuck felt it woul
be better to have him on his side from the beginning. "H
was highly suspicious," recalls Zanuck. He called Steinbeck
into his office and announced, "We intend to follow the exac
book. But there are certain things we can't show. We can'
show the baby sucking the woman's breast. These things car
never be passed by the Hays office." Then Zanuck added, "
never have been satisfied with the last scene, when Joad
leaves. I have the feeling I'd like to hear from the old mar
and lady."

"I don't know about that," said Steinbeck.

Suddenly Zanuck's secretary buzzed him on the intercom. "Mr. Zanuck, there's been an accident on one of our sets!" she said excitedly. "Shirley Temple has lost her tooth, and . . ."

"Her *front* tooth?" interrupted Zanuck.

"Her front tooth," affirmed the secretary.

"For God sakes, tell 'em to do something," said Zanuck.

"They feel it's such an important event you should come to the set," said the secretary.

During the exchange, Steinbeck listened silently. Finally he said to Zanuck, "Don't bother about me. *The Grapes of Wrath* is unimportant compared to Shirley Temple's tooth."

"Just get the best dentist," ordered Zanuck, "and close down the company!" Then he turned to Steinbeck and continued the conversation.

From the beginning to end Zanuck worked closely on the script with Nunnally Johnson, expanding, cutting, revising. Johnson, a colorful, critical ex-newsman, is unabashed in his admiration for Zanuck as editor. "He was the *best* editor in chief," he declares flatly. "His greatest value, his greatest talent was that he could read a script. In a page and a half, some kind of buzzer says to him, something is dull here; it's not moving. We would go over a script, line by line. He would always ask what could be done to improve it. If you came up with another solution he was quite flexible about it. To me he was a collaborator on anything I ever did. Every script I wrote was improved by his editing."

With crusty John Ford as director, one might expect an enormous clash of personalities. If there was any, it has been forgotten through the years. To Ford, Johnson, and Zanuck, the memory of *Grapes* is one of complete communication and common purpose.

Once the script was written, Zanuck left Ford alone, for the most part. His suggestions were usually to improve, not to change, or embellish nor to distort what Ford was doing. Says Ford, "One of his greatest assets was to supply the proper music—and sound effects. He held music down to a minimum. And with sound effects, he was absolutely uncanny. He'd put things in I'd never dream of. In *Grapes of Wrath* there was a scene with an itinerant preacher [John Carradine] and a swamp under a bridge, and Darryl put in the sound of crickets, and you *knew* you were in a swamp. Later there was this English picture [*The Third Man*] with one instrument, a zither playing all the way through it that they talked a lot about, but it was not the first time that was done. In *Grapes* Darryl used a single, lightly played accordion—not a big orchestra—and it was very American, and very right for the picture."

Actually the most important change Zanuck made on the picture, and the most controversial, was that new end that he had wanted, and Zanuck made the change after Ford had finished the picture. Originally, in the end, Tom Joad leaves his family to become a labor organizer and activist, to do something not only for the Joads but all oppressed workers. Zanuck wanted something tidier, and he wrote a speech for Ma Joad. As she and the remainder of her family leave the government camp, which had provided the first stability they had known since Oklahoma, and headed once again toward the promise of jobs, she said to her husband, "For a while it looked like we was beat . . . We're the *people*. Can't nobody wipe us out . . . We'll go on forever 'cause we're the people." This ended the movie on a note, many considered, of forced sentimentality, but Zanuck was—and is—proud of the speech (especially proud that some people, including critics, assumed it was directly from the book—which proves of course, to his way of thinking that it should have been in the book in the first place). Ford explains the inclusion: "This picture ended on a down note, and the way Zanuck changed it, it came out on an upbeat." But Ford had no objection.

Ford went to Honolulu, and Zanuck supervised the cutting, ordered the movie released. He was so convinced of the movie's quality and importance that for its premiere in New York he invited what he considered would be its stiffest audience—scions of industry, socialites, dowagers, board members of Fox—and they loved it. So did the critics. The movie was a tremendous hit, Fox's biggest success of the year, and it proved, in spite of warnings (mostly within the industry), that controversy could be profitable. Viewed again today, it is still quite an effective picture. It is not as dense nor as harsh as Steinbeck's book, but as a movie it is surprisingly successful, full of evocative moments that speak much longer than their duration on screen, full of character detail that is as true as it is sensitive. A lot of it is due to performance: Fonda, and, in the small part of the preacher Casy, John Car-

radine, perhaps the most touching of all as he forsakes his
profession until he can find his calling, at the receiving end
of a club.

In *The Grapes of Wrath*, Zanuck has taken an urgent problem (as he was to do later with racial discrimination, religious
prejudice, and insanity), and dramatized it, making it palat-
able to a wide public, not by softening it but by humanizing
it. In 1939 it took considerable daring and courage for
Zanuck to film *The Grapes of Wrath*—while it was hot—and
to do it so faithfully and movingly.

One month after *The Grapes of Wrath* was released Zanuck
bought the rights to Richard Llewellyn's *How Green Was My
Valley*, a sudden best-seller at the time. Whereas *Grapes* was
a social protest, *How Green Was My Valley* was something
of a pastoral romance—with a social point, of course. Perhaps
because of the foreign setting, perhaps because of the success
he had to follow, probably because of the price he had to pay
for it, Zanuck felt he was taking a risk. He assigned Ernest
Pascal, a Llewellyn enthusiast, to write the script, and in May
offered a criticism of the work to date. "I am disappointed in
the script, mainly because it has turned into a labor story and
a sociological problem story instead of a great human, warm
story about real living people. I think we should take a
revolutionary viewpoint of the screenplay of this story and
we should tell it as the book does—through the eyes of Huw,
the little boy. We should do much of the picture with him as
an off-stage commentator with many of the scenes running
silent and nothing but his voice over them. And then, of
course, from time to time we will let the voice dissolve into
scenes.

"If we use this technique we can capture much of the
wonderful descriptive dialogue of the book, particularly when
the boy talks about the valley and about his father and
mother . . .

"This is a revolutionary type of story; therefore, our treatment should not be revolutionary. Now it fumbles around and
I get the impression that we are trying to do an English
Grapes of Wrath and prove that the mineowners were very
mean and that the laborers finally won out over them. All
this might be fine if it were happening today, like *Grapes of
Wrath*, but this is years ago and who gives a damn? The smart
thing to do is to try to keep all of the rest in the background

and focus mainly on the human story as seen through Huw's eyes."

Except for his social conservatism and his cynicism about the relevance of the Welsh miners' problems, the memo made a great deal of sense, and displayed a clear understanding of just what story he wanted to tell. And as it turned out, his concept of May 1940 remained the concept of the movie through its script transformations. Pascal was replaced by Philip Dunne, William Wyler was named director. In November 1940 he read the "present script," cut it, and wrote Wyler, ". . . After reading the last half of the story and studying it, I am more than ever convinced that the boy, Huw, should never grow up . . . Now is the time for us to start talking in terms of drama and audience. I was bored to death by the repetition of the strike business and of starving babies, etc. etc. It all seems old hash to me . . ." Finally, by April 1941, the script was finished to Zanuck's satisfaction, the cast was complete, the picture scheduled, and then shelved. When it was activated again Wyler had gone to another project. John Ford was signed as his replacement and production began in June. *How Green Was My Valley* became very much a John Ford picture, a perfect complement and contrast to his previous year's, and previous collaboration, *The Grapes of Wrath*. But taken together, *Grapes* and *Valley* showed a new face of Zanuck, one that really did value story first.

Several years later Zanuck allowed himself some second thoughts about turning novels into movies, specifically *The Grapes of Wrath, How Green Was My Valley*, and *The Song of Bernadette*. ". . . You cannot ever hope to put an entire novel on screen. Just as it does in the dramatization of a stage play, it becomes a matter of selection and elimination. We were very successful . . . with the critics and the public, yet we never attempted to do anything but dramatize a certain portion of each book. Many entire sub-plots and certain leading characters were totally eliminated, yet the films carried the true spirit of the books, and we were enabled to expand and dramatize the incidents and characters we retained . . . In *Grapes of Wrath* we had to make a very vital decision . . . whether to tell the story of the Okies as a whole or the story of one isolated family. This meant the elimination of the flood which took four chapters of the book. It meant the elimination of the fights with the police. It meant the dropping of certain characters very important in the book and writing an entirely new last act. It succeeded and received the endorsement of everyone, including Steinbeck." And then about *How Green Was My Valley*, "When I think of what I got away with . . . and won the Academy Award with the picture, it is really astonishing. Not only did we drop five or six characters but we eliminated the most controversial element in the book which was the labor and capital battle in connection with the strike."

For Zanuck, *The Grapes of Wrath* and *How Green Was My Valley* were not really social documents but family pictures of a very special kind; movies about families in stress. That they were both commercially successful proved that artistry and controversy need not be antithetical to box-office receipts. As for Zanuck, not since *The Public Enemy* and *I Am a Fugitive from a Chain Gang* had he revealed such an adventurousness about subject matter, such a willingness to experiment outside the Hollywood formula, and such an ability to stir the public's conscience. The sad thing was that it was to be several years before he did it again.

4.

Showmanship

What we need on the payroll is a combination of P. T. Barnum and Buffalo Bill Cody.

—Darryl Zanuck

Even before it hit the rest of America, World War II hit Hollywood. In one blow it eliminated the European market. Zanuck mobilized his machinery, cutting back on his number of personal productions (although he did hire a few new producers including Mark Hellinger and Willian LeBaron, and directors Jean Renoir, Fritz Lang, and his old compatriot from Warner Brothers, Ernst Lubitsch). The negative situation gave Zanuck a chance to re-evaluate his position and consolidate his theories of moviemaking. In April 1940, he addressed himself to his producers:

"Our industry is in the throes of a revolutionary period . . . Today more than ever this business is a business of *showmanship*. Audiences do not go to the movies out of habit or just to pass the time. They *only* go when there is something playing that they definitely *want* to see. We pay entirely too much attention to good scripts—and not enough attention to good *subjects*.

"Audiences certainly appreciate fine writing and fine technical qualities but, after all, they do not pay for these things or think about these things when they decide what movie they are going to see . . . But not the greatest cast in the world can make them go to see a subject that they don't like or a subject that seems slight, empty or hackneyed.

"It may sound stupid to say so, but I would rather have a bad script on a great subject than a great script on an ordinary subject . . . Star power is valueless no matter how big the personalities or even if they are Clark Gable and Joan Crawford combined, unless the subject matter in the story stands the test.

"What do I mean by subject matter? I mean stories that are about *something*. I do not mean that every story has to be *Western Union* or *Brigham Young,* but at least these are stories that deal with something more than the usual formula output of most studios."

The following May, he further defined his position:

". . . box-office receipts throughout the nation have taken an alarming decline . . . No film, regardless of its size or quality, is getting what it deserves at the box-office. Therefore, the selection of story material becomes our Number One problem at this time. Of course, it is always a Number One problem—but now, before we purchase a story or start working on an original idea of adaptation, we have got to be doubly certain to the best of our ability that the ingredients of the prospective picture lend themselves to top-grade production . . . We should not buy any play or book regardless of how promising it seems as a popular attraction unless we feel that it *also* contains the ingredients of a popular moving picture, whether or not it ever becomes a best-seller or a stage hit." And then Zanuck announced that he was stopping work on seven or eight properties. "If we don't stop we suddenly find that we have fifty or sixty thousand dollars tied up in a story and then, knowing that we have all of this money invested, we are inclined to put it into production regardless of its *actual* merit—and then, of course, we pay for it later on . . ."

Certainly much of Zanuck's reasoning was a response to his rivals. MGM had the stars. Fox didn't. Therefore the subject, not the star, was the star. But it was a legitimate point, and proved prophetic. Today subject and story are the star. What he said about abandonment was also prophetic, in light of *Cleopatra,* and even *Dr. Dolittle,* and *Star!* A statement like, "It is pretty difficult to spoil a great subject or a great theme," seems naïve, especially considering all the greatness Hollywood has messed up. But what Zanuck probably meant was that it was easier to spoil a *lesser* subject or theme. The truth is that in the early forties, more often than not he did not follow his own advice. His picture were not marked by subject matter. They were in fact mostly formula pictures.

But as Zanuck perfected it, the formula was almost an exact science.

Zanuck's formula films fell into two major categories, Remakes and Sequels, both founded on the premise that if you've got a good thing, do it again. As an attitude it was directly opposite to Zanuck's stand in the late twenties and early thirties at Warners, when he began cycles—and stopped them. Certainly in the late thirties and early forties he was not the only offender. Remakes and Sequels were popular throughout Hollywood, but nowhere were in such abundant evidence as at Fox. A Partial Remake usually took only one ingredient, but a main ingredient, of a successful picture, such as the re-use of a plot device. Zanuck's favorite, which he first used in *Lloyds of London*, he described as "the story of two young boys who loved each other . . . and then . . . parted; one became a famous man and the other became more or less insignificant, but the insignificant one made possible the greatest victory of the famous one." A Total Remake meant a complete change of scene and transposition of character. Only relationships and plot remained the same. The theory was that there were only a limited number of plots in the first place. *Love Is News,* which Zanuck made with Tyrone Power and Loretta Young in 1937, was about an heiress who falls in love with a reporter who has been criticizing her. Zanuck remade it as a musical, *Sweet Rosie O'Grady,* in 1943, with Robert Young and Betty Grable, and again, in 1949, as a straight comedy again starring Tyrone Power. He briefly considered naming it *Love Is Still News,* but changed his mind and called it *That Wonderful Urge.* Gene Tierney played the girl. Actually the relationship is at least as old as *It Happened One Night,* which wasn't Zanuck's, and was made in 1934. A typical variation was in the musical *On the Avenue,* in which Dick Powell played a singer-playwright who satirized an heiress (Madeleine Carroll) in his latest play. Another favorite Zanuck theme was the hick who shows up the city yokels (as in his *Telephone Girl* episode, *Sherlock's Home*). He used it in *Thanks for Everything* (Jack Haley in 1938) and in *The Magnificent Dope* (Henry Fonda in 1942), although it had already been done, by Columbia in *Mr. Deeds Goes to Town* (Gary Cooper in 1936). *The Bowery* in 1933 moved across the river in 1943 to become *Coney Island,* and both were really *What Price Glory* in civilian dress. Zanuck's *Kentucky* of 1938 moved all the way to Rio de Janeiro in *Down Argentine Way* in 1940, taking its horse farm with it, although leaving Walter Brennan behind. Probably the most durable Zanuck Remake began in 1935 with a movie called *Folies Bergere,* in which a *Folies-Bergère* star (Maurice Chevalier) is mistaken for a Parisian financier (Maurice Chevalier). The movie co-starred Merle Oberon as the financier's wife and Ann Sothern as the star's girl friend. In 1942 Zanuck moved *Follies* to Rio de Janeiro and made *That Night in Rio.* Don Ameche played a Brazilian financier and an American vaudevillian, with Alice Faye and Carmen Miranda as the wife and the girl friend. In 1951, Zanuck dug up the property again and sent it *On the Riviera.* Danny Kaye played a French flying ace and an American entertainer and Gene Tierney and Corinne Calvet were the wife and the girl friend. Actually it all began with the French play, *The Red Cat.* Sometimes the theory of Remakes was stretched to ridiculous lengths, on at least one occasion by Bryan Foy, who was in charge of Zanuck's B pictures in the forties. He assigned Henry and Phoebe Ephron to remake *To the Shores of Tripoli* as *Rip Goes to War,* with a dog playing the John Payne part.

Zanuck was aware of his rivals' successes as he was of his own, and although he preferred to capitalize on his own, he was not averse to using someone else's. Usually the new film was not so much a copy as a contrast. If they could do it black, why couldn't they do it white. The success of MGM's *Meet Me in St. Louis* inspired Fox's *Centennial Summer,* and for a time Zanuck even considered calling it *See You in Philadelphia.* The Ridiculous Length Award again goes to Zanuck's B department. The order went out one day from Bryan Foy, "Do you know anybody at Warner Brothers? Can you get him to steal a script of *Air Force?* I want to do *Air Force* in a submarine." When Jack Warner found out about the projected thievery, he supposedly said, "Tell him to take the script of *Crash Dive* and *Up Periscope.*" On another occasion, Fox's A department bought a property, started to make it, and then discovered that Foy had already stolen it for his Fox unit and was making it with Sonny Tufts.

Zanuck's big hit of 1939 was *Jesse James.* Since Jesse died in the end, Zanuck couldn't bring him back, but there was still his brother Frank, and the following year he produced *The Return of Frank James.* Many preferred the Sequel to

Series cycle: The Cisco Kid was always riding again. The Jones Family (Jed Prouty and Spring Byington as a small-town druggist and his wife), who were often directed by Zanuck's old Rin Tin Tin partner, Mal St. Clair, traveled almost as much ground as Carmen Miranda. Charlie Chan (whom Zanuck had inherited from William Fox) went from Shanghai to Reno, and inspired another oriental eye, Mr. Moto. In 1939 Mr. Moto gave his *Last Warning* in January, stopped by *Danger Island* in April, then took a *Vacation* and never returned. By 1941 The Cisco Kid and the Jones Family had died, unmourned. Only Charlie Chan had one more place to visit, Rio, some five months after Carmen Miranda had been there.

At least partly because of the similarity of pictures, titles assumed an enormous importance. By the choice of title, an audience could be led to expect a certain kind of picture. For example, in 1941, Zanuck thought *Hello, Frisco, Hello* a great title, and decided to make a movie out of it. Then he memoed: "Someone [probably Zanuck himself] who heard that I was writing this note made the following suggestion, which may not be entirely wrong. They said that instead of trying to write a new story about Frisco, which, after all, can never be very original, why not take the plot of *In Old Chicago* and place it in San Francisco—even going so far as to replace the fire with the earthquake. Instead of telling the story of the O'Leary family, which was the basis of *Chicago*, we tell the story of another family who came to San Francisco in the early days, and instead of telling the story of a mother who raised a family we would have the mother die in the prologue and have the father raise a family of three girls instead of three sons . . . I don't know how we can parallel the situation that developed in *Chicago* when brother turned against brother, but with a little thought this might be arranged . . ."

Somewhere along the line, Zanuck decided that *Hello, Frisco, Hello*, instead of being a Remake of *In Old Chicago*, would be a Remake of *King of Burlesque*. And it was.

Actually Zanuck believed not only in the importance but in the interchangeability of titles. A typical exchange: on January 13, 1941 Zanuck wrote producer William LeBaron, "For the second time I am taking a title away from you on the same picture. I am stuck for a title on *Lazy Galahad*, and I am going to have to call it *Strictly Dynamite*. Therefore, we will have to get another title for your musical, and anyway, I don't think *Strictly Dynamite* is such a good title for a musical. Until we find a title, you can call it *The Prizefight Musical*." On the same day he informed producer William Perlberg, "We have got a great title for *Lazy Galahad*. We will call it *Strictly Dynamite*. This is a title that I had on one of the other pictures, but it can easily be made to fit *Lazy Galahad*." On January 19, he wrote both Perlberg and Le-Baron, "We have again changed the title of *Strictly Dynamite* and will call it *The Magnificent Jerk*. I am returning the title *Strictly Dynamite* to William LeBaron to put on the picture that we originally took it from, which is the prizefight musical." But LeBaron was not to have it again for long. On February 23, Zanuck informed him, "We must get a new title right away for *Strictly Dynamite*. This does not sound like a musical and this picture should have a title that has as much color and glamour as the story has." So that night Zanuck sat down and wrote some titles. "Do any of these appeal to you?" he asked Le Baron, and suggested, *Broadway Serenade, Footlight Serenade, Main Stem Serenade, Orchids for the Champ, Lovely to Look At, A Million to One, Orchids for You, Front Cover Girl, The Chorus Girl, and the Champ*. Eventually the Perlberg picture was called *The Magnificent Dope*, and the LeBaron *Footlight Serenade*.

Alice Faye was fading, but Zanuck had a number of young girls on the rise—Maureen O'Hara, Anne Baxter, Brenda Joyce, Linda Darnell, Cobina Wright, Jr., Kay Aldrich, and Gene Tierney, and, most important, Betty Grable.

After a brief dead-end movie career at RKO and Paramount, Miss Grable turned to the stage, scored a major success in *DuBarry Was a Lady*, and was picked up by Zanuck. She became Miss Faye's successor, both as Fox's blonde and Fox's musical star. She proved one of Zanuck's most durable stars, lasting until the next big blonde (of another sort) came along years later, Marilyn Monroe. In 1943 Betty Grable was named the number one star by the movie exhibitors, the first woman so honored. She was the number one box-office star during the war; in 1947 and 1948 she was the highest-paid woman in the country, earning $208,000 a year. For thirteen years, she was among the top ten box-office personalities, a record unmatched by any other actress. It was estimated that she brought in $5 million annually to Fox. She was the No. 1 pinup girl of World War II.

Even as Zanuck ground out the sunshiny musicals, he was very much aware of the approaching World War II. With film as his weapon he soon began to fight the cause. In October he decided to make a movie called *The Eagle Squadron,* about an American test pilot who enlists in the RAF. As Zanuck dictated the story outline the pilot is "a fellow like Tyrone Power played in *In Old Chicago.* He is a cocksure know-it-all, a breezy, brash young guy," who gets killed in the first big German air attack on Britain. Within a month, the movie was called *The Eagle Flies Again.* In January, at the unofficial request of British officials, Zanuck agreed that the American should live. And it was decided he would get the girl (Betty Grable), and that the movie would be called *A Yank in the RAF.* The movie went into production with Tyrone Power as the Yank, as Zanuck had originally intended. As the movie progressed Zanuck was so happy with it, he was already considering a sequel, about an American woman soldier in England *(A WAF in the RAF?).* The next month he changed his mind and thought about a reverse reverse English, *A Tommy in the U.S.A. A Yank in the RAF* opened in September, produced by Zanuck, directed by Henry King, written by Darrell Ware and Karl Tunberg, "based on an original story by Melville Crossman," and although it received severely qualified notices (the kinder critics emphasized that it was an entertainment) it became a solid hit.

Almost a year before Pearl Harbor, Zanuck came down with a case of war fever. In January 1941 he was commissioned a reserve lieutenant colonel in the Signal Corps, and whenever possible he spoke in favor of America's joining Great Britain in fighting the war. He gave many speeches including one to the National Convention of the American Legion in September 1941. "If you charge us with being anti Nazi, you are right," he told the Legionnaires, "and if you accuse us of producing films in the interest of preparedness and national defense again you are right." Just before America entered the war, Zanuck's military awareness got him in political trouble. Lord Halifax, who was then British ambassador to the U.S., was touring the country to raise money and support for Britain, and Zanuck decided he was doing a bad job of it. One day, while changing planes in Bermuda, Zanuck ran into his old friend Lord Beaverbrook, who was Britain's Minister of Aviation, and when they were both laid over they had dinner together. Zanuck began talking about Halifax. "Jesus Christ, I wouldn't say this except to you, Max, but he's doing more harm than good." Then suddenly it dawned on Zanuck that Beaverbrook would have loved to become ambassador to the U.S., and he suggested it to him. The next day Zanuck flew to London, via Lisbon. His first appointment was with Foreign Minister Anthony Eden, who asked him to spend the weekend at his house. Then Zanuck said, "As an American, I may be out of line, but you know we're not being helped by a very brilliant man, by Halifax. I'm a motion picture man. I know how to make an impression. If you want to favor the Indians you get a great Indian lead. If you want to favor the cowboys, you get a great cowboy lead." And then he suggested Beaverbrook as a great ambassador lead. "What I didn't know was that Halifax was one of Churchill's most loyal friends. He had supported Churchill when he was out of office. I went back to Claridge's and received a telephone call from Anthony Eden's office. Eden said, 'I'm sorry I have to cancel that invitation. A matter of great secrecy and urgency has come up and I have to go out and spend the weekend at Chequers.' I sensed something went wrong . . . then maybe not." Beaverbrook was back in London and because he had a cold, had gone to the country. He was staying at Pamela Churchill's house. She called Zanuck and invited him for the weekend. Beaverbrook greeted him, "What in God's name did you tell Eden?"

"What I thought about Halifax," said Zanuck.

"Oh, Christ," said Beaverbrook. "All hell has broken loose." Churchill was "absolutely livid. This American coming over here, meddling in our problems . . ." It was some time before the flap blew over.

In the last few months of 1941, Zanuck began applying showmanship to battle, and turning his company into war production. After Pearl Harbor, he was practically a defense industry. Zanuck made among others, *Secret Agent of Japan, To the Shores of Tripoli, This Above All, The Pied Piper, Berlin Correspondent, Manila Calling, Thunder Birds* and *China Girl*, both from stories by Melville Crossman, *Im-*

mortal Sergeant, Chetniks!, Tonight We Raid Calais, They Came to Blow up America, and *Crash Dive.* Then Zanuck took a leave of absence, and, like a breezy Tyrone Power character, he went to war. And so, as a matter of fact, did Tyrone Power.

5.

A Yank in the Signal Corps

Why don't you send him to school and make a real officer of him?

—Senator Harry S. Truman

In January 1942 Zanuck was promoted to full colonel by order of General George C. Marshall, Chief of Staff, and was sent to London to co-ordinate training films. He was there during the Blitz, living in Claridge's. He was dying to see action, and finally when he was assigned to Lord Louis Mountbatten's commandos as an observer, he was allowed to go on a British night commando raid across the English Channel to blow up a radar interception center in St. Valery. The next month Zanuck was assigned to the Aleutian Islands to make a movie about the U.S. military operation there. "There's a hell of a war up there," he said on his return to the States. "Two wars really—one against the Japs and the other against the weather." The soldiers, he said, were "itching for a fight." And so apparently was Colonel Zanuck. As motion picture adviser to General Dawson Olmstead, the chief signal corps officer of the U. S. Army, Zanuck was assigned to make a documentary movie about the North African campaign. He made the movie, released as *At the Front,* and he also kept a diary, which was later published as a book called *Tunis Expedition.*

On November 8, Zanuck was in Gibraltar waiting to fly to Algiers, when the Allies began their invasion of North Africa. Annoyed at missing the landing, he talked his way on to a flight the next day with General Mark Clark and his aides. Zanuck was armed with a Tommy gun, a Bell and Howell 16 mm. camera, 120 rounds of ammunition, and ten film

99

magazines. As the plane flew in over Algiers, they suddenly found themselves in the middle of an Axis air attack on the Allied ships in the Algiers harbor. They became the target for all the ack-ack from miles around. Dodging the fire, and firing themselves, they headed for the Maison Blanche airfield. "The sky is alive with colored tracer bullets, like a Fourth of July fireworks display," Zanuck wrote later. "A Nazi plane crashes nearby. Another explodes in the air and floats down, a mass of brilliant yellow and scarlet flames . . . I still can't seem to understand that this is really a battle and I am in it. The excitement of it was like the thrill that possesses one who looks at a dangerous polo spill or a thrilling bullfight and yet is entirely safe on the sidelines." But Zanuck was not on the sidelines. He was in the thick of the battle, and as observers have indicated he could have very easily been killed.

Some of Zanuck's Signal Corps men had already arrived and billeted themselves in the former German embassy. They anxiously and somewhat skeptically awaited the arrival of their "Hollywood colonel." "We were confident he would be rank happy and obnoxious," recalls Robert Gordon Edwards, a staff sergeant at the time. "He turned out to be neither. He was dynamic, aloof, full of nervous energy, and anxious to get into battle. One got the impression these were the most exciting days of his life until then, and he was determined to live them at the utmost pitch." His first night in Algiers, Zanuck immediately won the affection of his GIs by unselfconsciously spreading his sleeping bag on the floor alongside their blankets. It was, however, noted Edwards, a "monumental sleeping bag . . . the sort of tubular comfort Abercrombie and Fitch would undertake to supply to only the right White Hunters on safari, and in a peacetime world would inevitably have found its way to the noggin of a native bearer slogging through the Congo." Zanuck's boxes of cigars slept in his bag alongside him. A musette bag was his only other piece of luggage. He wore a .45 automatic on his waist, and later began carrying that Tommy gun. Several days after his arrival in Algiers, Zanuck attended and photographed a ceremony at which Clark was promoted to lieutenant general. Eisenhower made the presentation. "Ike, as was his style, greeted Zanuck warmly," remembers Edwards. To his surprise and pleasure, Zanuck introduced Edwards to the general. "Zanuck demonstrated a certain deference to Ike, which I later decided had nothing to do with rank, but was based on admiration. This was a man from whom he even enjoyed taking orders. There couldn't have been many like that in his life."

John Ford, then a commander in the U.S. Navy, was one of the men assigned to Zanuck. When he arrived in Algiers Ford greeted him, "Can't I ever get away from you? I'll bet a dollar to a doughnut that if I ever go to Heaven, you'll be waiting at the door for me under a sign reading, 'Produced by Darryl F. Zanuck.' "

Vehicles were difficult to come by, but Zanuck managed to "liberate" a late-thirties model electric blue Chevrolet coupe, that was once the property of the Italian consulate. Remembers Edwards, "The Chevy served us well, and damn near got us killed any number of times. How, after all, could a Kraut fighter pilot miss seeing a bright blue Chevy coupe on a dusty road, and once having seen it not be determined to twenty-millimeter the hell out of it? I have sometimes wondered if it ever entered Zanuck's mind to paint the damn thing olive drab, or had he promised to return it to its owner in its pristine condition . . . or did he just get a charge out of driving a Chevy coupe into war?" With Edwards, Zanuck drove to the local Twentieth Century-Fox office, which, according to Edwards, "was deserted and had been given over to the charge of a French caretaker who almost made water publicly upon the arrival of the great man from Hollywood. Zanuck's coming was clearly a matter of far greater importance to this type than the landing in Algiers of the Allied forces. Zanuck entered those silent halls and strolled about his fief with all the sureness of the sovereign in his own bit of extraterritoriality in a foreign land."

Then Zanuck embarked on his primary mission. He sent a detachment of his men, including Edwards, ahead by boat to Bone, and with a truck following him, he drove his Chevy overland to the same destination. Soon after his arrival, in the bar of the Hotel d'Oriente in Bone, Zanuck had drinks with Captain Randolph Churchill. Zanuck spotted Edwards across the room with some friends from Number Six Commando, invited him over, and introduced him to Churchill. They chatted informally, mostly about military things, and then one of Edwards' commando friends decided he wanted to meet the famous Hollywood producer, and tipsily swaggered over to the table. He saluted Churchill, because he was an officer, and extended his hand to Zanuck, saying, "I'm Berisford, Number Six Commando, and I want you to know this bloody Yank [Edwards] is the best fooking soldier in the whole fooking Yank army."

Calmly Zanuck replied, "My name's Zanuck and this is Captain Churchill, and we would be pleased if you joined us." It was an impetuous, unmilitary gesture, and it disarmed the sozzled sergeant. He sat and chatted about movies with Zanuck. Then he rose with a drunken waver, snapped to attention, and saluted both officers firmly, stomped his heel, about-faced, and marched away. Back at the bar he confided to Edwards in a roar of a whisper, "Fookin' good bloke, that Zanuck. And the other one's all right, too. What's 'is name?"

The next day Zanuck packed up his forces and drove out of Bone on the heels of the advancing Allied forces. At Souk el Arba, a village of mud huts, they were besieged by an air raid. "I let go with my Tommy gun and used up a full clip," Zanuck later wrote. "I fired three clips in all, and while I know some of my lead hit home I probably did no damage, yet there was always the chance that a lucky shot might strike a vital spot . . . At last I was shooting at a German— doing very little damage, I am sure—but I was still shooting." The group drove to within one hour of Tunis, and put up at a farmhouse, where they stayed for some time while making daily photo checks on the fighting—Zanuck driving the blue Chevy and one man standing shotgun on the running board. At the farm, Zanuck hardly ever slept inside the house. Mostly he stayed in the granary with the enlisted men until the rats chased them out or under or inside a camouflaged truck. (Sometime after the Americans left the farmhouse, the Germans burned it and then blew it up. After the war the owner of the farm wrote Zanuck about his loss. Zanuck sent him money to rebuild the farm.) During a period when German tanks were outweighing and outmaneuvering Allied tanks, Zanuck watched from an observation post and was furious at the distance of the battle from him. He vowed to tie two men to the Chevy and, driving himself, to plunge right into the action. To his men's relief, he changed his mind.

Zanuck spent about two months filming at the front under fire. Some of the time he was with John Ford. "He and I were in advance outfit," says Ford. "All the jeeps and camions and tanks were bunched together and we agreed it was a pretty good place for the Germans to strike, so we went down the hill by a beautiful old church and were going to take pictures of it. We were about twenty yards from this church and I asked Darryl if he had any cigars left, and he said, 'I gave you one this morning, and I have only one left.' And I said, 'Cut it in half.' And he said, 'O.K., but first why don't you go up in the steeple of that church and take pictures? I'm not Catholic, but you are, and what greater place for a Catholic to get killed than in a Catholic Church?' And just then a bomb came and blew us over a cliff and into some rocks. And I said, 'Did it hurt the cigar?' And he reached in his pocket, and it was there. The cameras were blown to bits. The blast didn't hurt us much—it didn't help us either—we felt each other, and there were no broken bones. Our clothes were torn and we were bruised up pretty good . . . Later in the day I saw him and he was covered with blood. He'd been helping the wounded, and he was smoking a full cigar. And I said, 'You lied to me,' and that was the only argument we had for years."

Finally Zanuck really was running out of cigars, and when orders for him to return to Britain came through, instead of protesting he accepted the decision—and what the future promised in terms of cigars. "We were sorry to see him go," says Edwards. "He was a good C.O. who looked out for his men and asked no special favors for himself because of rank. To our collective surprise, we found that Zanuck was a man of considerable personal courage. Now it is one thing to be brave at twenty, and quite another to be bold at forty, which was Zanuck's age. In any number of quite perilous moments I never saw him run, break, hesitate or even show signs of deep concern.

"We were, by this time, close to him but never friendly. I don't think it is in his nature to be intimately friendly with anyone, but I really don't know him that well to justify such a flat statement . . . I often had the impression he was looking on all this from afar, filing it all away for future use when seated at a typewriter."

At some point during the action, Zanuck had told his men, "I don't want any of you guys coming to me for jobs after the war. The reason is that they are still coming to me from the last war and the studio can support only so many wars."

"Colonel," answered Edwards, "like we say in Ohio, you will be the last son of a bitch in the world I will come to for a job when this is all over." Zanuck laughed. After the war Edwards went into the movie business and during moments of unemployment, thought about walking up to Zanuck and saying, "Why, hello there, last son of a bitch in the world," but he never did.

In his blue Chevy, Zanuck drove over the Atlas Mountains back to Bone and with General Jimmy Doolittle hitched a plane ride to Gibraltar, then after a nine-day delay because of the weather, flew to Dakar, from there to Trinidad, and from there to Washington. He never got to London, but presumably there were cigars to be found in Washington. On the trip back he had read his diary and elaborated on some of the notes. In the U.S. he showed it to Clare Boothe Luce and Nunnally Johnson, who suggested he publish it. For security reasons the government spliced some forty pages out of it and in three months, it was published. Damon Runyon wrote the foreword. "I consider this book one of the finest pieces of reportorial work that has so far come out of World War II," he said. "It is the story of the United States' most tremendous adventure in arms, set down by a man whose capacity for observation is as photographic as the cameras he operated for the Signal Corps in North Africa and whose knack of telling the tale of a moving event in swift, simple language will make every managing editor wish he had one like him on his staff." Then Runyon compared Zanuck to Richard Harding Davis. He considerably overstates the book's importance and Zanuck's talent, but the style is generally spare and clean, a direct contrast to his previous prose. Best of all, the writing is not self-conscious. It is like an informative letter home. Since Zanuck was after all a professional producer on loan he does not hesitate to use a movie image when he feels like it. He was in a sense living a war movie, and he cast it as he went along. Mark Clark was "an American version of Basil Rathbone." One British major looked and talked "like a younger version of George Arliss," a French soldier had a "physique like Wally Beery's," and Zanuck himself felt "like a character in an Edward G. Robinson epic." The ironic thing was that Zanuck's movie,

At the Front (in which there were several glimpses of Zanuck, in one scene holding a Tommy gun), the purpose of the expedition, was not well received by the critics. John K. Hutchens, for one, took the book's publication as an opportunity to blast the movie. In the *Times Book Review* he wrote, " 'At the Front' was anything but extraordinary . . . feeble and even unprofessional job, the like of which would have meant—in Hollywood—an option not picked up. But here is a book by Colonel Zanuck, *Tunis Expedition*, a sort of diary of his trip and . . . this one has its points." Zanuck immediately responded with a letter to the editor, defending his picture, distinguishing it as a combat action film from documentary or propaganda films.

"If the process would not have violated strict War Department regulations concerning authenticity," he wrote, "I flatter myself in saying that I might have easily transposed *At the Front* from a straightforward piece of visual reporting to a bang-up documentary with propaganda overtones.

"Give us a couple of broken down tanks, a platoon of Beverly Hills infantrymen, a few smoke pots, turn us loose on the studio back lot and then permit us to inject this material into our authentic battle episodes, and the result would undoubtedly amaze the uninitiated as well as pep up the entire congregation . . . Somehow, however, I am pleased that we resisted the temptation . . ."

For Zanuck, the action really started when he returned home. Newspapers and magazines began doing stories on him, some of them derogatory, picturing him as a "Hollywood colonel" who had no business being involved in battles, and certainly had no business shooting off Tommy guns. Zanuck found that away from the front, "I was caught in a crossfire." At the height of the press controversy, and the nadir of Zanuck's popularity in Washington, President Roosevelt asked him to dinner and, as Zanuck remembers, "Practically his whole cabinet was there . . . and Frankfurter and Robert Sherwood. About twenty. We were all seated when the President was wheeled in and he spoke first to me: 'Hi Darryl! I want to say one thing: pay no attention to the press. Pay no attention. I know it's annoying but don't dignify them by answering!' " Zanuck tried to ignore the press, but Harry S. Truman, then senator from Missouri, decided to take up congressional cudgels against him. He launched an investigation of Hollywood colonels with his special Senate War Investigating Committee, commonly known as the Truman Committee. Hal Roach, Arthur Loew, Anatole Litvak, Frank Capra were each singled out for obtaining quick commissions, but Zanuck came in for most of the criticism, and precipitated most of the headlines.

On the advice of his friend General George C. Marshall, Zanuck asked to be placed on inactive duty and on May 31, 1943, the request was granted and he returned to Hollywood. In 1944 he was awarded the Legion of Merit for "exceptional bravery under fire," and several years later, when Truman was Vice-President, they patched up their differences and became friends. But when Truman was President, Zanuck had his one last brush with active duty. Secretary of Defense Louis Johnson wanted to make a movie explaining the Korean War to the American public. He ordered reservist Zanuck to active duty in Washington, and explained that he was appropriating a million dollars for the film and that it would be based on a scenario written by a captain on his staff. Zanuck read the script and decided "It was just a piece of crap," and that "the situation was so fluid that by the time it could be made and distributed, everything might change radically." As an alternative, Zanuck offered to make free a one-reel short from stock Fox newsreel footage of Korea. "I'll have it in the theaters in two weeks," Zanuck said. He rushed the reel to Washington and it was released nationwide. But Zanuck knew that as far as the Department of Defense and Secretary Johnson were concerned, he was in the doghouse. He consulted Colonel (later, Brigadier General) Frank McCarthy, and they agreed he might be called back to permanent duty on one excuse or another. As a reserve officer he was fair game to the Pentagon, and reluctantly he resigned his commission. It was the end of Colonel Zanuck's official military career. He cashiered in his uniform, but he saved his battle ribbons and citations. In 1969 he requested the Department of Defense to re-examine his military record. Within two weeks Zanuck was advised that he had been restored to his full rank as a colonel in the Army of the United States, retired.

6.

Politics and Product

. . . unless these two pictures [Wilson *and* One World] *are
successful from every standpoint, I'll never make another
film without Betty Grable.*

—Darryl Zanuck

Zanuck has always been politically aware, and at least behind
the scenes he has usually been politically active. But he has
had no political philosophy, except that he usually votes
Republican, and likes presidents whoever they are. He prides
himself on his friendships with presidents, and he has known
them personally from Franklin Roosevelt through Richard
Nixon, with varying degrees of intimacy. With Harry Truman
it was an on-again, off-again relationship. Dwight Eisenhower
he helped convince to run for the presidency—he was one
of a group of public figures to solicit his candidacy actively—
and through his years in office, and after, knew him intimately. John Kennedy he met on occasion—or rather on occasions. Their relationship stemmed largely from Zanuck's old
friendship with Joseph P. Kennedy. Lyndon Johnson he never
met but received a photo personally autographed to "My dear
friend, Darryl." Nixon he has known for sixteen years on a
"friendly and intimate basis," and also from his close association with William Rogers, who was on Fox's board of
directors when Nixon picked him for Secretary of State. Of
all the presidents, Roosevelt was nearest to an intimate of
Zanuck's. He visited him informally many times at the White
House, and has many stories to tell about him. He remembers,
for instance, once having dinner with President and Mrs.
Roosevelt and Harry Hopkins on a bridge table on the
second-floor hallway outside of the President's room. "Mary,

the cook, brought in the dinner and FDR said, 'My God, Eleanor! Not sweetbreads again!' She said, 'Franklin, you must realize there is a war on.'" On another occasion Zanuck was having lunch with Roosevelt, Hopkins, and Robert Sherwood. "A new law had been passed. No one could draw more than $25,000 on his income. You were not deprived of the rest of the money, and the law only lasted about four months before it was abolished. In the middle of our lunch in ran—frantic, but with her usual dignity and composure—Eleanor Roosevelt. 'Franklin, I've just been talking to Mrs. So-and-so. Do you know what that law means to my charities to which Mrs. So-and-so gives $150,000 a year? If she can't give, the charities will go out of business.' With an old-fashioned in front of him, FDR took his cigarette holder out of his mouth [Zanuck acts this out, imitates FDR almost passably, thankfully does not try to do an Eleanor Roosevelt], and said, 'Don't talk to *me,* Eleanor. Talk to Harry [Hopkins]. It was his idea.'"

The irony of the Zanuck-FDR friendship is that Zanuck actively supported Wendell Willkie against him. In fact, of *all* the politicians he has known, Willkie was the closest. He often stayed at the Zanuck house in Santa Monica and became a member of the board of Twentieth Century-Fox. In 1940 when Roosevelt narrowly defeated Willkie, Zanuck received a call at his home. "It was Jimmy Roosevelt calling from the White House," says Zanuck. "He said, 'You know that Dad is a great admirer of Wendell Willkie and we know of your connection with him. He'd like to talk to Willkie but he wants to be sure Willkie wants to talk to *him.* Can you reach him?' I got Wendell, I think at his home in Indiana, and told him that Jimmy Roosevelt called me. 'If the President wanted to see you, would you welcome that, or resent it?' 'I certainly would welcome it.' I called Jimmy back and said Willkie would be honored to visit the White House. So they met, and it ended in his trip around the world which was climaxed by Wendell's book *One World.*"

Zanuck has never let his politics influence his moviemaking. But the Zanuck who came out of the war was somewhat changed. For a combination of reasons—what he had seen at the front, his own battles with the military, his friendship with Willkie and Roosevelt—he became something of a peacemonger, but in many other ways he was still the pre-war Zanuck.

In one of his earlier memos upon returning to the studio, in response to suggestions for various films from Kenneth MacGowan, he revealed something of his current frame of movie mind. "I am not interested in the story of Masaryk, the first president of Czechoslovakia. I feel that these stories are terribly dated. I am sure audiences seeking entertainment are looking for more spectacular subjects. By spectacular, I mean sensational. I don't care whether it is a musical or a drama or a story of Wilson. It must be spectacular entertainment. A biography of John Philip Sousa, built around 'The Stars and Stripes Forever' and a biography about Masaryk are miles apart in the final result. One lends itself to spectacular entertainment—music, patriotism, a colorful period. The other, no matter how finely you produce it, has certain limitations. On a picture about Masaryk, you would strive and struggle to hide the contents of the story. You would immediately be afraid that the word 'Czechoslovakia' etc., etc., would chase the audience away.

"Any story about Germany or labor slaves appalls me. Every picture yet made dealing with occupied countries including *The Moon Is Down* has laid a magnificent egg with the public. I can imagine no subject less inviting to an audience than the subject of slave labor at this time. I wouldn't care if it was the greatest dramatic story written." And then Zanuck revealed the biography he was really interested in! "Show me how I can make a good story out of the life of Ernest R. Ball, and the great Irish songs he wrote," he said and then filmed Ball's life in 1944 as *Irish Eyes Are Smiling*.

"I have always loved biographies, and I have made some very successful ones, as far back as *Disraeli, The House of Rothschild*, etc., and I will always make them, but when you think what we could have had if we had put the same casts, the same money, time and energy, into popular subjects or potentially popular biographies, our success would have been tenfold."

After saying all this, apparently disregarding his own advice, he added, "You might ask why I am doing *Wilson*. First off, I am doing it because I think it is the right thing to do at this time. I think it will serve a tremendous purpose for our company, for our industry and for our country, and furthermore, I will not start shooting it until I am completely satisfied that I have the opportunity of making it a popular entertainment. I will at least be compensated by making an important contribution that has an opportunity of being significant and helpful . . ." And so saying, Zanuck undertook what was supposed to be his magnum opus and turned out to be his greatest failure.

To Zanuck, Wilson was an early-day Willkie, a peacemaker who placed humanity above politics, and by showing Wilson's antagonists and obstacles, he hoped to clear the path for peace in Zanuck's time. The movie was written by Lamar Trotti, directed by Zanuck's favorite house director Henry King, and was cast not with an eye toward the marquee but with a concern for believability. Certainly the practically unknown Alexander Knox was not going to shatter any box-office records as Wilson. "It will cost us close to $3,500,000 to make, which is gamble enough in any language," he wrote at the time. "The subject is vital and has already plunged me and the studio into enough controversy to last us for years." Zanuck was more involved in the production of *Wilson* than in any other movie he had made. "It was the apple of his eye," says Henry King. "It was the *only* time I saw him on the set." Day after day he watched the filming, occasionally rewriting parts of the script himself and giving them to Trotti. When he was finished, Zanuck was convinced that he had a masterpiece, a movie to stake a career, and perhaps a civilization, on. The reviews in the popular and trade press were almost unanimous in echoing Zanuck's optimism. "A commanding screen biography," said Bosley Crowther in the New York *Times. Variety* even made what in retrospect was an astounding claim for it: "It will mop up at the box office." Zanuck does get high marks for sincerity and seriousness, but by any standards *Wilson* is not an outstanding movie, and certainly not "precedential." The odd thing is that *Wilson* was probably hurt by overpraise. In proof of Zanuck's feeling in the powerlessness of the critics *Wilson* flopped at the box office.

Zanuck stubbornly supported his picture. As a sign of his confidence, in October 1944, he triumphantly bore a print of it back to Omaha for the Nebraska premiere, also carrying a trainload of Hollywood celebrities with him, and for a day he returned to Wahoo. It was an act of unmitigated nostalgia, but realist that he basically is, the hero's return woke him up. For one thing it shattered his sentimentalization of his childhood. "When I saw the Grand Hotel—it was only a small brick building. I drove out to the place where I had hunted. I remembered it as a monumental bluff, but it was only a 150-foot slope. Early memories can murder you.'

In honor of Zanuck, Wahoo shut its shops, dismissed Wahoo High School and Luther College at 2:30 so that the youngsters could watch the hero's return. Led by cowboys on horseback, and the Wahoo High band, Zanuck sat in an open convertible and waved to the cheering throng. As the flags waved and the trumpets played, it was a scene right out of a Zanuck movie of the thirties. Mayor O. H. Person introduced Zanuck as "A Wahoo lad who went into the world and made good," and Zanuck responded, "If my movies have reflected the spirit of America, the inspiration came from my boyhood days in Nebraska. I am proud to be a Nebraskan." As a cast of 1500 cheered, Zanuck made his exit.

For the premiere of *Wilson* in Omaha, the theater was packed. The next day there were only seventy-five people in the audience. Zanuck was shocked. The family doctor set him straight about the arch conservatism of the natives. "Why should they pay seventy-five cents to see Wilson on screen when they wouldn't pay ten cents to see him alive?" And there, in a sentence, was the death of *Wilson*. Discouraged, disgruntled, and, after three days, bored out of his mind, Zanuck decided to leave Nebraska. He wired his office in Hollywood to wire him: "Urgent: needed at studio." Immediately upon receiving the wire, he left, and except for a brief visit to Lincoln in 1957 to pick up an honorary degree of Doctor of Humanities from the University of Nebraska, he has never set foot in Nebraska since.

Wilson was nominated but did not even win the Academy Award Zanuck thought it deserved. Three years later, when Zanuck accepted an Oscar for *Gentleman's Agreement* as best picture of the year he reminded Hollywood of what he considered an injustice. "Many thanks, but I should have won it for *Wilson*," he said. It remains the one movie he has never changed his mind about.

Zanuck's second unsuccessful attempt to win the peace was a projected movie version of Wendell Willkie's book *One World*. He bought it for $100,000 and in January 1944 began mapping plans for its production. He had Lamar Trotti construct a fictionalized plot which would demonstrate Willkie's thesis and also have Willkie as a character in the cast, hopefully to be played by Spencer Tracy. In the picture Willkie was to tell a bereaved widow that the death of her husband in battle should *not* be greeted with heroism and patriotism. "If anything," wrote Zanuck in his notes, "she should be *mad* about it—damn mad—mad enough to see that in the future things like this do not happen again." Zanuck continued, "In every picture I have seen lately, someone always tells the mother or the father to keep their chin up, they have made a noble sacrifice in giving up their son or sweetheart to the war. This is nonsense . . . when we lose our loved ones, instead of walking around with a patriotic halo on our heads, we should be damned mad about it and ready to strangle the first jerk who gets up at the peace table and starts yammering about Isolationism or the preservation of the British Empire or anything that does not guarantee equality of opportunity for all . . ." But months later, Zanuck reluctantly shelved his *One World.* "By the time we got the first scenario, situations had changed—not into one world," he said. "By the time we could make it and release it, it would be a year and a half." And who knew how much the world situation might change in that time? But as late as November 27, 1945, he was still thinking about *One World.* On that date he sent a copy of the script to John Ford, with a note, "If ever the world needed a picture with the theories of Wendell L. Willkie, it certainly needs it now."

When Darryl Zanuck went to war, he had left William Goetz in charge of the studio. Fox thrived in his absence, not through any particular innovation of Goetz's, but because actually there was nothing much a movie company could do to lose money during the war years. Almost whatever was shipped out to the theaters was a box-office success. When Zanuck returned, Goetz left. Relations had always been strained between them, and in his absence, Zanuck felt Goetz had tried to swing too much authority. Goetz went to Universal, Zanuck countermanded some of his orders (among other things Goetz had ordered that Zanuck's steam room be painted a color other than Zanuck Green), and then turned his attention to the product.

For several years one of the men producing Zanuck's

musicals was George Jessel. Jessel was also something of a court jester and provided much off-screen entertainment for Zanuck. He is credited with the prizewinning candidate in the grovel-before-Zanuck contest: "When I die, I want to be cremated and have my ashes sprinkled on Mr. Zanuck's driveway so his car won't skid." His work for the screen quite often was met with Zanuck wrath. "I have just spent two miserable hours reading the first draft script on *Hello, My Baby*," Zanuck wrote Jessel on one occasion. "I don't know when any script has both shocked and disappointed me as much as this one does, especially in view of the fact that the last thing you told me before you went to the train was that you thought it was excellent, or at least had excellent possibilities.

"In my opinion this is the most frustrated conglomeration that it has been my misfortune to spend my time on . . . The dialogue is atrocious and with the exception of a very few speeches is the kind of wisecracks you find in a vaudeville act or a Monogram musical.

"No one regrets the writing of this note any more than I do as this story has to date cost us a great deal of money and I can see no way of salvaging anything without starting over again from scratch.

"When you were given this assignment I told you to study carefully the structure of three pictures—*Swanee River, My Gal Sal, Irish Eyes Are Smiling*. You totally ignored this recommendation or else you are blind."

And then the unkindest cut of all: "I do not intend to be facetious, but hereafter before you put Melville Crossman's name on a script I wish you would do him the courtesy of letting him read it first.

7.

Dead on Three Balls

Though a neophyte at the game, Zanuck has true croquet spirit. He trusts no one but himself, never concedes—no matter how far behind he may be—and hates his opponents with an all-enduring hate.

—Moss Hart

In late December 1941, during a practice polo match at the Uplifters Club, a ball came flying at Darryl Zanuck's face. He held up his mallet to protect himself. The ball struck his hand, breaking it, and smashed the mallet against his face, fracturing his nose and turning his face into a mass of bruises and welts. Dripping blood, he returned home. He calmly walked in. There was a party in honor of William Powell in progress and Zanuck might well have joined it without giving his accident another thought except for the fact that one of the guests was a doctor who insisted that Zanuck needed medical attention. He set his nose, taped his face, affixed a cup to his face to catch the blood, leaving slits in the bandage for his eyes, his mouth, and his cigar. Looking like a mummy, the mogul in the plaster mask, Zanuck, as usual, went to the studio the next day, and conducted business as if nothing had happened. This accident, probably the worst Zanuck ever suffered, may not have been the only reason he lost interest in polo, but almost coincidentally with it, he made a magnanimous, patriotic gesture that few could duplicate. He donated his Argentine polo ponies—all twenty of them—to West Point, the academy insisting on giving him one dollar for each pony as token payment. After the war, he took up polo again, briefly, on a modest scale, with only five ponies, and then gradually drifted out of the sport.

Zanuck turned to croquet, presumably less of a blood sport than polo, but one that is bitterly competitive—a highly emotional, highly vocal, exacting, exciting science of a game. It was also much more accessible to the weekend player. Zanuck could create competition simply by asking people over to his house and he could control competition by deciding the rules of order. He played right in his own front yard. The lawn at Zanuck's house in Palm Springs became in the late forties the croquet capital of California, and Zanuck was its sovereign, as well as chief umpire, critic, and croqueteer.

The house was one Zanuck had purchased from Joseph Schenck, about the time that Schenck was jailed for four months for tax evasion (the imprisonment, though short, all but finished Schenck's career in Hollywood; when he began his term he was chairman of the board of Fox, when he returned he was one of many "advisers" at the studio). The Zanucks renamed the house Ric-Su-Dar in honor of their three children. Actually there were two houses on the property, one for the Zanucks, and a large guesthouse to the rear—in back of a swimming pool and in front of a tennis court. The main part of the guesthouse was an enormous, high-ceilinged room, which looked like a hunting lodge and served as a living-party-dining room. The walls were lined with African animal trophies, the tables with other trophies (mostly for movies and polo). Off the main room were, on each side, a pair of guest rooms, each with an interior and an exterior entrance. The double entrances were at least partially discretionary. Because of frequently changing partners, says one guest, "The Zanucks had to have a suspense file of who was going with whom. They tried to avoid any embarrassing encounter."

In season, the Zanucks drove down almost every weekend, usually leaving Santa Monica very late Thursday night, arriving early Friday morning. All day Friday Zanuck would sit in the sun and work on scripts. The people would begin arriving for the weekend, a cross-section of Hollywood society, sprinkled with some international celebrities. Some of them were there for work: producers, directors, and writers were called down for weekend consultations, and stayed for play. Most were there just for play. Among the frequent visitors were Mike Romanoff, Henry and Skip Hathaway, the Walter Wangers, the Douglas Fairbanks, Jrs., Aly Khan and Rita Hayworth, Tyrone Power and his wife or lady friend of the moment, Clifton Webb, Reginald and Nadia Gardiner, Rex Harrison and Lilli Palmer, Joseph Cotten, the Vincent Astors, and, as almost permanent fixtures, Gregory Ratoff and Elsa Maxwell, who would stay on even when the Zanucks weren't there. In the guest book, the Henry Luces, frequent visitors, inscribed a bit of doggerel:

> Some speak of Arizona and some of Wai ki-ki
> Of Nassau and Bermuda and places where they ski
> But of all the sun-kissed heavens there's none
> That can compare
> With the zestful, restful, guestful
> Home of Zanucks, pere and mere.

Moss Hart and Kitty Carlisle remembered Ric-Su-Dar as the place they came soon after their wedding—and stayed after she had a miscarriage. They commemorated that fact in the guest book in a poem, which also extolled their host and hostess, and groaned a bit about the serious gamesmanship:

> . . . This is a roundelay, this is a song,
> Of lunches late and dinners long
> Of bitter croquet and games at the table
> Of hitting the ball when you're hardly able
> To see your partner, much less the wicket,
> Of hiding from Darryl way up in some thicket
> Of starting at noon and playing all night
> Of knowing your strategy *never* is right . . .

The Zanucks were known as great hosts, and invitations for weekends were much coveted. Socially it was a very relaxing time. Everyone dressed exactly as he pleased. Zanuck usually wore tiny bathing shorts, the size of the briefest bikini. Everyone followed his own pleasure—reading, sleeping, drinking, playing tennis, swimming. Henry Luce, for one, was known to spend much of his time sitting by himself and reading the comic sections of newspapers. Dusty Negulesco always kept a quart of milk by her bedside, gulped milk all night, and didn't arise until two in the afternoon. Howard Hughes was a frequent house guest—sort of. He never stayed the night. Once he announced that he would love to meet Norma Shearer, so Virginia asked her down. They were introduced.

Hughes said, "How do you do?" and then left. On another occasion, Hughes had a very different request, also filled. He asked Mrs. Zanuck if "your man" couldn't get him a half gallon of gas so that he could drive to the airport. Sam the Barber, who was present that weekend as usual, was drafted as "your man" and asked to fill Mr. Hughes's tank. The next time Hughes visited, he announced, "I owe you some money. I only wanted half a gallon."

Breakfast was whenever you wanted it, which for Ratoff was frequently. He would be the first one awake in the morning. At dawn he would sneak down, wolf a large breakfast, then as others awoke he would suggest, "Let's have breakfast." Several breakfasts later he would have lunch (lunch generally was at two and informal) and then in the middle of an after-lunch croquet match he would sneak inside and have another lunch. If it was a hot day, over dessert Darryl or Virginia would often ask a newcomer, "Are you warm?" If he answered yes, led by the Zanucks, the regulars would ritualistically throw their ice cream at him. Mack Sennett would have been pleased at the scene—and the newcomer had to be, if he wanted to become a regular, at which time *he* could throw his ice cream. Dinner was not until nine (could Ratoff wait so long?), and was a great festive occasion. After dinner, movies would be shown. There would be parlor games like Murder, much stimulating conversation, and many pranks. Guests remember the time that Darryl and Virginia, fully clothed in formal dress, walked calmly into the pool, followed by all their guests.

For all the fun, there was one game that was serious business: croquet. Croquet hours paralleled Zanuck's work hours at the studio: all afternoon, and then after dinner until four or five in the morning. "Croquet players were under strict orders from Darryl and *had* to play at night," recalls Kitty Carlisle. With a few exceptions, such as Mrs. Vincent Astor and Mrs. Richard Rodgers, who were considered as good as the men, women were not invited to participate. Miss Carlisle was called upon only "when they had their backs to the wall and needed someone." The ladies were generally content to play Scrabble and canasta, and to retire early. Guests remember the time that Olivia de Havilland came out of her room at three in the morning, dressed in her nightgown, and demanded that her husband stop playing croquet and come to bed. After a moment of stunned silence, the game continued.

Before Zanuck took it up, croquet was already a big sport among the famous (Alexander Woollcott, Herbert Bayard Swope, Harpo Marx, Moss Hart). It was Hart who introduced Zanuck to the game. "Until then," says Zanuck, "I always thought of it as a kid's game. I was soon to realize it was one of the most difficult and scientific sports in the world. Strategy is much more important than accurate hitting. It's like chess. The game is not just to go through the wickets but to cripple your opponent." Zanuck pitched into croquet with his characteristic unquenchable enthusiasm. He converted the huge front lawn on his Palm Springs house into a full-size croquet court, with wickets sunk a foot into the ground. At Zanuck's instructions, his head gardener cut the field every other day, constantly watered it with a roving sprinkler, until it was a model lawn—smooth as velvet, neat as a golf course. At first, for night games cars were placed in the driveway and headlights directed toward the field. Since that was unsatisfactory, and, worst of all, unprofessional, Zanuck had high floodlights erected. At night, the temperature often plunged to zero, so he purchased army surplus in enormous quantities and in a variety of sizes, insulated boots, coats, pants, and stocking caps. Except for the absence of snow and the presence of croquet equipment, Zanuck's front lawn at night looked like *Ice Station Zebra.*

To Zanuck's house came the expert Easterners and the improving Westerners. Louis Jourdan was the best of the regulars, but Tyrone Power, Mike Romanoff, Howard Hawks, Jean Negulesco, André Hakim, Samuel Goldwyn (Zanuck's rival as Croquet Czar), and Zanuck himself became very accomplished and adamant about their expertise. Balls were imported from England. Each aficionado had his own mallet. Zanuck had his initials inscribed on the top of the leather handle, and he cherished it, like a lucky bat. "Polished," he remembers, "it was a beautiful thing." Between strokes, Hawks would take an occasional whiff of oxygen from his portable dispenser. Drinking was discouraged, at least among the active players, although Ratoff, for one, would dart off frequently, if not for another lunch, for a belt of brandy.

Competition was explosive. "The most violent fights!" recalls Zanuck. "The most violent fights! Nothing like polo.

I saw more than one friendship broken. People would pick up in the middle of a weekend and leave. I remember Jean Negulesco being so violent—more than once. Jesus, he was cunning—like all Rumanians. He was always complaining that a foul was committed on his ball. Sam Goldwyn and Mike Romanoff practically broke with each other over croquet. I've seen players break a mallet in anger." Everyone was so suspicious that finally when they went to lunch they began marking the place of each ball with a tape. "People would not really cheat, but they would take terrific advantage of someone else." The most heated arguments were about deadness. "The slogan," says Zanuck, "is Dead on Three Balls." It is the croquet equivalent of checkmate. "If you're Dead on Three Balls, the situation is hopeless—unless a miracle happens."

The arguments over deadness were apocalyptic. Zanuck and Moss Hart, who were friendly in all matters except croquet, frequently approached physical violence over the matter of deadness. Kitty Carlisle remembers on one occasion sitting with Mrs. Zanuck and some of the other ladies around the pool as the men tussled through croquet on the other side of the main house. Suddenly the servants came running. "Mrs. Zanuck! Mrs. Hart! Come quick!" They both ran, discovered their husbands facing each other with raised mallets, arguing relative deadness at the top of their voices. "I thought someone was going to be murdered," says Miss Carlisle. Finally in an effort to limit the violence, Zanuck installed a scoreboard on the lawn. Colored chalks were used to differentiate players. As Moss Hart later wrote in *Life* magazine, "In the East croquet always is played without a scoreboard, for the players trust each other's memory. Not so in Hollywood. There no one is trusted by anyone and sometimes even the scorekeeper is a suspect."

Ratoff was one of the better players, and also the most nervous, probably because he was often Zanuck's partner, which meant that he was heckled, prodded, threatened, and, at least once, pushed into the fish pond in the center of the court. When Ratoff would make a mistake, Zanuck would snap at him, "Go back to your position!" and Ratoff would vow, "I vill do vell now, Derrill." On one occasion, taunted beyond endurance, nervous, rattled, frazzled, and desperately hungry, Ratoff accidentally stuck a lighted cigarette in his pocket, igniting a pocket full of matches. Ratoff flared up like a fat Roman candle. "Not only can't you play croquet," yelled Zanuck, "you're on fire!" "Help, help," shouted Ratoff, and jumped into the fish pond.

As word of Zanuck's court spread, croquet players came from miles around. André Hakim, a close friend (and later, for a time, a son-in-law), came all the way from Paris, equipped with his personal mallet. Before Zanuck permitted him to enter competition, he was forced to demonstrate his ability. He was so nervous that he fell into the fish pond. Later, says Zanuck, "He became a top player, but with an Arabic instinct to 'cheat.' Any well known player who happened to be on the west coast would phone me immediately, and I would ask him for the weekend. Once Averell Harriman, a great friend of mine, flew down from San Francisco on a government plane. He landed at Palm Springs, played until four in the morning, got up at eleven, played until two or three in the afternoon, then flew back to his political assignment in San Francisco."

At least during the day, the gallery filled with watchers. Howard Hughes, for one, would sit on the lawn and watch croquet for hours. "He would never pick up a mallet," recalls Zanuck. "I tried to coax him into it. He said, 'It's too damn complicated.' " Another non-player was Rex Harrison. Says he, with aplomb, "I would sit and drink." Some of the ladies too were in the audience. "I watched Zanuck playing croquet," says Miss de Havilland, "and I learned all about him. He was the strategist. He was not only superb in terms of strategy, he was awfully good as an individual player. He ran the game like a military operation. He took the initiative, the responsibility. As he saw it, he had an absolute right to his position. He knew where every ball was. He would outwit his opponents in advance. As I watched him, I saw the whole shape of the man."

8.

Ric-Su-Dar

*The night that Richard was born I sent Darryl a telegram
saying that he had just thrown off a Xerox copy of himself.*
—Sy Bartlett

As his children lovingly describe him, Darryl Zanuck sounds
like an absentee father. They, and he, deny it. The point
they make is that although he did not spend much time with
them, his presence was always felt—just as his presence was
felt on the set of every picture he made, whether he ever
appeared there or not. "When I was old enough to go to
school," says Richard, "from kindergarten on, I was out of
the house by the time he was up and I wouldn't be up
when he got home. We didn't really have in that sense a
family, a normal kind of family, things where parents are
there for dinner, and have breakfast together. We didn't
operate that way. But I would see him of course on weekends, although he was always reading scripts. We would
throw a football around and swim together. During the week
I would see him mostly when I would come into his office
from school." At work he always found time to talk to his
son. When his son entered, he would automatically stop
whatever conference he was having. It didn't matter who else
was in his office.

Mostly he kept in touch with his children as he kept in
touch with his producers and directors, through memos. They
weren't formal, typewritten memos, but scraps of paper he
would scribble on. He would comment on school grades and
on other things they had done well or badly and he would
leave the notes for them in the house. He always signed
notes (and later, letters and wires) to them, "Love, Z. See

you later," just as instead of saying good-by he would say, "*À tout à l'heure, à bientôt,*" French for "See you later." After school, the children would read the correspondence and write answers—and he would read them when he returned. They each had calling cards with their names embossed on top: Darrylin, Susan, and Dickie, and occasionally they used them for their notes. One from Dickie read, "All the luck in the world to the best father in the world. Your Dickie. I love you," followed by twelve circles and twelve crosses. Darryl kept it under glass on his office desk.

When the children were young, Darryl used to make up stories about Gippy the Monkey, a naughty monkey who made mischief of one kind—and another. The monkey really was, so its creator confessed, Darryl F. Zanuck. Later he was to tell Gippy stories to his grandchildren, and they to this day call him, affectionately, Gippy.

"We were all kind of a little scared of him," says his son. "He had a quick temper and would get very irritable if we were making too much noise or that kind of thing. I think the only time he really physically struck me was one time when I was nine or something. I was up on a roof at the house at the beach, and I hit some passing car with a bean. I was using a curtain rod as a beanshooter. The car swerved. It didn't hit anything. The driver stopped the car and saw me up on the roof. I think he was a high-ranking officer. DZ beat the bejesus out of me with the curtain rod."

For his part, with no apparent provocation, Zanuck had a terrible fear that his children would be kidnaped. Perhaps he had read too much about the Lindbergh baby. He hired a full-time bodyguard who still is in his employ; he is now the night watchman at the Santa Monica house. "We used to pull his gun," says Susan, "and stick it in his back." As a precaution, as well as a convenience, he had the children chauffeured to school in his green Cadillac.

There was also a governess, Alma, "my Alma," as Virginia Zanuck calls her, who remained long after the children grew up. When they were little, Alma guarded them closely but allowed their father one privilege. Whatever odd hour he came home, she let him go in the nursery and pick up the babies. When they were adolescents, she was if anything even more strict. Once she barred the door to a shaggy, besandaled young actor who had come to call on Susan; he was Richard Burton.

Zanuck had always prided himself on his physical fitness— perhaps some of the Bernarr Macfadden rubbed off on him— and to make sure his children, particularly his son, were healthy and active, he hired a physical instructor for them, a man named Paul Nass. The kids called him Captain Nass and every day he would come to the beach house, have a game of badminton with the elder Zanuck if the weather was good, and instruct and play with the children. He taught all three how to swim, and as Dick says, "We all became good swimmers." Like most young Californians the younger Zanucks lived on the beaches, grew up bronzed and surfing. On Sunday nights the Zanucks would show movies in their home, usually two or three, and the children were allowed to stay up for the first. If it was a boring picture, Darryl would reach over to Dick and start wrestling. "He always won," recalls Dick, "until the last time. I was about fourteen and I got him in a neck lock and that was the end of the wrestling."

Even when Dick was very young, and he was a healthy tow-haired child, his father wanted to be sure he was tough. At first, Dick took piano lessoss—at the suggestion of his mother. "I became quite good," he remembers, "and played once at the Coconut Grove. They said I was a child prodigy as far as my piano was concerned. I had to practice every morning. I remember one morning, he got up early and said, 'What the hell are you playing the piano for? Why aren't you out on the beach playing football?' Shortly thereafter I got sick and gave up the piano and can't even play a note." Later, when Dick was at Harvard Prep, a military school, his father used to go to all the track meets and football games he was involved in. "He'd bring a whole gang from the studio, his whole staff, who couldn't care *less* about it, and they'd all be in the bleachers watching the football game." Similarly, for his daughter Susan, Zanuck had Gregory Ratoff work up a night club act with her (singing, dancing, jokes), and for two weeks they played the El Rancho Club in Las Vegas. The proud, indulgent father flew a planeload of friends over for the opening. "It probably cost Darryl $25,000 to put the act together," says Charles Feldman, "and we lost a fortune gambling." It was Susan's only appearance on the professional stage. For Susan's coming-out party, her father was supposed to dance the first dance with her, a waltz, and he didn't know how to waltz. Clifton Webb was volunteered as instructor. Behind locked doors, with Jules Styne playing the piano, Zanuck and Webb, doubled-over so that he was his boss's height, danced cheek to cheek, Zanuck puffing his cigar during the entire lesson.

Although the emphasis was on the physical, Zanuck did not entirely neglect his children's intellectual pursuits. He decided that Edward Leggewie should teach the children French too. They preferred Captain Nass's activities and responded to Leggewie's tutorship by tying him up and locking him in the bathhouse. "We used to torture Edward," remembers Susan. "We put bugs on him, anything we could think of." Once Zanuck himself put Leggewie on a wild horse, which threw him, breaking Leggewie's leg. With the indomitability of Job, Leggewie survived all the deviltries and harassments, and years later became head of Zanuck's Paris office.

Slowly Dick became aware of his father's position and power. Almost from the first, "I realized that we had money and he was in charge of a big corporation, that he made pictures. But I wasn't terribly interested in the business part of it. It was a kind of slow awakening to that. I didn't wake up one day and say, 'Gee, Dad is a big movie mogul.' There were always motion picture people around. They'd come to see him on weekends [in Palm Springs as well as Santa Monica]. Gregory Ratoff and George Jessel and Ty Power were drifting in all the time and we kids went about our own business. It didn't seem to be any big deal. It may have impressed my sisters a little more, having Tyrone Power walk into your house, a big star like that. But mostly he had writers and directors and those kinds of people."

When Dick was nine, he began selling the *Saturday Evening Post,* and he picked a good place to sell them, the Twentieth Century-Fox studio—a captive market if there ever was one. "I sold a lot of magazines. I used to stand outside the cafe during lunch time and sell *Posts* and go to every office in the building. Practically everybody bought a *Saturday Evening Post.* One thing: I was never allowed to take tips. I could only sell magazines for exactly what they were worth. I could have made an absolute killing if I had been able to take tips because I was the boss's son." Why did he sell magazines?

"I guess I was probably ambitious. I wanted to make money, although that money was very little really. I felt it was a constructive thing to do. You know it was a little ridiculous. I'd be picked up at grammar school—I was in the fourth or fifth grade—and be driven by chauffeur in a Cadillac to my little stand where I would sell *Saturday Evening Posts*. You know, it was ludicrous. I had a little money belt with dimes and nickels and quarters, a little thing where you could make change. Every Wednesday they'd deliver them in a truck. It must have been 800 or 900 copies each week right at the studio, and I'd sell every last one of them. I got to know everybody. I saw a lot of stuff happening. That was my first real exposure to the lot itself"—and one way to be introduced to the movie business. By the time he was in sixth grade Dick had graduated from magazine salesman to script reader. Darryl would give him scripts he was working on and ask him what he thought about them. "He was not interested in my opinion as such because that wouldn't mean anything to him, but in getting a youngster's opinion which reflected perhaps many many youngsters' opinions. And then I would sit in when he was showing rushes sometimes. He was always very interested in what my age group would think of certain pictures. He would show me rough cuts and stuff like that. When I got a little older he would bring me into story conferences."

Once, when Dick was twelve or thirteen, his father took him on a hunting trip with him and Sam the Barber. "It was just a total fiasco," recalls Dick. "We took a station wagon from the studio and drove down to Mexico, about fifty or sixty miles across the border. In those days DZ was very rugged. He'd go into these little huts with dirt floors, one room where twelve people were living, with kids and pigs. DZ would eat right out of their pots. Sam couldn't stand it. It was just like eating garbage, and DZ would rave about it. He was very rugged. Anyway the trip was a fiasco. He was convinced that I was going to shoot him—accidentally. Every five minutes he would say, 'You got your safety on?' I said, 'Yeah, I got my safety on.' When we'd go through swamps and underbrush and everything, he'd always make me go first because he was afraid I'd shoot him, you know, stumble and shoot him in the back. And he was always dramatizing. 'Your mother's home and the phone'll ring and they'll bring me in

on a stretcher.' It was freezing cold and he and Sam had
these tremendous, fantastic sleeping bags he and Sam had
used, I guess, on earlier hunting trips. All I had was a little
Boy Scout sleeping bag. He was worried that I'd get a cold.
So he made Sam get into this little Boy Scout bag. It was way
too small for him. I remember him throwing a shoe at Sam
early in the morning because Sam was snoring a great boom
across the camp. I did eventually shoot a hole in a little
dinghy and we started to sink. He got so excited. He said he
had warned me about the goddamn safety. But I had the
safety on. Back at the studio we had this prop shop for war
pictures. They examined the gun and it did have a faulty
safety." That was the last father-and-son hunting trip.

Once a year he took his whole family with him to Sun
Valley, and several times he took them all to Europe with
him. Susan remembers at thirteen going to the Lido in Paris
as a family outing. "I was shocked by the naked girls," she
says. "I put my napkin over Daddy's eyes."

One day, when Dick was thirteen or fourteen, Sam Silver
suddenly showed up at the beach house and said, "I want to
take you for a little ride."

Dick said, "Where?"

Sam answered, "We're going to the studio. I have something to show you."

They drove to the studio and went to the apartment of
commissary manager Nick Janios over the studio cafe.
Recalls Dick, "There's this gorgeous dame. And I was scared
to death."

Dick turned to Sam and asked, "What am I supposed to
do?"

Sam said, "Well, just talk to her for a while . . ."

Blackout.

"That was my first experience," says Dick, "and on the way
home I was kind of shell-shocked."

Finally coming out of it, he said to Sam, "Jesus, Sam, don't
you think you're taking a helluva chance? If DZ ever found
out about this, he'd crucify you."

Sam answered, "Jesus, you don't think I'd do a thing like
this without his instructions."

Says Dick, "DZ never once said a word about it, nothing.
I know that he was very worried, not worried, concerned
about me. He never took me aside and explained anything,

but he wanted me to be straightened out." On the other hand he was strict with his daughters, forbidding lipstick until he thought they were old enough; they would put it on after they left the house.

As it turned out, Dick's sex life was the least of Darryl Zanuck's worry about his son. It is generally agreed that as a teen-ager he was fast on his way to becoming a juvenile delinquent. "He was a little bandit," says one family friend. "He grew himself up. He resisted any kind of coddling." Dick freely admits, "I was very much of a brat all the way until I got out of college. The day before my sixteenth birthday he asked me if I knew how to drive. I said sure. I didn't. The next day DZ and my mother got me a car as a birthday present. Three days later I had a terrible collision." He smacked into another car, sending its occupants to the hospital. "DZ had one of those flashing temperaments that would flare out of control. He had a fantastic facility for getting back control and completely forgetting it in five minutes. This time he flared up. He said, 'Driving eighty miles an hour down Coldwater Canyon!' I said, 'I can't drive.' He blew up. He gave me the biggest tongue lashing in the world. I would have to take a taxi to school the rest of my life. I was in tears. He paused, panting, and there was silence for two or three minutes and he said, 'Do you brush your teeth up and down or sideways?' I said, 'I brush them sideways.' He said, 'The studio dentist says a lot of people who brush them sideways have trouble with their teeth.' "

During his freshman year at Stanford he got involved in a bloody knife battle in Palm Springs, which landed him in jail and his name and picture all over the newspapers. As Dick tells it, "There was this wealthy Indian in Palm Springs who invited me over to his house for a party. Before I even got there, he left. I came in with two or three friends from Stanford. The people there thought we hadn't been invited. And they started shoving and everything. There was this terrible scuffle. Knives were pulled. And everybody got cut up pretty badly. I called DZ from the hospital. He was in Palm Springs with guests. I called him and said, 'I'm in kind of a little trouble here. You better come down to the hospital.' Of course the guys that pulled all the knives were rounded up and arrested. But they tried to sue and it became a big affair. It made the newspapers and was a scandalous thing.

DZ kind of cringed at all this terrible publicity. He was goddamn mad at me. There wasn't a great deal he could do. He took away my car for three months. That was about the only form of punishment he could think of."

During vacations Dick became something of a travel bum. "I was a surfer and I traveled all over Europe, several times with my parents, by myself, and many times with one or two of my classmates. We would take motorcycles and run all over the place." He decided he wanted to be a writer. "I felt that this love of mine for traveling and moving around fit in with being a writer. All I needed was a typewriter. I would go to Honolulu and surf and when surfing was up, I would write. But I never did do any serious writing or anything." But somewhere between surfing, he began to settle down. During vacations he worked around the studio on the labor gang and in the story department and in the New York office, writing advertising copy. One summer he worked in the cutting department.

In 1956 he graduated from Stanford with honors and his father and mother came up for the ceremony. They stayed overnight at the Fairmont Hotel in San Francisco. Darryl started shaving, then asked his son, "Where shall we have dinner?"

"Let's go to Ernie's," said Dick, naming one of San Francisco's best restaurants.

"Great," said his father. "Call up and make a reservation. It's eight o'clock. Tell them we'll be over in half an hour."

As his father continued lathering, Dick called Ernie's, and was told, "Impossible. Absolutely impossible. We're fully booked. The earliest would be ten o'clock."

"Forget it," said Dick and then told his father.

"Wait a minute," said Darryl. "Give me the number," and with shaving soap all over his face, a cigar clenched firmly between his teeth, he called the number. "This is Darryl Zanuck," he announced. "I saw Ernie last month in Los Angeles and he said that any time I wanted to come up to his restaurant, he would do *anything*, that he could have a table for me on five minutes' notice. I want one in half an hour."

The lady on the other end of the phone laughed. "Mr. Zanuck, come on over in half an hour and we'll give you a table, but Ernie's been dead for twenty-five years."

9.

The Director's Studio

There was only one *boss I believed in and that was* me.
—Darryl Zanuck

In the middle and late forties, Zanuck ruled supreme, at Fox and in Hollywood. "Every creative decision was either authorized, or okayed, or created by me," he says. "Every script! There was no individual, no executive between me and the back lot. I was The Executive. I decided whether we made something or didn't make it. I was a One-Man Show." Nominally Spyros Skouras was, as president, the chief executive officer of the firm, but he was completely divorced from production matters. "I've never sent him a script in my life," declares Zanuck unequivocally. "Never! I showed him pictures, pictures that were edited, scored, and finalized." Zanuck himself became the number one studio. As one of his writers phrased it, "Fox knocked Metro out of the box." Zanuck did it, oddly enough, by making good movies. He made good movies by choosing exciting subject matter, hiring creative writers and directors, and guiding them into a mutually rewarding collaboration. For good reason Sixteenth Century-Fox became known as The Director's Studio. In a way it was also The Writer's Studio (just as it never became an Actor's Studio). John Ford, William Wellman, Elia Kazan, Henry Hathaway, Henry King, Otto Preminger, Lewis Milestone, Ernst Lubitsch, George Seaton, Joseph Mankiewicz all directed for him. Writers were bought, or brought out, by the planeload: Robert Riskin, Joel Sayre, St. Clair McKelway, F. Hugh Herbert, Henry Ephron, Jo Swerling, Sally Benson, Robert Sherwood, Moss Hart, Philip Dunne, so many of them New Yorkers and New York wits that they could have started a Round Table. Just as Zanuck gets the blame for the imitative and formularized pictures he produced, particularly in the thirties, he gets the credit for the adventurous, explorative films he produced in the forties. What are the reasons for the change of face? For one thing, Zanuck matured, artistically, in the forties; perhaps he became bored with the formula. On the other side, he found that controversy was commercial, so that making artistic pictures did not run counter to his commercial sensibility. He also had much better people working for him, and he took more chances with them, hiring novelists like Millen Brand, who had never written screenplays, stage directors like Elia Kazan, who had never directed movies, and letting screenwriters like Joseph Mankiewicz and George Seaton direct as well as write. Mostly he took chances in terms of material: not just one movie about the Okies, but many about anti-Semitism, racial violence, Negroes passing for white, insanity and mental institutions, lynching, marital infidelity, war crimes, and the psychological pressures of battle. During this time, Zanuck also had pictures that failed, but his record for producing quality pictures with a purpose, movies that were not only entertaining and profitable, but also provocative, and in some cases important, is unmatched by anyone in Hollywood.

The surprising thing is not only that he made these pictures, but that he made them in such an atmosphere of mutual respect and trust. His directors and writers, even those who hated him personally, admire him as a producer. At the very least they rate him very highly as an editor of scripts and a cutter of film.

"Darryl Zanuck was the best working producer in the history of our trade," says Philip Dunne, who wrote for Zanuck, among other scripts, *How Green Was My Valley, Pinky* (with Dudley Nichols), and *The Ghost and Mrs. Muir.* "To work with, he was exacting, demanding, stimulating, often irritating, and always rewarding. He was the boss, but he always treated you as an equal in discussion. Above all, he respected professionalism. As an editor he had few weaknesses. He never lost sight of the basic point of the picture. He might tend to overedit in an effort to speed the script, to get to the main point sooner, but always gave you ample opportunity to defend what you had written. And he never tried to rewrite you himself.

"His greatest strength was his decisiveness. Right or wrong, he made his decisions quickly and firmly. He never vacillated. Next to this I would put his innate ability to handle people, this being the hallmark of every great executive, and he would have been an outstanding executive in *any* line of business. He knew which writer or director best responded to iron discipline, which to sweet persuasion. He stood behind his own work and the efforts of those who worked under his orders.

"Next among his assets I would place his enthusiasm. Sometimes he carried this to somewhat ridiculous lengths; it was a standing joke on the lot that every current picture was the greatest picture ever made, but I think he did this deliberately." As weaknesses, says Dunne, there was one that was "a by-product of his decisiveness: sometimes he would decide too firmly and too fast and thus trap himself into error. And when he made a mistake it was a beaut."

The chain of command was Zanuck to everyone else. "In Darryl's time," says Dunne, "writers did not write scripts for directors; they wrote them for Darryl. Directors were assigned as writers and actors were assigned: by his decision." For both *How Green Was My Valley* and *Pinky*, Dunne wrote the scripts before the final director was assigned, and he insists they shot the script exactly as written (although with a few minor changes in *Valley*). Between Mankiewicz and Dunne it was more of a collaboration, both being assigned at the same time, along with producer Fred Kohlmar. "We worked together happily and, for me at least, rewardingly, but, as always, the dominant figure was not Joe, not Fred, not I, but Darryl Zanuck . . . To his way of thinking, there could only be one boss on a picture and that boss was Darryl F. Zanuck. This held for the Fords and Kazans as well as for journeyman directors. They seemed to thrive on it. The system produced at least five Academy Awards for direction."

Later Dunne became a director at Fox but his career "unhappily began almost coincidentally with Darryl's departure from active direction of the studio. I can only say that I wish he had stayed. I made some successful pictures, but I can't help feeling that they would have been better and more successful if he had still been there."

Not all Zanuck's collaborations were successful. There were occasional dissatisfactions and conflicts and even acts of violence. Sally Benson was so upset about *Come to the Stable,* that she systematically broke all the pencils on producer Sam Engel's desk and then in a fit of pique kicked Zanuck's door. Zanuck and Alfred Hitchcock had their disagreements over *Lifeboat*—Zanuck wanted to speed up the action—and it was the only time Hitchcock worked for Fox. Some of the collaborations were just not very creative. Fritz Lang passed through Zanuck's hands, briefly, in the early forties, and then made better picures elsewhere. Zanuck hired Jean Renoir, even though "his English was almost non-existent," carefully chose his first picture, which became the murky *Swamp Water,* and then Renoir made better pictures elsewhere. But as Renoir describes it, there was no disagreement between them. "My acquaintance with Darryl Zanuck lasted only a short time," says Renoir, "and I remember it as an extremely pleasant experience. Darryl Zanuck is a great producer and it is always exciting to work with somebody as dedicated as he is. I don't know him well but I am sure of one thing, it is that he loves sincerely and deeply the 'cinema.' "

In 1947, when Preston Sturges arrived at Fox, after a brilliant career making comedies mostly at Paramount, Zanuck still thought "we had a great coup in getting him." He made two pictures for Zanuck, *Unfaithfully Yours* and *The Beautiful Blonde from Bashful Bend,* both of them disasters at the box office, the second having the dubious distinction of being Betty Grable's first unprofitable picture—and this during the time that she was still Zanuck's number one star. "He crucified her in it!" remembers Zanuck. "We previewed it in Pomona and I walked around the block ten times. God, I didn't know what to do." *Unfaithfully Yours,* on the other hand, although not truly Sturgean (more farce than satire) has been generally underrated, even by Zanuck himself. Oddly enough, it was Zanuck's ordering of the sequence of twists that give the movie its funniest moments. There is an uncharacteristically physical (and hilarious) performance by Rex Harrison as a wildly successful, slightly stuffy orchestra conductor who suspects his wife (Linda Darnell) of infidelity and fantasizes what to do about it. Harrison remembers the movie and the director with great fondness. Sturges, he says, was "a most extraordinary and ingenious creature. The whole thing was like a party. He directed in a red fez. He would have a Doberman pinscher on set with him. Before he would start, he would stuff a handkerchief in his mouth to stop from laughing."

Zanuck honestly admired Sturges and his memos to him are filled with words like marvelous, magnificent, brilliant, and comedy masterpieces. Perhaps Zanuck liked him too much. According to Harrison, Sturges was one of those directors, like Lubitsch, to whom Zanuck gave total autonomy. He saw the dailies but otherwise he let him follow his own lead. The truth was that Sturges had problems that were distracting and ultimately debilitating. "He had a restaurant," remembers Zanuck, "and it was losing a bloody fortune, a boat company which was losing more and more. He was brilliant in conversation but he was drinking like mad. I got him at the end of his career."

It is difficult to imagine Otto Preminger as a boy wonder but that is exactly what he was when Joseph Schenck discovered him in 1935. A stage director in Austria, with a quickly accumulated reputation, Preminger at twenty-eight was both unknowing and curious about the movies. One of the first Hollywood personalities Preminger met when Schenck imported him to America was Zanuck, and he impressed him very much. "He was really to me—from Vienna, a soft, European city—the personification of everything American. He was terribly efficient, outspoken. He is probably the most organized executive that ever existed. His capacity for work at that time was tremendous, unbelievable." Then he adds, "It was difficult for me to follow Zanuck, who speaks very colloquially." Since Preminger still speaks very Germanically, the difficulty in communication was mutual. "Watch how pictures are made," ordered Zanuck, and for six months Preminger watched. Then Zanuck let him practice with a low budget. He made *Under Your Spell* and *Danger—Love at Work,* and then he was given his first big film, Robert Louis Stevenson's *Kidnapped.* "I read the book and script and I didn't understand it. Kilts and Scotland don't particularly appeal to me. I told Gregory Ratoff, 'I turn this down!' Ratoff said, 'If you do this, he'll never talk to you again.' "

So, reluctantly, Preminger went ahead with the picture—until he and Zanuck had an argument about Freddie Bartholomew's dog. After seeing the rushes, Zanuck said, "Why didn't you have the boy speak to the dog as the script called for?" "But this is not in the script," said Preminger. "You think I don't know my own script?" answered Zanuck. "The next day," remembers Preminger, "I was on the back lot." He hung around for almost a year watching how pictures were made. Zanuck couldn't use him and no one else would either. He wasn't considered important enough to employ or to worry about. Preminger worked his way back to Hollywood as an actor. He was on Broadway in *Margin for Error* while Zanuck was in the Army. Goetz wanted him—as an actor—for the Fox movie version of the play. Preminger wanted to direct again so badly that he offered to take a cut in salary, and work for a week on trial. Goetz hired him, and he directed, and acted in the movie of *Margin for Error,* and signed a seven-year contract with the studio. Shortly thereafter Zanuck returned and severed his relations with Goetz. Having been fired by Zanuck, and hired by Goetz, Preminger had two huge strikes against him, and was in imminent danger of being fired a second time. But then Zanuck informed him coldly, "You will produce, but you will never direct." Preminger thought, "Here I go again," another eleven months in purgatory. Instead he was assigned to the last circle of hell, Bryan Foy's B-picture unit.

Then Preminger discovered a story called *Laura,* and sent it to Foy. "I don't like it," said Foy. "You didn't read it," said Preminger, who knew that he had given it to an assistant, David Stevenson, to read. "I get one thousand dollars," said Preminger. "David gets seventy-five dollars. Why don't *you* at least read it?" The next day Preminger saw Foy in the elevator and Foy pretended he had read it. "David's right," he said. "Give it to Zanuck," insisted Preminger. "Zanuck will let you do something else," responded Foy. Finally the script was given to Zanuck and he called Foy and Preminger in to discuss it.

"You don't like the script, Brynie?" asked Zanuck.

"No," said Foy.

"Why don't you like it?"

Foy explained why he didn't like it. He talked and talked, waiting for Zanuck to interrupt him and agree with him.

But Zanuck just sat back and listened. Then he announced coldly, "Well, *I* like it," and he turned to Preminger and said, "Report to me from now on."

Preminger wanted to direct *Laura* himself, but Zanuck wanted him to find someone else. Preminger hoped that everyone would reject it, so that Zanuck would have to turn to him, and for a while it looked like they might. Lewis Milestone, among others, turned it down, but Rouben Mamoulian accepted it. When Jennifer Jones turned the part of Laura down, it was given to Gene Tierney. At Preminger's insistence, Clifton Webb was signed to play opposite her. Soon, with Zanuck in New York, the movie began shooting. The rushes were terrible. "Everything was blamed on me," says Preminger. "Webb was not good. Dana Andrews had no sex appeal. Then Zanuck came back. Then, as he did with Bryan Foy, he put me on the spot. What was wrong with the picture? Being an actor, I acted it out. He said, 'Why don't you explain that to Rouben?' 'Rouben doesn't listen.' " They started filming again, and "after three days, the rushes were no better." Then in the executive dining room, with all the producers and directors sitting in attendance, Zanuck announced, "I think I'll take Mamoulian off the picture." After lunch, walking down the hallway with his producers following him, Zanuck waved Preminger on with his polo stick, and said simply, "You're on." Unencumbered, Preminger directed *Laura*, wrapped it up, then showed it to Zanuck. He didn't like the ending, and the next day started to dictate a completely new one: everything was a dream and now we're going to tell the truth. Reluctantly, Preminger shot the new ending, then he and Zanuck watched the movie again, with Zanuck's friend Walter Winchell and a lady friend of Winchell's in the back row of the screening room. The two guests laughed at Clifton Webb's funny lines, then were silent. When the movie was over, Winchell shouted, "Bigtime! Bigtime, Darryl. But the end—I don't get it. You're going to change it?" Zanuck smiled, and said to Preminger, "After all these arguments, you want the old ending back?" Preminger nodded. "If this is a big success," said Zanuck, "it will be all to Preminger's credit."

Laura was, of course, a huge success, and was the beginning of a long relationship between Zanuck and Preminger. For him, Preminger made all sorts of pictures. He finished

A Royal Scandal when Ernst Lubitsch got sick, and again, *That Lady in Ermine*, when Lubitsch died. He made comedies on his own, such as *The Fan*, a version of *Lady Windermere's Fan*, which Lubitsch had filmed so superbly for Zanuck at Warners. He made musicals (*Centennial Summer* and later, in 1954, *Carmen Jones*), romances (*Forever Amber, Daisy Kenyon*) and melodramas (*Fallen Angel, Where the Sidewalk Ends*). Sadly, none of Preminger's subsequent pictures were anywhere as good as *Laura*, although he and Zanuck kept trying to repeat that success.

Looking back on his years with Zanuck, Preminger says, "I think Zanuck basically is one of the fairest men. He inspires a certain loyalty and following. He has a group of people, and I'm one of them, who would do anything for him. When we had an argument, there was nothing malicious about it. In spite of, or because of, everything, I have a warm feeling for him. It might not be unconditional admiration, but it is great admiration. More than Mayer or Warner or Cohn, he was a professional. He is a tremendously vital showman. The amazing thing about Zanuck is his flexibility. He is probably the most realistic man I know. He adjusts to a situation." And Zanuck on Preminger: "I fired him, hired him, fired him, hired him. I had him as an actor, producer, director. A great talent, but he has to be controlled."

Elia Kazan was a young stage director of commanding reputation and skill in 1945 when Zanuck hired him to direct his first film *A Tree Grows in Brooklyn*. Today the move would be a natural one, but in those days Hollywood still looked to its own, and since Kazan's success was with Tennessee Williams, then still considered too immoral and outspoken for the movies, merely for employing Kazan Zanuck must be praised. Kazan was very much one of Zanuck's hired directors, but more than most of them, he seemed to make pictures of a generally consistent level and type. He was not caught in the studio mill at all—no musicals, no costume epics or program fillers. Professionally their relationship was one of trust and admiration, although always each would be a little suspicious of one another for obvious reasons: Kazan of Zanuck because of his commercial reputation, Zanuck of Kazan because of his artistic reputation. Zanuck's wariness of

Kazan was expressed early in his employment in a memo to Louis Lighton, who was producing *A Tree Grows in Brooklyn*. He said that he felt that Kazan had thrown Lighton off the beam. "In his searching for illusive moods and inner emotional motivations there is the danger that we may talk ourselves into a perfect psychological story that is emotionally magnificent but lacking the true elements of entertainment that will appeal to the masses . . . Perhaps it is because I am naturally suspicious of deep thinkers in relation to motion pictures. They sometimes think so deep that they miss the point . . . I don't believe any story as good and as obvious as *A Tree Grows in Brooklyn* should be too difficult to construct and write."

As it turned out *A Tree Grows in Brooklyn* was a happy experience for all concerned. Kazan had accepted it originally because of his admiration for Lighton, which continued unabated through the filming. As for Zanuck, the picture has remained one of his personal favorites through the years. *A Tree Grows in Brooklyn* was filmed almost entirely in the studio, but for his next picture *Boomerang!* Kazan went on location—to White Plains and Stamford. This was one—and one of the best—in a number of "semi-documentaries" Louis de Rochemont co-produced for Zanuck (most of which were directed by Henry Hathaway, including *House on 92nd Street, 13 Rue Madeleine,* and *Call Northside 777*).

On the strength of these two successes, Kazan was called upon to direct *Gentleman's Agreement*, which probably more than any other is the definitive Zanuck movie of the period, in terms of subject matter (anti-Semitism), source (a best-selling novel), approach (a social situation studied through a human relationship), timeliness, controversy, and quality packaging. Seen today, it seems outmoded, but compared for instance, to a 1967 slick protest film such as *Guess Who's Coming to Dinner*, which was dated even before its time, *Gentleman's Agreement* seems a model of complexity and subtlety. There are all forms of discrimination in it—country-club snobbery, corporate quotas, Jewish anti-Semitism—except for violence (which Zanuck left to RKO's *Crossfire,* the rival anti-Semitism movie of the moment). The movie was a personal production for Zanuck, and he was in charge from start to finish. He convinced Moss Hart to make a rare trip to Hollywood to write the screenplay. Since Kazan was involved in the stage production of *A Streetcar Named Desire*, Zanuck and Hart did most of the preliminary work, preparing a script from Laura Hobson's book (Miss Hobson herself was at the studio for much of the filming). As Hart's widow, Kitty Carlisle, remembers, "Moss liked Darryl enormously. They wound up the best of friends. They enjoyed each other as people. He felt Darryl had great courage to do the picture. There was great pressure from some not to do it. Moss did it as a labor of love." Kazan echoes the point about the Zanuck-Hart friendship. Kazan and Zanuck never had that kind of personal relationship, but professionally they never were closer than on *Gentleman's Agreement*. "We saw very well eye to eye on *Gentleman's Agreement*," says Kazan. "He was energetic and vociferous. I was strong willed. We'd argue a lot. He was a combination of very lively energy and impersonality. Like all executives who operate on a large scale, he kept everyone sort of at arms' length. But I felt a warmth stirred up by the work itself. His actions made him seem like a warm person. Lots of rich Jews in Hollywood didn't want *Gentleman's Agreement*. Don't stir it up! He didn't pay attention to them. To the Catholics who got after him—they told him the leading lady couldn't be a divorced woman— he said in effect go fuck yourself. Those were the days of censorship—fantastic and prurient censorship. *Gentleman's Agreement* was not terribly daring," admits Kazan, "but at the time it marked a step. It made a clear commitment against anti-Semitism."

Kazan wasn't satisfied with one scene he had filmed and told Zanuck immediately that he wanted to shoot it over. "When?" asked Zanuck. "Tomorrow," said Kazan, and the next day he reshot it. As Zanuck explained in a letter to Hart, "I would rather get it good *now* than have to chop it up and try to trim after the picture is finished. These things are to be expected, particularly in a film where you have eighty per cent talk and twenty per cent action. Rest assured that to the best of our joint abilities we will eliminate nothing that is essential or significant to either the story or the theme, but I am sure you agree that by all means we must not make a dull picture even though it be significant and important . . . It is a double challenge to me. The subject on one side and the utter necessity for an exciting lively drama on the other side." The movie, released in 1947, won Academy Awards all around, Zanuck's first Oscar since *How Green Was My Valley.*

After *Gentleman's Agreement* Kazan went back to Broadway and then Zanuck called him for an emergency rescue mission on *Pinky,* Zanuck's entry in the Negro discrimination sweepstakes. *Pinky* was based on Cid Ricketts Sumner's novel *Quality.* John Ford had been directing *Pinky* but suddenly "became sick and quit." Ford also had apparently had a conflict with Ethel Waters, who was starring in the picture. Zanuck says, "It was a professional difference of opinion. Ford's Negroes were like Aunt Jemima. Caricatures. I thought we're going to get into trouble. Jack said, I think you better put someone else on it. I said, finish out the day and I took Ford off the picture. Some directors are great in one field and totally helpless in another field." Zanuck called Kazan in New York and asked him to fly out, didn't even tell him what the script was about. Kazan asked to see it. Zanuck said he would send it and that Kazan should read it on the plane coming out. Kazan took the plane, read the script, scrapped Ford's two weeks of photography, and shot the entire picture in eight weeks. In the title role, that of the poor southern girl who passes for white in the north and returns home to regain her balance after a whirlwind courtship by a white doctor, Zanuck cast Jeanne Crain, who by that time was Fox's Miss Homespun America. Probably the only "whiter" actress on the lot was Betty Grable. The choice certainly would be attacked. Today a Negro actress would get the part. But there was a curious courage in the casting of Miss Crain, for her as well as Zanuck, for her because of whatever injury playing black might do to her career (none as it turned out—she got the best reviews of her life), for him because by putting the wholesome Miss Crain in the part, he put the lie to the whole color double standard. The other characters in the film, like the people in the audience, couldn't believe Miss Crain was a Negro, but because she was supposed to be that was enough to subject her to prejudice. If this could happen to Jeanne Crain, Zanuck seemed to be asking his audience, couldn't it happen to anybody? And weren't Negroes anybody, too? Zanuck insisted that he was interested, as usual, in "an individual and personal story. We are not trying to solve a general problem in this picture. We are dealing with a specific story and a specific problem of one girl and what happens to her." Although there are occasional glimpses of other sides of the problem: the shabbiness of Niggertown, the passivity of southern Negroes, mostly this was the story of Pinky. *Pinky* seems like a romance, and the well-designed moments of sadness and sentiment reinforce that semblance. But there is a hard core to this picture. Even today, *Pinky* is a surprisingly relevant movie, and in 1949 it was nothing short of a shocker.

Kazan continued directing for Zanuck into the early fifties. In 1950 there was *Panic in the Streets,* "a good experience," says Kazan. "It was done away from the studio in New Orleans with lots of non-actors. The most fun movie ever made. The only thing I didn't like was the title. It was half winging, a pseudo-, or semi-documentary." In 1952 came *Viva Zapata!* with a script by John Steinbeck. It was, says Kazan, his idea, and Zanuck gave the go ahead because of the success of *Gentleman's Agreement* and *Pinky.* Once committed, Zanuck attacked it with his usual enthusiasm, but in this case also with naïveté. "This story . . . is a spiritual adventure," he wrote. "We must not ignore any opportunity to include the elements of suspense and tension. I would like it to be the kind of picture that a ten-year-old kid could look at and like and that a professor of philosophy would also think highly of . . . It is really a Robin Hood story with an ideal." Eventually Zanuck ran into political trouble with the Mexican government, so he merely moved the location across the border and shot it in New Mexico. Kazan's final picture for Zanuck was *Man on a Tightrope,* which he says was not a happy experience.

In talking about Zanuck, Kazan prefers to minimize their later differences, and emphasize their earlier agreements. "I sort of like him personally," he says. "He was always straightforward when I was working with him. He didn't go behind my back. He's a dominant, aggressive man, but not a dishonest man. He was essentially a fair guy when he was not challenged in a competitive way. He often explained to me that you have to make popular or program pictures in order to afford the others, the pictures he had to nurse, shepherd, and look after. He was a tough little guy with a narrow, intense vision. I was completely consulted, but I didn't have the final cut. Either you do or you don't. Zanuck prided himself on being a great cutter." His forte was "chase and detect.

Will he fuck her or won't he? Will he catch her or won't he? He had a strong feeling for external plot. There's a validity in that because the plot carries it through. But anything with ambivalence or the subtler qualities . . . He worked very hard on a script, very hard. He didn't duck a problem. I'd want to sleep on it and he went for an immediate direct attack. He would never double deal. There was no production chicanery. He'd work days and nights, night after night. He saw every foot of film shot on the lot. He is an excellent executive. His studio was a well-run, well-managed organization. A one-man organization."

Anatole Litvak read Mary Jane Ward's *The Snake Pit* in galleys and bought it for $75,000, then went out to Hollywood and tried to get a studio to back him making a movie out of it. "You're crazy," he was told. "Why do you want to do a picture about mad people?" After several rejections, he went to Darryl Zanuck "in desperation" because at the time Fox was not known for making independent deals. But Zanuck was an old friend. Litvak had made *This Above All* for him in 1942 and through Zanuck's intercession had gotten a commission in the Signal Corps during World War II. "I always thought of him as a very hard-boiled executive," says Litvak, "but I found that he was a very nice man. There was something terribly warm, a deep devotion to his friends, covered by a lot of sarcasm and kidding around. Down deep he's deeply considerate of the people he's cared for." As Litvak remembers about *The Snake Pit*, "He was kind of scared of the whole thing, but he felt that subjects of this kind should be made. Zanuck has the tremendous quality and ability of making quick decisions. He would act, sometimes, in fifteen minutes, not several months later. He said, 'Put it down in three pages. I don't want to read the book.' " Litvak put *The Snake Pit* down in five pages. Zanuck called the next day and said, "Look, go ahead."

On *The Snake Pit*, Litvak was in charge more than most directors (probably because the property was his inspiration and also because Zanuck trusted him), but the two worked closely together. And although Zanuck did not work much directly with the screenwriters, Millen Brand and Frank Partos, Litvak was his pipeline to them. As with all his important movies (important either in a commercial or artistic sense), Zanuck worked carefully, line by line, scene by scene on the script. In looking back over his script suggestions, it is clear that not only were they accepted (after all, they had to be) but they were intelligent and justified. All of his good films benefited by Zanuck's emphasis on clarification and pacing of the plot, but perhaps none more so than *The Snake Pit.* It was, after all, in almost a classic Zanuck sense, the story of one woman, through whom is revealed a situation of greater importance than herself. But the focus is on that woman, and her problem, and Zanuck did not let anyone forget it.

When the movie was deep in production, Zanuck studied the script "from the viewpoint of entertainment and economy. The feeling of suspense and urgency has not carried me along," said Zanuck, and through cutting and manipulation he hoped to increase that suspense and urgency. He (and Litvak and the writers) succeeded. *The Snake Pit* is not only a compassionate psychological probing of one woman and an indictment of medical shortcuts and malpractices, but it is an exciting movie, full of "suspense and urgency," with a marvelously sensitive and controlled performance by Miss de Havilland. Zanuck was proud of the reviews, the grosses, and the controversy. One of his happiest boasts is that because of *The Snake Pit,* new legislation covering state mental hospitals was passed in twenty-six states.

As a screenwriter, Joseph Mankiewicz wanted most of all to direct his own films. But his longest-running superior officer, Louis B. Mayer, said he should first become a producer. Finally in 1943 Darryl Zanuck said that if Mankiewicz came to Twentieth Century-Fox, he could direct, produce, and write. During his eight years with Zanuck, Mankiewicz made two masterpieces of sophisticated movie comedy (*A Letter to Three Wives* and *All About Eve*), another comedy of only slightly lesser charm (*People Will Talk*), the bluntest of the racial dramas (*No Way Out*), an exciting thriller (*Five Fingers*), and seven other pictures of great variety and varying distinction (including *Dragonwyck, The Ghost and Mrs. Muir* and *The Late George Apley*). More than any of Zanuck's resident directors, Mankiewicz put his stamp on his pictures. Even Kazan did not really mark his movies as his own (something he was able to do on stage even when his author was

1. Sign outside Wahoo: top billing

2. The Man behind the shades: Zanuck at Cap d'Antibes, June 1968

3. Frank Zanuck: father

4. Louise Torpin Zanuck: mother

5. Henry Torpin: grandfather and hero

6. The Wahoo Kid at age eight; see inset upper right corner

7. A boy and his gun: hunter and trapper

8. At fourteen, boy soldier

9. At the front with Private Zanuck

10. Darryl F. Zanuck in office, c. 1930

Back from Europe
Pasadena – feb 19-'28
Darryl and Virginia Zanuck

11. Home from abroad, 1928

12. Zanuck ranch in Encino: Darrylin, Susan, Richard

13. Father and mogul: Zanuck with Shirley Temple and daughter, Darrylin

14. With Virginia Zanuck at Sun Valley: a daring skier

15. Darryl, Virginia, and rhino: on safari

16. Hollywood horseman: a tough competitor at polo

17. Outwitting the bull in Pamplona

18. Flying mogul on a trapeze at a party at Ciro's in 1954

19. Office at the studio: trophy room

20. Conference in DZ's office, c. 1939, with Eddie LeBaron and Mark Hellinger

21. Grand Cross of French Legion of Honor: Admiral
Richard E. Byrd (left), Will Hays (center), Walt Disney
(right)

22. Ric-Su-Dar, Palm Springs: (top to bottom), tennis court, guesthouse, pool, host's house, croquet court

23. The children: Zanuck with Susan, Richard and Darrylin

24. Henry King; Claudette Colbert; Zanuck; Louis Mountbatten, Earl of Burma; and Douglas Fairbanks, Jr.

25. World War II colonel: Zanuck with Jack L. Warner and Field Marshal Montgomery

26. Political idol: "One World" Wendell Willkie

27. Rin Tin Tin (with Baby Mary Louise Miller in **Jaws of Steel**)

28. **The Public Enemy** with James Cagney and Edward Woods: the gangster cycle

29. **I Am a Fugitive from a Chain Gang** with Paul Muni: bum rap, fine film

30. **The Grapes of Wrath** with Henry Fonda and Jane Darwell; agony for the Okies

31. Top stars: Tyrone Power and Betty Grable in **A Yank in the R.A.F.**

32. **Down Argentine Way** with Betty Grable and Don Ameche: formula fun

33. Alice Faye: Nice in spite of it all

34. Tycoon in the sun: at Cap d'Antibes, June 1968

35. **Gentleman's Agreement** with Gregory Peck, John Garfield, Celeste Holm

36. **The Snake Pit** with Olivia de Havilland: compassion for the insane

37. **All About Eve** with Anne Baxter, Bette Davis, Marilyn Monroe, George Sanders: irony for the famous

38. Oscars for **Eve**: smiles all around

39. War waif: Juliette Greco in **The Roots of Heaven** (with Errol Flynn)

40. Resistance fighter: Irina Demick in **The Longest Day**

41. Rich man's unhappy wife: Genevieve Gilles in **Hello—Goodbye** (with Curt Jurgens)

42. Friend and Director: John Huston, at 52 Association dinner

43. Genevieve Gilles:
the lady with DFZ

44. Star and friend: Zanuck with Elizabeth Taylor

45. Darryl Zanuck: in 1970, the last tycoon

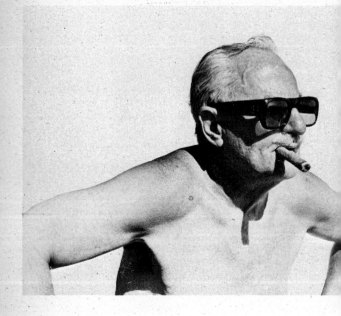

46. Richard Zanuck and Darryl Zanuck: the president and the chairman

47. Report to Stockholders, 1970

Tennessee Williams or Arthur Miller). Perhaps Kazan's screenwriters—people like Moss Hart and John Steinbeck—were stronger than his stage writers. Perhaps the difference was simply that Mankiewicz wrote his own (and with the exception of George Seaton there were not many of Zanuck's directors who won that privilege). And by winning double Oscars, in successive years *A Letter to Three Wives* and *All About Eve,* Mankiewicz proved he more than merited that freedom. Although his first film at Fox was an assignment (he wrote and produced *The Keys of the Kingdom,* a box-office disaster), within several years, as he recalls, "I could choose what I wanted to do."

With Zanuck, it was an interesting collaboration. Brilliant phrasemaker and house wit, Mankiewicz was one of several Fox directors (Preminger was another) who worshiped Lubitsch. But whereas Lubitsch had a long professional and personal history with Zanuck, Mankiewicz seemed much more the natural antagonist. The acidulous, intellectual Mankiewicz and the practical-joking Zanuck were never really friends. But in mutual trust and with a healthy degree of mutual suspicion they worked superbly together. Each honestly admired the other. Zanuck knew that there was no one better with dialogue on the lot and Mankiewicz knew that his outspoken comedies could not be made except in such an atmosphere of freedom as provided by Zanuck. Years later, long after Mankiewicz left Fox, he and Zanuck became not only antagonists but enemies. When Zanuck fired him as director of *Cleopatra,* it was clearly a case of cinematic castration. Even though, later, publicly some of their differences were patched up, Mankiewicz will never forgive Zanuck. He was, as few people of his stature have been, injured and humiliated by Zanuck. The surprising thing is that even Mankiewicz can't help give Zanuck his due.

On the one hand Mankiewicz calls him a megalomaniac and says, "Zanuck in the forties was Sukarno at his height. A tremendous security of power and success. Not for nothing was he called the Czar of the Rushes. He lived like a czar." And then, about Zanuck's success—"Not bad for a little man. The essence of Darryl is also the essence of Napoleon." On the other hand, Mankiewicz says, "Darryl was a talented man. I've worked for all the major producers, I can't think of anybody in those days I'd rather bring a play or movie script or novel to—not for over-all judgment, but for his editorial opinion in the first instance. He's a damn good critic and editor," adding with emphasis, "in the first instance." Then, as always with Mankiewicz on Zanuck, comes the demurrer, "The longer he is concerned with something, the worse he is. Just like his cutting—peak to peak to peak." (As Peter Viertel has described it, "He would very often take the nuance off the picture and leave the fast and the violent.") "This is style and substance today," says Mankiewicz. "In the days when character was developed more deeply, Darryl would break a director's heart and a writer's heart. He was impatient with anything cerebral. But . . . in the first instance, for that major elimination . . ." Perhaps the classic illustration of Zanuck's talent in the first instance is *A Letter to Three Wives.* The movie began as a *Cosmopolitan* story called, "One of Our Hearts," was retitled *A Letter to Five Wives,* and early in its metamorphosis into movie was abbreviated to *A Letter to Four Wives,* which is the number it stood at as Mankiewicz finished the screenplay. Zanuck read it and liked it "immensely," but indicated that he had "one violent and major criticism," and immediately got it off his chest:

"Insomuch as it is quite obvious that we are never going to get this script down to proper length without sacrificing or cutting some of the individual episodes," he memoed Mankiewicz, "I therefore began to study the script after I had finished the first reading with an idea of not cutting from the standpoint of economy or footage but trying to cut from the angle of dramatic interest . . .

"There is one episode in the story that by comparison bored me . . . I refer to the entire episode with Martha and Roger. The rest of the story is exciting, sexy, humorous, but when you come to the problems of Martha and Roger you start on a familiar downhill path . . .

"I do not intend here and now to defend my criticism, but I will go on record as saying that if you eliminate Martha and Roger entirely from this script you are going to have a motion picture that is one hundred per cent better . . . By dropping them out you will give the entire picture tempo and in addition to this will bring the picture down to a reasonable length." In other words Zanuck said, "Cut one wife." They did, and as both he and Mankiewicz knew, it made a much better picture.

Zanuck committed no such major surgery on *All About Eve*. After reading the script and praising it, he wrote Mankiewicz, reminding him of his last editing, "You will recall that on *A Letter to Three Wives* I astonished everyone including you by taking 40 pages out of the script and eliminating completely one set of characters. In this case I could do no such operation but you will have to go along with me and trust my judgment in this instance the same as you did then." And then he sent Mankiewicz nine pages of notes, detailing suggested changes and cuts. "I have tried to sincerely point out the spots that appeared dull or overdrawn. I have not let the length of the script influence me. I have tried to cut it as I am sure I would cut it if I were in the projection room." Most of the cuts were to keep the play moving. Some points of characterization bothered him: in "the scene where Addison overhears where Eve makes a pass at Bill . . . I think we drop Eve right down into the gutter and she never gets out of it. I do not mind dropping her in the gutter but when we do it this early then I think we are making a dramatic error . . ." A good many of Zanuck's revisions were included in the shooting script and made the screen. One was disregarded entirely. "On Page 32 I think the use of my name in a picture I am associated with will be considered self-aggrandizement. I believe you can cut it with no loss." Somebody convinced him otherwise.

"Zanuck, Zanuck, Zanuck," said Bette Davis to Gary Merrill. "Are you two lovers?"

As the movie became a classic, a camp classic among other things, with contraband copies of Mankiewicz's early uncut version being acted out at cocktail parties, each line assumed the shape of revealed truth. Would the same canonization have taken place for a movie called *Best Performance* starring Claudette Colbert? Actually Marlene Dietrich was one of Zanuck's early choices to play Margo Channing. Mankiewicz thought she would be all wrong, but both he and Zanuck agreed that Claudette Colbert would be right in the part. Happily, they also agreed on Bette Davis.

Just as RKO's *Crossfire* contrasted with *Gentleman's Agreement*, Zanuck's *No Way Out* contrasted with his *Pinky*. Where *Pinky* was about a sly, insidious sort of prejudice, *No*

Way Out was about racial hatred and violence, "the first time racial violence was shown on screen—except for *Birth of a Nation*—in modern times," says Mankiewicz, adding, "Darryl had all the guts in the world as far as subject matter is concerned." The violence of *No Way Out* is its strength; the brutal encounter between the eager-to-please young Negro doctor (Sidney Poitier) and the savage racist (Richard Widmark); the riot which is precipitated by the whites but actually begun by the blacks; the vicious epithets. In some ways it is a stronger picture than *Pinky* but in others a somewhat weaker one. One of the most curious things about *No Way Out,* and probably the best comment on the discrimination of its time is Poitier's sensitive, disciplined performance—his first in a movie. If he had been white, he would have rocketed immediately to stardom. Instead he took a back seat for another fifteen years.

Mankiewicz's last picture for Zanuck was *Five Fingers.* "I was leaving Fox," recalls Mankiewicz, "and Darryl gave me a script by Michael Wilson and said, 'This needs some rewriting. I don't want you to take writer credit.' I rewrote it and directed it and Otto Lang, a *very* nice fellow, produced it." The day before the movie opened, Mankiewicz heard that Zanuck had recut it. From New York, he sent a long night letter, full of fury, accusing him of butchering the picture. The next morning, he opened the *Times* and read a rave review of *Five Fingers.* Frantically he called his brother Herman in Hollywood (who worked for a time for Zanuck) and asked him to go to see Zanuck's secretary, Esther Roberts, and reclaim the angry letter before Zanuck saw it. Herman asked for it, and Miss Roberts answered, "I already gave it to him." At their parting, Zanuck remained one up on Mankiewicz.

Henry King worked more years for Zanuck and made more pictures for him than any other director. He was at Fox even before Zanuck, joining the company in 1930 to direct *Lightnin',* remaining through the merger with Twentieth Century, and lingering to direct more than forty films. It was his destiny to direct many of Zanuck's personal productions. The result was that . . . there is no Henry King. He became Zanuck's alter ego, with no definable directional personality of his own. King's best, which is not to say most Kingly, Zanuck films are *Song of Bernadette, Twelve O'Clock High,* and *The Gunfighter.*

Among Zanuck's good films, *Song of Bernadette* is probably the most uncharacteristic. It is actually the sort of film, at least on the record, that would have appealed more to Spyros Skouras. During the production, there was the one great problem of what to do about the Virgin Mary—whether put her on screen or off, and if on, how to visualize her. King wanted her on screen. George Seaton, who wrote the screenplay, wanted her off screen. Zanuck settled the question by naming Linda Darnell to play the part. Seaton was so upset that he showed scenes of St. Linda in blue to the author, Franz Werfel, who blew up. "If you release the picture with the girl in blue," he said, "I will write a letter to the New York *Times.*" The scenes were removed, and a soft, creamy, misty, indefinable non-actress was photographed instead. When the movie was shot, Zanuck had been on active duty in the Army. He returned, screened it, and decided that it was a mess. "Jesus, I fought with King and [producer William] Perlberg. The problem was length. They had literally taken the book. There were *hours* of her scrubbing the floor. She had blisters on her knees!" Zanuck took it into the cutting room, and in two days, tore it apart, for one thing cut down on the scrubbing, put it back together, and made it work. *Bernadette* turned out to be quite a good picture, a box-office hit, and won an Academy Award for Jennifer Jones as best actress.

In contrast to *Bernadette,* Zanuck was involved in the production of *Twelve O'Clock High* from its first false start (the movie was shelved for nine months) to its finish. He worked closely with Sy Bartlett on the screenplay and with Bartlett and King on the production. For the supposedly pro-military Zanuck, it was an unusual movie to make, showing as it did through General Savage (Gregory Peck) the insane psychological pressures borne by men in combat. *Twelve O'Clock High* was really a pro-peace movie, or at least anti-military-establishment, and one that took courage to make even in 1949. (Perhaps Zanuck was closer to it than he thought. As Sy Bartlett says, "He knew General Savage so well. In ways his life paralleled his. He ruled by rigid discipline," and later, like Savage, "Zanuck found he couldn't crawl into the goddamn cockpit.") *Twelve O'Clock High* was a huge hit.

In the beginning Zanuck had the highest hopes for King's next, *The Gunfighter*. To its producer, Nunnally Johnson, Zanuck criticized the script: "It could be made just as it is and it would be a hell of a good and rather unusual western. I do feel, however, that this can emerge as a real classic in the field . . . as powerful as *Stagecoach* . . . I have always been looking for a frontier picture to top *Stagecoach*. To my mind *Stagecoach* was the best of them all. *Ox-Bow Incident* was great from an artistic standpoint but the lynching theme rendered it unpopular." He felt that *The Gunfighter* would be a classic depending on the direction and the casting and if "we ourselves enlarge the scene and probe deeper and squeeze out every ounce of conflict that we can." Zanuck and King had one great disagreement on the picture: over Peck's handlebar mustache. "I would give $25,000 of my own money to get that mustache off Peck," said Zanuck, adding, "The picture's a Rembrandt but I don't know if it's box-office." The movie turned out to be a financial failure, but over the years has achieved an underground artistic success.

Looking back on their long association, King is full of admiration for Zanuck, the admiration of one professional for another, of an old-line commercial director for a nononsense administrator. "He was involved in the editing of every picture that ever went through the studio," says King. "He was one of the most astute film editors I've ever seen in my life. He has an uncanny instinct . . . He does everything by correspondence. You send him a note and you get an answer in an hour. He is a great executive, the type all young people should go to study How to Be an Executive. I've always heard people say Zanuck was a hard taskmaster, but to me he was the easiest man to make a picture for I've ever encountered. You see, Zanuck looks at the rushes every day and makes a report on them. It gives you confidence to have someone like that to see something that you don't see."

Unlike Henry King, John Ford was a strong director with a strong personality, one who could easily stand up to Zanuck. In the late thirties and early forties it was Ford, not King, who made Zanuck's best movies—*Young Mr. Lincoln, The Grapes of Wrath, How Green Was My Valley*—even though King directed many more, including many more of Zanuck's supposedly major productions. Considering their closeness then, and during the war, it might be assumed that Ford and Zanuck would continue their collaboration after the war. Such was not the case. *My Darling Clementine* in 1946 turned out to be something of Ford's valedictory to Zanuck. He did make two brief unsuccessful revisits to the studio, *When Willie Comes Marching Home,* in 1950, which Ford remembers as "a very funny picture," and a curious remake of *What Price Glory* in 1952, which had music added during its production and then subtracted when it was released. As Zanuck said about it later, "Our picture was a flop because it was neither fish nor fowl. It was not the powerful *What Price Glory* of World War I that everyone loved and remembered—and it was certainly not a good comedy." *My Darling Clementine,* on the other hand, was an *homage,* a valentine. It was a compendium of all western clichés. But it was expertly made and had an unforgettable performance by Henry Fonda, and even a strong one by Victor Mature, not a great Western, but a pure Western. After *Clementine,* Ford went elsewhere, everywhere. Why? "More money. Better offers," Ford answers laconically, like a Ford cowboy hero. "Darryl and I parted very amicably, the best of friends. But you can outlive your stay at one studio, and my contract was finished so I just went elsewhere."

Ford remains one of Zanuck's greatest admirers. "Darryl's a genius," he says flatly, "and I don't use the word lightly. Of course in this industry every idiot nephew of some executive producer is a genius, but he actually was. He was head and shoulders above all other producers. The only other I'd compare him to, who I would also use the word 'genius' to describe is the late Irving Thalberg . . . Darryl and I never had a disagreement. We talked it over. He knew I hated to go into the projection room, so I had this tacit agreement that he would cut the picture. If it was up to me I'd cut everything out. He'd say, 'What do you think of it?' and I'd say, 'It's just another picture.' He was a great cutter, a great film editor . . . I never look at rushes. You see, I'm not very proud of my own work," he says, with a deadpan expression. What Ford is omitting of course is that he cuts as he shoots. Once shot, there is not much room for cutting. Like a good tight novel, in a Ford film, all the pieces fit, interlock, intertwine, and it is not easy to edit without totally remaking the picture. Zanuck did cut Ford's movies, but obviously as part of their agreement, Zanuck knew that with Ford there was just so much he could do, and Ford could sail off firm in the knowledge that the movie would not be corrupted. "We had an ideal relationship," says Ford.

In the fall of 1968 Zanuck decided "In reviewing all the work of the many directors I have finally come to the conclusion that John Ford is the best director in the history of motion pictures. I have disregarded D. W. Griffith as he was basically a technical creator of outstanding brilliance but worked in another age long before the advent of sound. The reason I select Ford above William Wyler, Frank Capra, René Clair, Ernst Lubitsch, Leo McCarey, George Stevens, David Lean, George Cukor, Robert Z. Leonard, William Wellman, Gregory La Cava, Erich von Stroheim, Michael Curtiz, Joe Mankiewicz, Frank Lloyd and Alfred Hitchcock is that Ford was unique in that he visualized motion pictures in purely visual terms and I believe any director on this list would agree that Ford could get more drama into an ordinary interior or exterior long shot than any director and that his placement of the camera almost had the effect of making even good dialogue unnecessary or secondary. The fact that we won two Oscars together as producer and director, namely, *The Grapes of Wrath, How Green Was My Valley*, does not influence me in my choice as he won his first Oscar with *The Informer* which was a visual masterpiece almost unparalleled in cinema history. The names I have listed after Ford are not in order of their talent as all of them made at least two or three outstanding films but Ford was the master." It is an interesting, but curious list in some of its inclusions as well as its omissions. For one thing, most of his favorite directors never made movies for Zanuck.

"Jack Ford was the greatest for many reasons," he explained. "Ford had that enormous sense of the visual. He makes the camera act. If you look at the end in *My Darling Clementine* . . . he built a fence, a wooden fence, a crossbar fence, one half mile long, down a dirt road. In the last scene, as he [Henry Fonda] looks at the gravestone on Boot Hill—a skimpy four, five, or ten graves—you don't see the fence but you see his expression and when the camera pans with him, you see the fence running into the endless distance. The musical score on a harmonica plays *My Darling Clementine* and Fonda walks away until he's a dot in the distance . . . When it came to staging a fight scene, Ford was better than anybody. It was always done as funny as hell. The first time I ever saw a bartender slide a beer down to a customer, twenty people away, and stop on a button was in one of his pictures . . . I think he made more outstanding hits than any other director—on all subjects. He was an artist. He painted a picture—in movement, in action, in still shots. He would never move a camera setup—move in or zoom in. You would look at the set and think, maybe you need a closeup, but you didn't. He was a great great pictorial artist. He was a motion picture director!"

By 1950 Zanuck had made his major contribution to the movies: the sophisticated comedies, the semi-documentaries, and especially the pictures with social content. Zanuck's detractors credit his success to luck or cynicism. Many of his best pictures of the period were perhaps more journalistic than artistic (if one can think of the two adjectives being opposite poles) but with a purpose. They were, for the most part, contemporary, meaningful, and in some cases precipitous of reforms. And if Zanuck was not exactly leading the country into social action, he was at least leading Hollywood.

In June 1950 *Time* magazine put King Zanuck, crowned in celluloid, on its cover, and called him the "pacesetter for the U. S. Cinema." But for all his growing artistic and social awareness, he never forgot first principles: profits. By the end of 1950, with the Korean War in progress, he rejected the idea of making a movie about an alcoholic called *John Barleycorn*. He noted that *Panic in the Streets* was losing money, doubted that *The Lost Weekend* and *The Snake Pit* would have made money if they had been released then, and said, "Today audiences seem to be shopping for anything that sounds like adventure or escape. They want to get out and away from the gloomy news of the moment." Almost immediately the flow stopped and Zanuck was back in business.

10.

"Artists"

Do you realize, Darryl, that when I was a baby you used to dandle me on your knee?

—Elizabeth Taylor

Zanuck's weak points are actors and actresses. Partially this is a question of casting. On occasion he has cast his important pictures well, sometimes brilliantly: Jennifer Jones in *The Song of Bernadette*, Olivia de Havilland in *The Snake Pit*, Bette Davis in *All About Eve*. Ironically, each of those three was not a regular Fox contract player, but borrowed for the assignment. Consider who might have played the parts if the choice had been limited to the Fox list: Betty Grable, June Haver, Linda Darnell? At best it might have been Gene Tierney or Jeanne Crain. But here of course something must be said in favor of Zanuck. Who, except for Zanuck, would have thought that Jeanne Crain had a *Pinky* in her, or that Gene Tierney, one of the most beautiful ladies on the Fox lot, would turn into such a fine actress, as in *Laura* and *The Razor's Edge*, that even Linda Darnell had such a sense of comedy (as in *A Letter to Three Wives*)? Occasionally Zanuck had a sudden success with a newcomer: Richard Widmark in *Kiss of Death*, Paul Douglas in *A Letter to Three Wives*. Or with an older player: Clifton Webb in *Laura* and then *Sitting Pretty*, Edmund Gwenn in *Miracle on 34th Street* and *Mr. 880*. But the tendency was toward typecasting, Widmark as the psychopathic killer, Webb as the prissy babysitter. In the absence of stars, too often Zanuck created types, so that when Tyrone Power went to war, there was John Payne to be the cocky heel-with-a-heart. As the sincere hero, in place of Don Ameche and Henry Fonda, there was Dana

Andrews. As one associate says, "A star to him is a civilian who has been elevated in show business." They were names on file, to be flipped into a picture, and another, and another, or to be traded—but not for keeps—to another studio, like bubble gum cards or comic books. One Tyrone Power picture at MGM for a Spencer Tracy at Fox. It was all a big board game.

From the early days at Warners, Zanuck has let many of the big ones get away, and they have become stars in spite of Zanuck. In the early forties, his daughter Darrylin wanted him to discover one of her playmates, a beautiful, raven-haired, violet-eyed English girl, but Zanuck said, "You and your friends!" and let Elizabeth Taylor go to MGM. He fired Rita Hayworth and later Marilyn Monroe. Subsequently he hired Miss Hayworth back for *Blood and Sand* and Miss Monroe for a series of mostly terrible Cinemascope extravaganzas, such as *River of No Return, Niagara, Gentlemen Prefer Blondes.* In some cases Zanuck didn't so much lose, or abuse a talent, as simply neglect it. Anne Bancroft languished at Fox for many years as a sort of latter-day Linda Darnell. In one of the worst of her Grade B melodramas, *Gorilla at Large,* she played the title role, a homicidal girl who donned a gorilla suit whenever she committed mayhem.

On the other hand he frequently worked an actor beyond his merits. Glenn Langan was one of the several faceless players who popped up with regularity in Fox productions in usually interchangeable parts. One measure of this facelessness, even with Zanuck's biggest names, is how many have been forgotten, even by Zanuck. "Who's Glenn Langan?" he asks. Can you imagine any Fox actor except Fonda deserving a film festival. Dana Andrews? Dan Dailey? A William Lundigan Film Festival?

When faced with someone who obviously had talent, such as Rex Harrison and Richard Burton, Zanuck still didn't always quite know what to do with them. He hired Harrison directly after World War II, and put him in *Anna and the King of Siam* (the two first choices were James Mason and Robert Montgomery) and couldn't very well typecast him as an Oriental potentate. So Harrison got the hand-me-downs, parts that might have been better done by everyone from Cary Grant to Clark Gable. In the late forties the choicest male leads still went to Tyrone Power. Of all of Fox's top movies of the time Harrison had a crack at one: *13 Rue Madeleine.* He turned it down and the part went to James Cagney. The fact that he was English certainly was one limiting factor. Generally, he was put in period: *The Foxes of Harrow,* or otherwise wasted—with the exception of *Unfaithfully Yours,* which no one saw anyway. Looking back at his indenture at Fox, Harrison says, "I'm not ashamed of anything I did," but he doesn't seem particularly boastful either. Of all Zanuck's actors, however, Harrison was probably the most independent, not only questioning assignments, but scripts. "The independent attitude was not regarded as highly then as now," says Harrison. "I must have been rather a nuisance in those days." In one sense Hollywood was waiting for this outsider to fall from grace, and when Carole Landis committed suicide over him, he was driven out of town like a villain in a Victorian melodrama. Harrison retreated to Broadway and became, and stayed, a big star, returning in the late fifties and sixties to Fox. "Through all kinds of vicissitudes," he says, his relationship with Zanuck, "is a very friendly one. I've worked at Fox more than any other studio."

Several years after Harrison, Richard Burton passed through Fox, and was also wasted. He made seven pictures in seven years for Zanuck, and says Burton, "Most of them were pretty bad. There were two and a half possible ones. *My Cousin Rachel* was sort of all right. *The Desert Rats* was sort of all right. *The Robe* was at least commercial. *Prince of Players* has become a collectors' item. You have to look hard to find it." Although in retrospect Burton is quite critical of his days at Fox, at the time he was quite content, especially as his salary began to escalate. "All I wanted to do was live," he explains, "to pick up a new Jag and to act at the Old Vic." And his Fox contract left him time for the Old Vic. But didn't he care that his movies were bad? "Of course I cared, enough to say to my friends, 'Don't go to see that picture.'" And then he remembers that his career at Fox almost ended before it began. "At first Darryl didn't want to employ me because I was too fat." He adds with a laugh, "I was a stone lighter then."

Actually Zanuck had little direct dealing with actors, except for the few, such as Tyrone Power, Clifton Webb and Reginald Gardiner, who became friends. Webb, for no known reason, always called Zanuck "Bud," his only recorded nickname. Says Gardiner, "Darryl is a loner. He doesn't need anyone. He's a dynamic incredible little man." More cynical was someone like Dan Dailey, who hardly ever saw him. "He didn't have a lot of truck with the men actors," says Dailey. "He was a very distant little man, very arrogant. He walked down the street followed by the high muckymuck producers—like a bantam rooster." Discussing Dailey, Zanuck says, "I forced him into leading roles over the objections of my staff producers who admitted he had great comedy talent but couldn't play a love scene or a serious role. He was a superb dancer, but whenever he had to kiss the leading lady, the audience laughed."

As one actress remembers, "He was a master of political technique, the Lyndon Johnson of the movie business. It was a gift that was extremely necessary in Hollywood. Most artists who were serious artists distrusted him completely as a great blown-up phony. Some executives are very impressed with Darryl. He has a great technique for puffing on his cigar and saying, 'Cut this' and 'Cut that.' That was also necessary. He could impress them on a creative level. His technique was bluff. They had a respect for him. He had no respect for them. His talent had nothing to do with creativity, but it was necessary to business. He had a gift for sizing up men of talent. He would pick their brains. He had a nose for what might, in general terms, work. People who have immense power automatically alienate me. 'He's seen the rushes!' And you always waited to see what he had to say. You were always *aware* of his presence."

11.

Sex in the Studio

Certainly most movie executives were making love to star-lets. But so were most of us actors.

—Richard Burton

Some of the greatest upheavals in Hollywood, besides the corporate and technical ones, have been over matters of sex and morality, which in Hollywood were traditionally considered opposites. The coincidental cases in 1922 of Fatty Arbuckle being charged with rape, the killing of William Desmond Taylor, and the dope addiction of Wallace Reid triggered off the institution of the Hays Office. At first, Will Hays, then later Eric Johnston, as chief censor, codified conduct on-screen. The code became largely an obstacle course of restrictions that producers tried to circumvent. Suggestion and snigger became the order of the play. During the forties, the Johnston Office breathed heavily down the neck of Hollywood, so that not a touch of immorality would sneak into a picture (which did not leave room for much more than a touch of sophistication). More than any studio head, Zanuck stood up to censorship, and in matters not concerning sex he was the most daring and outspoken. When it came to sex, Zanuck's attitude was to try to convince the censors of the rightness of his position, and when all else failed, to ignore the censors as long as he could. Finally he was often forced to capitulate. In the light of the freedom one finds on the screen today, it is amazing how petty things once were. Zanuck had trouble not only with movies like *Forever Amber*, but with ones likes *My Darling Clementine* and *A Letter to Three Wives*. To the prurient minds that decided what Hollywood could and could not do, apparently everything was sacred.

When it came to a steamy best seller like Kathleen Winsor's

Forever Amber, Zanuck knew of course—from the time he purchased it—that he would have trouble with the censors. In a memo, Zanuck considered some of the possible problems: "I believe we will be severely criticized if we definitely prove that Amber does not sleep with every man she is supposed to sleep with. But why do we have to prove it? We are not going to actually see her get into bed with these men but we do not have to prove that she *didn't* get in bed with them.

"In a hundred pictures we have suggested an affair between two unmarried people without ever showing it or proving that there was an affair . . .

"It would be a crime to whitewash Amber and mathematically and statistically *prove* that she is a perpetual virgin . . . There should be nothing in our script which can be used as concrete evidence one way or the other . . ." But the censors still had suggested cuts in the script. As Murray Schumach has pointed out, Zanuck disregarded the cuts, hoping to slide by, but when the Legion of Decency and the local censors in thirty-six states protested, he was forced to add a prologue and epilogue which stated among other things that "the wages of sin is death." And the wages of making a movie about sin, without sin, is a dull movie.

When *My Darling Clementine* was questioned by the censors, Zanuck defended it on historical grounds, as a "picturization of an era," like *Wilson.* And, said Zanuck, "we cannot avoid the inescapable fact that whiskey drinkers, gun toters, and prostitutes were as much a part of this era as singing waiters and dance-hall gals were a part of the Bowery . . . It would be very easy for us to cheat . . . and call our girls hostesses in the saloon, but . . . nobody is fooled." Since *Clementine* was not basically about prostitutes or dance-hall girls, the exercise of the censor's authority was not as injurious as in the case of *A Letter to Three Wives,* whose humor depended completely on a mature attitude toward matters of morality. The censors were offended by the "unacceptable amount of drinking, drunkenness, and discussion about liquor" in that film and suggested striking such lines as "There's nothing like having a cocktail before cocktails." Also they asked for the elimination of kissing that was "prolonged, lustful or open-mouth," and Lora Mae's line, "Funny you should mention my heart, it's the one part of

my body you never showed any interest in." Toned down,
Three Wives was still daring by forties standards. The important thing to the local censoring boards was apparently not
that a movie get away with anything, but that it didn't break
any of the specific rules, which were often different in different states or cities.

The attitude of the official, and unofficial, censors toward
what appeared on screen was reflected in the hypocritical attitude toward what happened off-screen. What was not known
was not censorable. What *was* known was punishable by
moral outrage and occasionally banishment. Movie stars were
expected to be cleaner and purer than anyone. One victim of
outraged puritanism, says Zanuck, was Carmen Miranda. She
had made her first appearance for Zanuck in *Down Argentine
Way*, which was, as he says, "an en*orm*ous hit." Then, as
Zanuck recalls, her career at Fox ended suddenly and dramatically. "There was a big scandal when Carmen danced and
didn't have any pants on under her skirt," says Zanuck. "I
don't think she ever wore pants when she danced. She was
not a tart by any means. A real lady. A real professional. It
was a matter of her freedom of body movement. But one
time a free lance still photographer had a camera set at a low
angle as she danced. It revealed *everything*. Millions of her
pictures were suddenly being sold. We had the FBI trying to
trace who was behind it. It was the finish of her. We claimed
is wasn't the end but I don't think we used her again. It was
one of those Hollywood periods where the women's organ-
izations ganged up on us, those pressure groups. Those super-
puritanical pressure groups." Years later when Fox faced a
similar situation with the proliferation of Marilyn Monroe's
nude calendar picture, the studio momentarily worried that its
star's career was finished. Quite the opposite was true. The
calendar was the turning point in her career. Says Zanuck,
"It promoted her rather than hurt her."

As Zanuck rightly sees it, it was not so much any single
performer but Hollywood itself that was the sex symbol in
the mind of the general public. "It was a kind of dirty word,"
he says. "We were really under attack." But beneath the cliché
there was an enormous truth. The movies, an industry founded
on commercialism, nurtured by egotism, and aimed at exhibitionism, *were* sexier than the rest of America. Studio press
agents were also anti-press agents, uprooting items as well as

planting them. Today, says Rex Harrison, in contrast to those days, "You can live quite openly even though not married and no one gives a hoot." Fox's longtime Hollywood press chief Harry Brand is more succinct about the change, "Today a goddamn star could fuck an ape and it might create a vogue."

Earlier, there was a peculiar kind of double standard. What was frowned upon for the underlings was favorite sport for the bosses. Seduction has always been a way of life in Hollywood—especially at the top. As Sy Bartlett says, "Temptation is ever present when you're dealing with beauty. It's bound to affect any man." It is Bartlett's prudent, perhaps singular, judgment that "if a man is a polygamist, the least he should do is take it out of town." Tell that to the moguls! Certainly there have been some producers who were more insistent and some actresses more pliant, but because of the nature of the profession and the relationship to talent, practically all producers have had reputations as seducers. What is hearsay and what is performance? In Zanuck's case the line is particularly hard to draw. The stories, and everyone who has ever worked for him has a handful of them, are generally couched in hyperbole. They are tales of wild exhibitionism and satyriasis. But most of them are second- and thirdhand. For obvious reasons the parties most directly involved are not talking—especially if their ascension to stardom depended upon their accession to sex. Because of his reputation, which probably exceeds that of any other producer in Hollywood, Zanuck could easily claim supremacy. Who would argue? But he is surprisingly discreet and even enigmatic.

First the stories. The scene of the liaisons was Zanuck's office—the front office for the Pre-game Run-around, the back trophy room and adjacent bedroom for the Touchdown. As one Hollywood folk tale has it, if a girl left by Zanuck's front office she had had it and there was no reason to "cover up." If she went out through his side door it was because it was the quickest route, there was no consummation. Some got away, including one nubile starlet. During the "prologue," Zanuck allegedly asked her, "How old are you?" "Seventeen. Please, Mr. Zanuck, I'm younger than your daughters." "Forget it," said Zanuck, dismissing her through the side door. One story is often repeated, each time with a different actress playing the lead. Whoever she was, Zanuck was chasing her around his office, grabbing at her breasts. Finally she stopped, reached into her bodice, removed a pair of falsies, and threw them at him, saying, "If you want 'em so bad, take 'em."

As with many Hollywood producers, there are rumors about Zanuck. One Hollywood watcher observed, "Zanuck probably screwed almost every actress on the lot. It was never that blunt that you couldn't get on the lot without it. It was never a condition of any kind. It was just one of those things."

Zanuck flatly and angrily denies the stories. Then he adds: "It was too big a gamble, and a payoff meant a contract or exercising an option. I never touched a soul." He says this not in shock or outrage but as a simple statement of fact. "There was a *great* rumor about a certain big star and me. A great great rumor. I swear I never even knew if she was a man or a woman off the screen. And Linda Darnell. I never knew Linda Darnell from Adam as far as that was concerned. Not even Marilyn Monroe. I hated her. I wouldn't have slept with her if she paid me. I had a pretty fixed rule with people under contract—born out of fear. I got mixed up with a girl under contract at Warner Brothers during those early days. She turned out to be impossible as an actress. When I came to the conclusion she didn't have it, she suddenly started to undress, getting out of her dress and panties faster than a man could unzip his zipper. She scared the hell out of me, but I was saved by the bell. The buzzer on the 'private line' rang. I answered. My secretary said, 'Urgent—the White House calling.' "

If false, how do the stories arise? "Anybody in my position —Dick Zanuck, L. B. Mayer, Jack Warner, Harry Cohn— I don't care who it is. The only production head there was not any scandal about was Irving Thalberg. From B. P. Schulberg on, everyone has had these stories told about them. I wouldn't deny that some of it may be true, but I'd hate to be on the witness stand and asked to prove it. From poor old Walter Wanger up and down, you're too big a target in essentially what is called a sex industry. I can speak for myself . . . there isn't one starlet that I ever had an affair with. Any of my indiscretions were"—a long pause—"with *people*, not actresses."

One thing that needs stressing is that Zanuck, unlike the prototypical lecherous studio boss forcing his attentions on talentless nymphets, is attractive to many women, sexually attractive, and many are easily compliant. His supposed deficits —his lack of height, his rudeness—are more than offset by his air of magnetism and masculinity, his strength and his confidence. He is single-minded in his devotion to duty, whether work or women. When he focuses on someone, he excludes everyone else, which is why he has not always endeared himself to wives of friends. He can sit next to a lady at dinner, and if he is not interested in her, sexually, he is oblivious to her to the point of hostility. If he is interested, then the courtship begins. Helen Gurley Brown, an analyst of sex, and a good friend of Zanuck's in recent years as a result of her husband's association with him, explains that women like Darryl Zanuck because: "Darryl loves women. He never exploits them. He likes pretty young women. He's a very masculine man, in the traditional sense of what a man is—in this country. Polo-playing. Skiing. A lean, handsome body. Sports oriented. Plus money. He spends money on his girls, I don't think he cares about money. What turns them on is the full flower of his drive. In addition, he's . . . Darryl Zanuck! He has the mystique of being who he is. Women find power sexy. I do myself. I'm very attracted to him because he's a very powerful man. It never bothered me when Jackie married Onassis because—that's the sexiest! In addition, Darryl is a movie mogul. There's not anybody who doesn't want to get in the movies."

A statement like "Sex is very important to Darryl Zanuck, isn't it?" is always greeted by loud laughter. To the question, Zanuck answers, "I have a normal interest, not abnormal. Virginia and I never had any sexual relationship prior to our marriage. We had a normal married life. I was busy working like hell at night. A relationship is important to me. I don't believe in separating the sexual act from the emotional act. If the emotion is not right, then the sexual act is not right."

Zanuck is adamant about that position, but others are equally adamant about his extreme sexual pride and drive. Says one former employee, "Every afternoon he had to have his virility assured. It was a compulsive thing." One director sees sex as the symbol, the chief motivating force, of Zanuck. "He's an emotion. He lives in a frenzy." And he adds, with utmost seriousness, "The single most important thing in Darryl Zanuck's life—bigger than movies or success—is sex."

12.

The Wide Screen

We're hoping to establish a hallmark of the highest in entertainment. We want the public to say there never was a bad CinemaScope film, just like they'd say there never was a bad Cadillac.

—Spyros Skouras

In the early fifties, as television began making serious inroads on America's movie-going public, theater screens fairly writhed in anguish and desperation. They stretched, yawned, and popped right into the laps of viewers. Cinerama, with its early concentration on auto races and low-skimming airplanes gave front-row patrons a serious case of the bends. Three-D, hurtling balls, knives, and actors directly at the camera, was turning moviegoers into a crowd of duckers and dodgers. Hollywood searched for the perfect screen that could enfold an audience like a security blanket. Business was hurting at Fox as much as anywhere, and CinemaScope was, at least for the present, the company's salvation. "I went through the only two great revolutions in movies—sound and wide-screen," says Zanuck, "and I was with the two companies that started them both. The only other revolution was when Edison made the camera. I missed it!"

CinemaScope, or rather the anamorphic optical process that became CinemaScope, was invented in the 1920s by Henri Chrétien, a professor at the Optical Institute in France, and optioned by the Rank organization in Great Britain. When Rank's option lapsed, Spyros Skouras picked it up, and led by Earl I. Sponable and Herbert Bragg, the company's New York Technical Directors, and Sol Halperin, executive director of photography, Fox developed the process into Cinema-

Scope. Scanning his product, Zanuck decided that *The Robe* should be the first movie made in CinemaScope, in spite of the fact that it had been shooting for four and a half weeks in the standard 35 mm. process. He announced "Hollywood will rise or fall on the success of *The Robe*."

Lloyd Douglas' best seller had first been brought to Zanuck's attention by producer Frank Ross. Zanuck was in Europe on vacation and Ross showed up with the book and a script. "The book is great," said Zanuck, "but I don't like the script at all. You've done it like a cheap piece of melodrama." Zanuck sat down with Ross and over a period of four or five days, wrote in broad outline a new continuity. Budgeted at $8.5 million, production began in Hollywood. Then, as Zanuck says, "Christ, comes this device. They showed it in a demonstration to me, and I went for it. It was the goddamnedest thing! I was overwhelmed. I took the greatest gamble. I stopped *The Robe*." The immediate problem was that there was only one CinemaScope lens and Sponable thought it would take Bausch and Lomb five months to make a second. Nevertheless Zanuck decided to go ahead, and begin *The Robe* all over again. He took one precaution: he assigned a detective to guard the lens. Bausch and Lomb worked overtime and in five or six weeks had constructed a stand-by lens. "Ross saw the potential of CinemaScope, but he was also the first one to scare me. One day he said, 'Where is this picture going to play?' " No theaters were equipped for CinemaScope, and in deciding to switch, theater owners had nothing to go on except faith in Fox, and a sales pitch from Skouras and Al Lichtman, the head of the sales department. "Every theater man had to tear down his projection system," says Zanuck. "He had to reconstruct his booth. We had a different ratio. He had to change the size of the screen! Sometimes they had to take out eight or twelve rows of seats." To convince theater owners Lichtman and Skouras used every ploy imaginable, from promises to threats. Says Zanuck about Skouras, "About pictures he couldn't tell a good one from a bad one, but on business manipulations he's a master. He did a great job on this. He led the crusade as he called it. 'This will save the movies!' he told them. The whole Bible-stumping bit. I think the fact that he was able to mastermind the exhibitors of the country to switch to CinemaScope was Skouras' greatest moment of triumph."

It was Zanuck's idea that if he could sell rival studios on CinemaScope then exhibitors would buy it as well, and "If they were against it," he realized, "then why would theaters change their entire system?" He prepared a four-reel demonstration short. "It was spectacular," he says. "Today it would look like nothing," and he staged a series of screenings, inviting the presidents of the various companies and a selection of top directors to view it. Many were visibly impressed. After the last screening, Cecil B. de Mille got up and said, "Fox, I congratulate you . . ." but before he could finish, Y. Frank Freeman, president of Paramount, cut him off by announcing, "We're having a conference back at the studio," and leading his men, he stalked out. Eventually most other studios, including MGM and Warners, leased CinemaScope from Fox—with the outstanding exception of Paramount which, within two years, developed its own wide-screen process, Panavision. Zanuck later realized that "CinemaScope was all wrong mechanically. We cut too low and too circular. Visual experts told us—not then—but later, that the correct proportion is Panavision. Panavision is the perfect proportion to fit the eyes." But CinemaScope was first, and it, as Zanuck said, "electrified the world," or at least the part thereof that he was most concerned with. In February of 1953, before *The Robe* had even begun CinemaScope shooting, Zanuck and Skouras announced that they were converting their entire output to CinemaScope. Zanuck was cutting the number of pictures almost in half and spreading them all out in wide screen.

The Robe opened to mixed reviews and enormous business. In its first week at the Roxy in New York, it grossed $264,000, and the remaining reluctant theater owners began converting. *The Robe* was followed by *How to Marry a Millionaire,* the first CinemaScope Marilyn Monroe, and *Beneath the Twelve Mile Reef,* which had the first underwater CinemaScope scenes. Not Zanuck, but CinemaScope, seemed to be in charge of the company. Properties were bought, movies produced to fit the width of the screen. Zanuck himself realized this, and announced: "It is my conviction that we can use CinemaScope only for the very best type of quality pictures and that if we violate this policy we will reduce the potential box-office value of CinemaScope. In other words, I believe that every picture must at least have the stature of *Sir Walter Raleigh*. If it is a Western it must be *Call Me Madam* or nothing else . . . We have got to in almost every instance strive to get so-called 'name' subjects for CinemaScope. The only other pictures that we should make are pictures like *Twelve Mile Reef, Hell and High Water* and *River of No Return*." There was to be no room on the Wide Screen for a *Snake Pit*, a *Twelve O'Clock High*, a *Gentleman's Agreement*, but only for big properties. Fox made half as many pictures in 1953 and 1954. They were at least twice as big, and about half as good.

One picture Zanuck could have made (and should have made) but didn't, was *On the Waterfront*. Elia Kazan, as director, and Budd Schulberg, as screenwriter, brought the idea to him. He considered it, then rejected it. "He was interested in the new medium of CinemaScope," recalls Schulberg. "The most charitable thing I could say about him was that he was like a child with a new toy." After Zanuck turned *Waterfront* down, Kazan and Schulberg tried selling it to every other studio, and they all turned it down. Finally Sam Spiegel produced it outside of the commercial glare of Hollywood. It was easily the best movie of 1954, the kind of controversial, timely, exciting picture that the old Zanuck would have given anything to call his own.

13.

Polish Roulette

If you said to Darryl, "Why don't you use Garbo in The
Egyptian?" *he would say, "You're crazy. I've got Bella
Darvi."*

—Charles K. Feldman

In June of 1952 Darryl and Virginia Zanuck were in Paris
and ran into Alex d'Arcy, an actor friend, sitting at a sidewalk cafe on the Champs Elysées. D'Arcy was with an
attractive young woman, and she caught Zanuck's eye. He
suggested that the four of them have dinner together. In the
course of the evening the Zanucks discovered that the girl's
name was Bella Wegier. She had been born in Sosnoviec,
Poland, emigrated to Paris with her parents when she was an
infant, and grew up in the shadow of World War II. At
twelve, she had been placed in a concentration camp, and
survived, apparently with no physical scars although there
were some psychological ones. In 1950 she married a rich
businessman named Alban Cavalade, and, as his wife, began
to be noticed at various Riviera resorts. Within a year and a
half they were separated, and a year later divorced. On meeting
the Zanucks, she was almost a free agent. That first evening
they ate, drank, danced, and both Zanucks were thoroughly
charmed with the girl. The next day in reciprocity Bella
sent flowers to Mrs. Zanuck.

For Mrs. Zanuck, Bella became something of a best friend
and favorite niece. They went shopping together and almost
every day lunched together. For Mr. Zanuck, Bella was a
"girl."

Very early, in Paris, according to Bella, she and Darryl
began having an affair. The day after the affair began, they

met by arrangement in the Calvados at 3 P.M. The cafe was deserted. Bella explained her financial problems: she was in debt, banned from the casinos, and on the verge of being forced to sell her extensive wardrobe. Two thousand dollars would free her. The following day Zanuck delivered the money to her. In Paris, the Zanucks suggested that Bella visit America. In November, 1952, she showed up in Hollywood, and at the invitation of both Zanucks, she moved into their beach house in Santa Monica. With Darrylin married and Richard away at school, Bella shared an annex of the beach house with the Zanucks' younger daughter Susan. The two of them did not get along from the very first moment, but the relationship with the elder Zanucks continued with unabated cordiality. Virginia and Darryl introduced her to the Beverly Hills social whirl, and as almost a member of the family, she was invited to the Zanuck house in Palm Springs for weekends.

One day in Palm Springs, Zanuck announced, "We have a surprise for Bella. She's going to make a film test." According to Bella, that was the first time Zanuck had ever talked about the possibility of a career. She took a screen test and apparently it was good enough to win her a contract— or at least it was not bad enough to lose her a contract. In preparation for stardom, her name was changed to Bella Darvi.

The publicity department went into action. Typical of the rarified reportage appearing on Miss Darvi was the following story in the New York *Journal-American*. On July 11, 1953 INS correspondent Emily Belser wrote:

"A newly-arrived French doll by the name of Bella Darvi, who has a voice like Marlene Dietrich, eyes like Simone Simone and the allure of Corinne Calvet, is hitting Hollywood with the impact of TNT.

"She's got zip, zoom and zowie and in parlez-vous she's ravissante, chi chi and très élégante. In any language, that's hot stuff.

"Still slightly stunned by it all, Bella planned to ankle back to France.

" 'Then eef they still like me,' she says modestly, 'I will come back.'

"La Bella Darvi is what is termed in movietown as a 'personality.' She never would stop traffic a la Marilyn Monroe. Yet she is beautiful in an exotic way."

All the front-office publicity couldn't stop the zip, zoom, and zowie from fizzling. Darvi made two small duds, *Hell and High Water* and *The Racers*, and she was a dud in them. Zanuck, stubbornly convinced she had talent, cast her in a big CinemaScope production, the movie version of Mika Waltari's best seller, *The Egyptian*. She was to play Nefer, the courtesan, not the central role, but an important one. Zanuck signed his old friend Michael Curtiz to direct and Marlon Brando to play the star role. Several days before shooting was scheduled to begin, Curtiz called the leading players together for a reading. Zanuck listened. That night, about nine o'clock, back in his home in Santa Monica, Zanuck received a call from Brando's agent, informing him that Brando had left for New York. Zanuck was stunned. "Why?" he asked.

"He doesn't like Mike Curtiz," answered the agent. "He doesn't like the role. And he can't stand Bella Darvi."

"You can't do this to me," protested Zanuck.

But he did. "It took about four hours," says Zanuck, "but we borrowed Edmund Purdom who was under contract to Metro. We filed suit for damages against Brando, and then we compromised. He made a picture for us free [*Desiree*]." *The Egyptian* was a colossal bomb, and so was Bella. Even *Variety*, traditionally more lenient than non-trade publications on expensive productions, said, "A weak spot in the talent line-up is Bella Darvi who contributes little more than an attractive figure. Her thesping . . . is something less than believable or skilled."

Zanuck began behaving uncharacteristically—like an adolescent instead of a powerful tycoon. On January 18, 1954 he and some four hundred guests, many of them famous, welcomed his daughter Susan and actress Terry Moore back from entertaining the troops in Korea, with a gala oriental costume party at Ciro's. After dinner there was a show. Al Jolson sang, acrobats performed on a trapeze, and then Zanuck got up, expressed his pride in his daughter, and unsolicited and nonscheduled, he asked that the trapeze be lowered. "I hope my publicity director isn't here to stop me," he said, and took off his oriental robe, his tuxedo jacket, and dress shirt, and in pants and cummerbund with his suspenders drooping and a cigar clenched firmly in his teeth, he tried to chin himself with one hand, a feat that he had performed frequently in the privacy of his own steam room. But now in public, obviously debilitated by alcohol, he was unable to raise his arm. Suddenly, as Zanuck remembers it, "Four hundred cameras came out of the woodwork," and starting snapping pictures. Actually, as the Associated Press reported, it was more like twenty-five. His friend Clifton Webb tried to persuade Zanuck to dismount, but Zanuck instead chinned himself six times with two hands, and then, as the audience counted, swung on the trapeze over the tables. Finally he came down—to applause—got dressed, and went home. Although Zanuck called his friend Henry Luce in New York and tried to have it stopped, *Life* printed a full-page picture of him hanging limply from the bar. "My wife and daughter were so furious," recalls Zanuck. "Oh God, I was really in the doghouse. I don't know what possessed me. I wasn't really that drunk. It was a moment of madness."

After a long intimate talk with her daughter Susan, Virginia Zanuck acted decisively. She threw Bella out of her house.

Bella returned to France, and eventually Zanuck followed. "I was still infatuated or sex crazy or whatever you call it," says Zanuck. "That was the beginning of the end of our marriage." It was also the beginning of the end of his career. "And it was all my fault."

For more than twenty years he had been head of production at Twentieth Century-Fox, and in recent years with the rise of television and the decline of the star system, the power of the studio and the power of the studio chief was weakened. Stars formed their own companies and became producers. Power shifted into the hands of agents, who could hold up a studio like bandits. The European market was more and more important to the survival of Hollywood and European filmmakers were showing signs of beating Hollywood at both the European and Hollywood games. Together with that was Zanuck's growing boredom with his job, particularly in the altered form it was assuming. "Sitting in that room watching movies, night after night," says Sy Bartlett, "I thought he would explode into a thousand fragments. The curtain had to drop." There also was the fact that, with the possible exception of *The Man in the Gray Flannel Suit,* he had not had a major hit either artistically or commercially in some time. On top of it all were his personal difficulties: his realization that he had ruined his marriage; at middle-age a sudden stirring of life. In his pursuit of ambition and accomplishment, had he missed something? A true adolescence?

"It wasn't Bella or any other girl. She was a sordid, forgotten memory. My separation and break-up from Mrs. Zanuck came at the same time as my divorce or break-up with Hollywood," says Zanuck. "Both turned together. Both came to head together. My mood was to escape, to get away from the scene, the social scene, the studio scene, and everything connected with it. I felt I didn't give a goddamn. I felt I never would be able to create anything again."

In 1956 Darryl Zanuck suddenly resigned as production head for Fox, just as twenty-three years before he had resigned as production head for Warners. At that earlier time he quit at the very top of his form, and immediately was the most sought-after producer in Hollywood. In 1956, although not quite at the bottom of his form, he was certainly descendant. But he was still powerful enough to name a successor, Buddy Adler, and to dictate his terms of departure. He formed his own company, DFZ Productions, with a contract with Fox, giving him carte blanche to make the movies he wanted, the only limit being one of money. Any individual film costing over five million dollars had to be approved by the Board of Directors.

Zanuck moved out of his disintegrating household, moved out of his office, left his wife, family, home in Palm Springs, croquet, steam room, and all the other trappings of his Hollywood kingdom. He went off to capture something he had lost—or something he never had. He was going to leave the past and live in the present. He was going to make pictures, individual pictures bearing the stamp of Zanuck. But what was the stamp of Zanuck?

III | *The Lost Tycoon*
1956-62

1.

The Sun Also Rises

I was subconsciously playing the role of Errol Flynn.
—Darryl Zanuck

As befitting a runaway, Zanuck was rootless and homeless.
Bella Darvi was compulsive about gambling. "Gambling was
absolutely a mania with her. She would win $150,000 one
night and the next day she would have to pawn her jewelry,
and then be back gambling again. I've seen her strip her rings
and jewelry off and throw them on the table to call a bet."
She was way over her head in debt to the casino and, for
non-payment, the government had seized her passport. (Casinos in France are under strict French law.) She cabled
Zanuck for help. Short of cash, Zanuck was himself in an
unhealthy financial situation. Whom could he turn to, to help
him help her? He called his old friend Howard Hughes, and
asked to borrow $50,000. "I would like it in francs," he said.
Zanuck thought Hughes could arrange for him to pick up the
money at Hughes' TWA office in Paris. The next night
Hughes called back and said, "You can have the money, but
not in francs. Are you going to France?" "Yes, tomorrow,"
said Zanuck. "You'll get it," said Hughes tersely.

The next day Zanuck boarded a plane in Los Angeles and
seated across from him was a man with a briefcase. The man
nodded at him. Zanuck stopped overnight in New York, and
the next day on the plane to Paris, there was the same man,
with the same briefcase and the same nod. In Paris Zanuck
checked in at the Hotel Rafael. He had been in his suite
barely an hour, when the concierge called to say there was a
man from TWA with a package for him.

"Send him up," said Zanuck.

It was the same man, but this time he had a suitcase, not a briefcase. He opened it and it was stuffed with crisp twenty-dollar bills. The two of them spread the money on the floor, and counted. There was $50,000. Zanuck put the money in a duffel bag and toted it to Cannes.

Bella puts the blame for the gambling mania on Zanuck. "When we first met, I had problems but *that* wasn't my problem."

With Bella finally out of his system, Zanuck began assembling properties for DFZ Productions. The first to be filmed was supposed to be *The Secret Crimes of Josef Stalin*. The title was changed to *I Married Josef Stalin*, and the movie shelved, as were *The Day Christ Died* and *Suzanne Valadon*, about a girl who had modeled for Renoir and Degas. Finally, he began working on two movies, both of seemingly great potential, but both of which grow dimmer through the years: *The Sun Also Rises* was Hemingway's masterpiece, *Island in the Sun*, Alec Waugh's latest best-seller. But because the theme of *Island in the Sun* was miscegenation, that was the one that was the immediate subject of controversy. The movie was threatened with boycotts, mostly by southern theater owners. The South Carolina legislature considered passing a bill which would fine any theater showing the movie $5000, and Zanuck announced that he would personally pay all such fines. The bill was not passed. As the movie neared release, Zanuck continued to churn up interest. "They've given me the same treatment before," he announced to the press. "They said I couldn't show *Grapes of Wrath* in Oklahoma and Texas, and I got scared as hell. All I won with that was an Oscar and a fortune. And the censors gave me the same business with *Pinky*, but the opposition never really materialized . . . People are reacting, I guess, because now for the first time we have Negroes playing Negroes, which we didn't in *Pinky*. But I'm not frightened of any opposition." This sounded like the old Zanuck talking, but it was not the old Zanuck producing. *Island in the Sun*, filmed on location in the West Indies by Robert Rossen, had little in its favor except for the first time in screen history, a white woman was kissed by a black, Harry Belafonte. Ironically, *Island in the Sun* was the only DFZ production, before *The Longest Day*, to turn a healthy profit, which probably proves that even inartistic controversy makes money. It cost $2,250,000 and grossed $8 million. Commercially, it was an auspicious debut for DFZ Productions, but as Zanuck himself admitted in 1963, "I never liked *Island in the Sun*. I didn't like it because they made me compromise the book."

The Sun Also Rises was much more a labor of love on Zanuck's part, particularly because of his personal friendship with Hemingway. Zanuck admired Hemingway as a man and a sportsman. He was the writer that Zanuck knew he could never be, writing about what Zanuck would have liked to write about—if he could really write. Zanuck and Hemingway knew each other over a period of years, from the time Peter Viertel introduced them in Paris and through shared experiences in Sun Valley where they both spent their winters. For most of their friendship, at least until Hemingway's crack-up, Zanuck's admiration was unabashed. "He was a great companion—eating, drinking, storytelling companion. He had great attraction for women, even during the period when he was overweight. He had style with women and his conversation was so good. We would have long long discussions on our African hunting experiences. Once I was at the bar with Hemingway at a party place called The Trail Creek Inn just outside Sun Valley and patronized by Averell Harriman and the elite of the colony. A mutual friend, a very rich New York society man, young, married to a very beautiful and lovely girl, came up to Hemingway. He was white, almost bursting out in tears. He said, 'That beast made a pass at my wife.' Hemingway said, 'Where?' 'See him sitting over there.' Hemingway took off his glasses, ready to go into battle. We both went to where the man was sitting. When we were within a yard of him, Hemingway stopped in his tracks and said to the husband, 'Jesus Christ, that's my best friend!' " And Zanuck and Hemingway turned and walked away.

In many areas—hunting and skiing, for two—Zanuck could certainly hold his own with Hemingway. Peter Viertel, who was an intimate friend of both, declares flatly, "Darryl is, physically, a brave man. Hemingway was not, physically, a brave man." And he adds a similarity. "Hemingway was another midwesterner not always wedded to truth when it comes to remembering. Zanuck and Hemingway. He eventually developed a chip on his shoulder about Darryl. He liked him . . . until *The Snows of Kilimanjaro*."

Inevitably Zanuck and Hemingway's professional relationship conflicted with their personal one. Over the years Zanuck has made more movies out of Hemingway stories than any other producer—— *Under My Skin, The Snows of Kilimanjaro,* and *The Sun Also Rises* (the last two directed by Henry King)—and although at least one, *The Snows,* was a hit critically, none, apparently, was a hit with the author. In the book *Papa Hemingway,* by A. E. Hotchner, Hemingway recalls the time that Zanuck called him in Sun Valley and said, "Ernest, we are in executive session here in my conference room, and we've been wrestling all day with a crisis that only you can resolve. We have made a truly wonderful picture of your wonderful story 'The Short Happy Life of Francis Macomber' and we're ready for distribution but we feel that the title is too long for the average movie marquee, so we would appreciate it very much if you could change it to something short with eye appeal—you know, a title that would create on-sight excitement—something that'll appeal to both sexes and make them feel they *have* to see the movie." Hemingway said he would think about it, and after killing some time and having a drink, he got back on the phone and said to Zanuck, "Now, you want something sort and exciting that will catch the eye of both sexes, right? Well, then, here it is: F as in Fox, U as in Universal, C as in Culver City and K as in R.K.O. That should fit all the marquees, and you can't beat it as a sex symbol." Zanuck denies the story categorically and with justification. It was not Zanuck, but Zoltan Korda who made *The Macomber Affair,* for United Artists, not Twentieth Century-Fox.

"The only dispute I had with Hemingway," he says, "was long after those days, or at least some time after. For instance, to show how close we were, he telephoned me from Cuba, urging me to put Ava Gardner in the role in *The Snows of Kilimanjaro.* Our dispute arose because he said he didn't like the picture. He said it should have been called *The Snows of Zanuck.* I traced back to see if the picture had played in Cuba [where Hemingway was living], or if there were any prints he could have seen. I confirmed he hadn't seen the picture. Someone had told him or he had read the reviews, *one* of the few unfavorable ones."

Now, for his *The Sun Also Rises,* Zanuck decided that Tyrone Power was made for Jake Barnes. Power was in a sense something of a symbolic Jake Barnes, to Zanuck, the truest, the handsomest, the best of the lot. He was a good choice for the part, except for his age—forty-three. Ava Gardner certainly was everyone's Lady Brett—even Hemingway's. Also signed were Errol Flynn, Eddie Albert, and Mel Ferrer. About the only place Zanuck's casting was open to question was in the part of the bullfighter. For some inexplicable reason he signed Robert Evans, a young clothing manufacturer whom Zanuck discovered dancing at El Morocco. (Actually, Evans had already been discovered—by Norma Shearer. He played her husband Irving Thalberg in *The Man With a Thousand Faces*, but it had not yet been released when Zanuck saw him. After *The Sun Also Rises*, he was in several more movies, then retired back into clothing. Eventually he returned to movies as a producer, and became production head of Paramount Pictures.)

The most important parts of *The Sun Also Rises* take place at the Festival of Pamplona, where, says Zanuck, "all the corrida episodes were staged and photographed with the entire cast." Pamplona eventually became a major tradition in Zanuck's life. When they filmed the "run with the bulls" episode, Zanuck, in characteristic fashion, made sure he could beat the bulls. He put on his tennis shoes and timed his run, found by pacing himself he could out-run them by a minute and a half to two minutes. With measured daring, he then ran *with* the bulls—and made it. After Pamplona, the film moved to Morelia, Mexico, "as Morelia is a physical double for Pamplona, but after the festival, Pamplona is a colorless and empty morgue."

In Mexico, filming continued and one feminine role, still uncast, seemed unimportant—until it came close to the time to shoot her scenes. Audrey Hepburn, who was on location with her husband Mel Ferrer, said she knew of someone who could play the part, the singer Juliette Greco then appearing at the Waldorf-Astoria in New York. They were personal friends. At Zanuck's request, Ferrer phoned her there. "How long do you need me for?" Greco asked Ferrer. "Four weeks here and two in Paris." She said, "I have another engagement, but I can cancel it." Finishing at the Waldorf, she boarded a plane and flew to Mexico City where the company had moved from Morelia, to shoot the interiors in a Mexican studio.

Juliette Greco was born on a farm in southern France, spent her adolescent years in Paris under German occupation. Although her mother and older sister were interned in a concentration camp by the Nazis, she managed to survive in Paris—although she was for a time in jail there. At fifteen she was living on the streets and stealing. After the war she fell in with a group of young artists in St. Germain des Prés, and as the Greco legend goes, one night they opened a night club—literally opened; the club was closed and locked before they broke into it. They lived and worked there, finally with the owner's permission. The club was called Le Tabou. It was a dark, smoke-filled cellar cabaret, and at first Greco was a headwaiter and bouncer. Then—one night—she sang. Dressed all in black—slacks and sweater—her black hair hanging down to her waist, her voice sad and passionate, she (and her club) soon became the symbol of postwar Paris. Her admirers included Jean-Paul Sartre, Albert Camus, Simone de Beauvoir, Jean Cocteau. "Juliette Greco reigned there by her simple presence," wrote Cocteau. "Everything rallied, organized, discussed, quarreled, danced and thought around her black silhouette, similar to those of the young girls on frescoes of Crete. It is true that the apparent shabbiness of her sweater hid a ruinous jewel which explains many things: her heart . . ." Greco and her friends became known as Les Rats des Caves, the cellar rats, and they moved from cave to cave. By the early fifties, she was one of the biggest stars in France—on records, in clubs, in concert. She had appeared in several plays and movies, including Cocteau's *Orpheus*, but without success. However, except for movies, she was, when she met Zanuck, at the very top of her career: she had just added America to her list of admirers. But her soaring professional life was in marked contrast to her private life. In and out of love, she had suffered a succession of unhappy romances, ending in divorce, violent death, and suicide.

Zanuck recalls their first meeting in Mexico. "I got in the elevator at the hotel and two floors below a brunette girl got on. I thought, Jesus she's got an awful nose! When we got out of the elevator, we bumped into Mel Ferrer and he introduced us." In a large group that included Viertel, Power, Linda Christian, and Gregory Ratoff, they had dinner. Zanuck found her "very amusing, very bright." She was unimpressed. "I couldn't stand him," she recalls. "I didn't know him. He was representing something very far away, very strange for me. It was The Industry. Zanuck sounded to me like Coca-Cola. There was something inhuman about the sound of his name." Then she adds, "But when he started speaking, you started listening." At first, as they filmed, she and Zanuck fought. Then, as she recalls, "One day he said to me, 'Yes, you may be right, but I know certain things you don't know. I've made six hundred pictures.'" This impressed her. They began getting along and Zanuck began expanding her role. "I'd give King bits for her, little things. I never left the set." Romance with Greco flourished.

When the company finished the Mexican sequences, they flew back to Paris. According to Zanuck, Greco suddenly told him, "There is a young boy madly in love with me. He'll be at the airport." "Are we through?" asked Zanuck. "No," she said. "I'll tell him frankly, I'm in love with you." The "boy" was Sascha Distel, whom she had been living with for the previous three years. In Paris she told him about Zanuck and he was very upset by the news. "It should have been a tipoff to me," says Zanuck, "She liked me, no doubt, but what happened to him could very easily happen to me. When we finished the picture I said, 'Let's get the hell out of here. Let's go to the south of France.' She said, 'I'll take my nurse and my child with me and put them up at St. Tropez and we'll go to the Hotel du Cap.' Just as our train was leaving, here came Sascha Distel running up and down with a bouquet. Just then, he got a flash of us. I seemed to take it stronger than she did. She shrugged it off. I couldn't. We dropped the kid and the nurse off and drove to Hotel du Cap." They vacationed in the sun and then went back to Paris, and says Zanuck, "I foolishly started looking for stories for her . . ."

2.

De Luxe Tour

*The picture never got made because the survey trip cost
more than the budget of the picture.*

—Richard Zanuck

While his Paris headquarters was being set up, Zanuck was
in a wide-open state of euphoria. He was not a tired fifty-five-
year-old mogul, but an adolescent embarking on an adventure.
It was time to skylark, to joyride. His choice of a property to
kick off DFZ Productions in Paris was, suitably, *De Luxe
Tour,* a skylarking joyride of a movie to be based on Frederic
Wakeman's novel. A script was written, and while it was
being rewritten by a succession of writers including Irwin
Shaw, Zanuck decided to take a scouting trip to choose locations. He cast it like one of those old all-male hunting expeditions in the Warner Brothers days. The only one missing was
Sam the Barber.

There was:

Richard Zanuck, who had graduated from Stanford University and gone into his father's business.

Robert Jacks, producer and first husband of Darrylin Zanuck, who had just gone into his father-in-law's business.

Frank Donahue, a stunt man, amateur cameraman, and
friend of Jacks', whose duties included watching over the luggage, and, at the request of Darrylin, watching over Jacks.

Jack Smith, head of Twentieth Century-Fox's art department, who was to make sketches of the trip as preparation
for the movie.

Paul Mantz, three-time winner of the Bendix Trophy, a
daredevil stunt pilot employed by Fox and other studios,
who was the pilot—assisted by a co-pilot.

Darryl F. Zanuck, commanding general of the mission.

The vehicle for the mission: A B-25 bomber, converted for peacetime use but still sporting World War II make-up, lent to Zanuck by his friend Howard Hughes. On August 17, 1957 a photograph of the two Zanucks, Jacks, and Mantz— looking like World War II flying aces—appeared in *Motion Picture Herald* as they embarked on what was called a round-the-world trip. They did not quite circle the globe, but in two months they fairly leveled Europe, Africa, and the Near East, scouting and often disturbing the peace from the North Pole to the Ngorangora Crater in Africa. "It was the greatest trip ever made!" says Dick, and it was one of the craziest, and most dangerous. For all aboard it was an act of outrageous hedonism. Whatever mad emotion Darryl Zanuck had, Mantz was there to carry it out, and, often, to top it.

The nose of the plane had been designed to accommodate a camera, and from it Donahue shot thousands of feet of 16-millimeter film. When Donahue wasn't shooting, Dick Zanuck was stationed there, an observer under glass. They named the plane *Smasher,* in honor of Mantz's second favorite pastime: drinking.

Flying and smashing down from Paris, Zanuck decided they should stop in Cannes, where they toured the casinos. The last night in Cannes he jubilantly threw a party and announced to his guests, "We're taking off at ten tomorrow. Everybody has got to be out on the beach." The next morning the beach was packed with bleary-eyed revelers and starry-eyed strangers. As the crowd watched, the *Smasher* buzzed Cannes. Mantz strafed the beach, flying a bare ten feet off the ground, whipping the sand, water, and people into an uncontrollable frenzy. Hangovers ceased immediately. Eyes popped open. Screams filled the air. People dove into the water, flew under the boardwalk, flattened themselves on the sand. And in the plane, the Zanucks gulped and Mantz laughed. At full speed he headed directly for an apartment house at the end of the bay. A woman was hanging laundry out of her window of the house. Seeing the B-25 head-on, she fainted dead away into her apartment. The pressure of the plane blasted out ten windows of the house, and at the last second Mantz swung the plane up and barely cleared the building.

They stopped in Rome and then, bored on a Sunday,

Darryl said, "Let's got out of here," and they headed for
Rhodes. Twenty minutes outside of Rome, the left motor of
the two engine plane caught fire. Zanuck was sitting in front
with Mantz and his co-pilot. Richard, Bobby Jacks, Frank
Donahue, and Jack Smith were in back. There was no direct
contact or passageway between the two parts of the plane,
except by phone. With smoke pouring in, Darryl gave the
order, "Get your parachutes on." A frantic call came back
over the phone from Dick, "There are four of us and only
three parachutes." Making the supreme sacrifice in the call
of duty, young Zanuck ordered his subordinates to tie him
and his brother-in-law together to one parachute. Meanwhile
Zanuck couldn't find any parachutes up front. Mantz coolly
refused to desert the ship. Assuming command, Mantz suddenly began climbing on one motor, up and up, then just as
suddenly, he cut the only working engine, then dove, straight
down, and just before he touched the ground, came out of
the dive, and made a perfect landing on the airfield. His
downward dive, he later explained, had blocked the flames
from enveloping the craft. As the Italian airport personnel
watched, the Hollywood cast and crew exited the still-smolder-
ing bomber: a stunt man, an artist, two pilots, a short smoky
man with a large cigar, and like clown tumblers, two young
men, bound face to face, bouncing and bobbing to safety.

Later, inspecting the plane at the airport, Mantz said,
"Boys, it looks like we're going to be stuck here a couple of
days. You go to Rhodes and I'll stay here and try to fix the
plane." Zanuck immediately chartered a commercial plane, one
that normally carried one hundred thirty people, and the sur-
viving members of *De Luxe Tour* flew first class, with two doz-
en seats apiece, to Rhodes. Actually Mantz had rigged the
engine, and caused the smoke, faking a fire, so that they
would be grounded in Rome. While his friends flew to
Rhodes, he had climbed back into the B-25, which was
actually undamaged, and flown solo to Catalina, California,
where he owned a restaurant and had a girl friend. In his
absence the girl was running the restaurant and he had
heard rumors about her behavior. Ten days later Mantz
caught up with Zanuck in Lebanon, and the survey continued.

They flew within two hundred miles of the North Pole, not
going further only because they had to stay within range of

a refueling station. Then they flew to Egypt, landing in Cairo where officials demanded their passports before they were allowed to disembark. Mantz, who had once had a difficult time regaining a passport when removed under similar circumstances, refused. He had it chained to him, and stubbornly stayed and slept on the plane while the others rode into Cairo.

Then, back on the *Smasher,* they flew up and down the Nile, stopping as frequently as if they had been in a motorboat. Although most of the villagers they visited had never entertained tourists before, they were more than adequately prepared for them. "We hit every dive on the Nile," says Dick. They dusted camel trains in Chad. "Some of them were on two-year trips to Nairobi or Khartoum," recalls Zanuck. Most of the flying was in short stops, which was at least partially precautionary. "DZ was getting restless," says his son, "and a little worried because Paul was drinking very heavily. So we decided to keep our trips very short. On extended flights he would be completely *drunk* by the time we landed." The farthest south they flew was to the lower end of the Ngorangora Crater. "We flew down below it," says Zanuck. "Down into it. We got in trouble with the British Government. You can fly over it, but not in it. It's a game reserve." They flew over the Serengeti Plain, stopping at "offbeat places, not even named, not on the map. We made a complete circle of Lake Victoria."

As they were landing in Nairobi, they hit a gust of wind, and Zanuck, who had not tightened his seat belt struck his forehead against an overhanging radio box. Bleeding profusely, in Nairobi he went to a doctor who took a few stitches and dismissed him. Weeks later, after the trip was over, in London, Zanuck's stitches began opening and the gash spreading. He hurried to the plastic surgeon Sir Archibald McIndoe, knighted for rebuilding the faces of World War II pilots. Sir Archibald sewed in twenty-eight stitches on Zanuck's forehead. For a month, Zanuck wore a cast on his head. (Paul Mantz died some years later while doing a daring stunt in a Fox film.)

All Zanuck had to show for the scouting trip, besides his injury, was Donahue's film, edited down to fifteen reels. Some of it was used as stock footage in several Fox movies; the rest of it is in a studio vault. For all practical purposes the de luxe tour was an absolute fiasco. "The cost of the movie was uncontrollable," says Darryl. Dick Zanuck clarifies: "We had a very bad script, and by the time it was rewritten and re-rewritten we piled up such a monumental expense that made it financially impossible to make the picture."

3.

Roots of Hell

. . . It's Box 99, "Roots of Heaven," Fort Archambault, French Equatorial Africa, and make a note never to come here if you can avoid it . . . This definitely is no place for anyone in their right minds.
> —Errol Flynn, in a letter to Beverly Aadland

De Luxe Tour was the movie that never was made; *Roots of Heaven* was the movie that should never have been made. The surprise is that it was made at all, for never has a movie been filmed under more adverse circumstances. The Romain Gary novel on which it was based is about a mad moralist named Morel, who, disillusioned with mankind, embarks on a futile, idealistic mission to save the elephant from becoming extinct. "The elephants are our largest and greatest friends on earth," says the idealistic Morel. "They are docile unless harmed. We slaughter them for their valuable ivory tusks. This must be stopped—with force if necessary."

Zanuck's decision to buy the book, in 1957, seemed justified from the standpoint of art and commerce. Gary had won a Prix Goncourt for the novel, and the best reviews of his sometimes distinguished literary career. The setting of Africa was something that appealed to Zanuck's viscera. The subject matter, the fact that this was not just an adventure but a story with an important theme, appealed to his social consciousness. In every sense, *Roots of Heaven* looked as though it would be a big picture, the sort of spectacle with a message that might be *the* Zanuck movie of the late fifties.

Initially, Zanuck's moves seemed correct ones. He signed John Huston to direct. Romain Gary himself and Patrick Leigh Fermor, an Irish novelist Huston particularly admired, were hired to write the screenplay. To play Morel, Zanuck signed William Holden, a reasonable if not inspired choice, and when Holden was unavailable he signed Trevor Howard, who from his past performances would seem the perfect actor to play the compulsive Morel. Also in the cast were Errol Flynn, who was so surprisingly good as a mock-Flynn in *The Sun Also Rises*, as an alcoholic British mercenary; Orson Welles as the big-time American broadcaster; Eddie Albert as the platitudinous photographer; Paul Lukas as the well-meaning public official. Even Juliette Greco seemed to have a part exactly suited to her personality. She was to be the sad lark of a concentration camp survivor, who finds in Morel's quest a sudden reawakening of her own dead spirit. Out of necessity the film had to be produced in Africa, for authenticity and for the elephants themselves. As it turned out, the location was the major reason for the film's failure, and succeeded in compounding other errors: script problems, personality conflicts. But at the heart of it was Africa.

Filming was done mostly in French Equatorial Africa. "The heat was terrible," recalls Huston. "It would be 135 in the daytime and never less than 100 at night." So he began shooting at dawn, and ended the work day at noon. Still, "people would fall down from the heat. It was so hot that whenever you relaxed you went into a coma." The actors sweated so much while working that, as Errol Flynn remembered, every five minutes they had to douse their heads in water and re-apply make-up. Heat was directly followed by heat exhaustion. The camp was decimated by sunstroke, malaria, dysentery, heart attacks, and several diseases of unknown origin. Actor Frederick Ledebur got an eye infection and spent six months in the American hospital in Paris. Juliette Greco came down with a strange blood disease and almost died. She also went back to Paris before the movie was finished. The 160 members of the cast and crew reported for 624 sick calls. Those who didn't come down immediately with a physical illness suffered some sort of mental collapse. "Half the people went off their rocker," says Huston. "I remember when we were filming on an island and a French transportation man would drive Darryl and me to location every day. He would always be smiling, but one morning he was not smiling. Then he closed up altogether. Then he disappeared. Then he called us on the walkie-talkie system saying, 'Get off the island. There's a storm coming.' We decided to stay on the island, and there was no storm. We went back the next day and the same message came over the short wave. Every day. He had gone crazy. He said he was going to make movies in Africa. He was writing out scenes in long-hand and giving them away." One member of the crew suddenly began directing traffic—where there was no traffic. Eddie Albert was the last of the principals to arrive on location. For the first day and night he refused to wear a hat. "I've lived and worked in the Mexican desert," he boasted, "I *worship* the sun." The next day he dropped. Then he disintegrated. "He began to worry about his wife," says Huston. "He hadn't heard from her. My God, we didn't hear from *anyone*." Adds Zanuck, "Eddie Albert was out of his mind for three weeks, completely out of his mind. When he was in the worst stages, he was lying naked on the cement floor of his hut. I told him this later and he didn't believe me. He'd refuse to go to the toilet. We got two boys to tie him to a pole and carry him to the toilet."

The company's major relief and outlet was drinking. They quickly ran through their initial supply, and from then on they airlifted alcohol from the outside—whenever they ran dry. Planes arrived carrying only whiskey and vodka. "In three months," recalls Marc Doelnitz who played a small part in the picture, "we had drunk all the reserve of whiskey for Africa." Zanuck makes one of his rare claims for the picture, "I think the liquor consumed making that picture has never been equaled in the history of the cinema." Zanuck stayed with beer, downing, by his estimate, ten or twelve bottles a day. "I'd go to bed with it," he says. Most of the others were drinking Scotch, after Scotch, after Scotch. Huston and Howard are famous drinkers, but Patrick Leigh Fermor outdid them. "Paddy could drink with the titans," says Huston, "but there weren't any titans around, so he drank by himself. And he would go drunken-walking. He'd walk in the jungle. There were maneaters around." (Some 160 poisonous snakes were killed in the camp itself.) As for Trevor Howard, "He fought microbes off with Scotch whiskey." One night, smashing drunk, Howard woke up Zanuck, and shouted, "Zanuck is a bitch!" The most blatant imbiber was of course Flynn. He brought twelve cases of vodka with him on location, drank it all, and sent for more.

"I remember going up to him at six in the morning," says Doelnitz, "and he offered me a drink from a large glass. I thought it was water. It was straight vodka." Recalls Huston, "He would sit all night with a bottle of vodka, and an open book, and a Coleman lantern, and never look at the book. He was never drunk when working but whenever we shifted to another location he would drink too much and to recover he needed drugs. Errol was on his way out of course. He was dying." And less than a year later he died.

Then there was Greco. As the only actress, and one of the few women, on the location she was the center of attention and the object of many male attentions. Jealousy surrounded Zanuck like the black smoke from his endless supply of cigars (at least they seemed endless—until they were destroyed by Greco's pet mongoose). To please Greco he had let her bring an entourage with her to the juungle, thinking that if she were accompanied by her friends, she might keep her mind on the movie. Marc Doelnitz, for one, was an old Paris friend of Greco's. Working on publicity was Anna-Marie Cazalis, a French journalist, and one of the first to discover Greco singing in Paris cellars. Cazalis was on location to calm Greco down, but the opposite seemed true. Finally, annoyed at her intrusions, Zanuck sent her back to Paris. Later, in obvious retribution, she collaborated with Juliette on her memoirs, which charted in embarrassing, unflattering detail the Greco-Zanuck courtship, romance, and break-up—all of which seemed to happen concurrently. In those memoirs Greco had one strange picture of Zanuck during the filming of *Roots of Heaven*. She wrote, "Imagine a man who is getting on in years and who, like so many Americans, is accustomed to the most potent sleeping pills, putting on a black mask to sleep and wearing a sort of male 'baby doll' nightshirt instead of pyjamas."

John Huston concludes, "I think Darryl and I were the only survivors. I don't think anyone else pulled through without some trauma—physical or mental," and then, "There were no bitter dregs that Darryl didn't taste."

The most bitter dregs were the disappointment and despair of the picture itself. Just as the principals started falling apart, so did the movie. And, sadly, the story of the filming finally was more interesting than the movie itself. The very reason why it should have been a magnificent movie—the complexity of the book—turned it into a disaster. What should be emphasized: the philosophy or the adventure, the elephants or the people, Morel or his followers? Originally the script was written by Romain Gary, and as he remembers it, Zanuck loved it. "He said he'd rather have his throat cut than change the script," says Gary. "I have 50 cables assuring me that there would be no changes." Then, says Gary, "He fucked it up."

For one thing, he adds, "They improvised according to the book of Errol Flynn," which may be the only time anyone blamed Flynn for the movie's failure. "The next thing was the premiere and only one line of my script was left," says Gary. And that's it for Zanuck's *Roots of Heaven.* Then Gary switches to Zanuck himself. "He's a person with tremendous enthusiasm. The trouble is he's the lousiest writer that ever lived—but he has a compulsion to write. He knows good writing in other people but not bad in himself. If only he could just be a producer, he would be fantastic, but he gets involved in writing and directing. Just one touch of Darryl and it begins to stink." Then again Gary's ambivalence, "I never met a movie maker with such genuine enthusiasm and love for movies. He's truly a great producer."

"I'm afraid it wasn't a very good picture," says Huston about *Roots of Heaven,* "or it could been an awful lot better. I take full responsibility for this. Darryl put on a writer I recommended, put all my people in. He went all the way with me. The script wasn't what it could have been. It called for a profound approach. As it turned out, it was a kind of adventure picture—which it shouldn't have been." Once when Huston was quoted as assuming the blame for the movie, "Darryl called me and said, 'What the hell do you mean by claiming you're the only one responsible for it not being a good picture?'"

Reflecting on *Roots,* Zanuck says, "It was the most difficult location in the entire history of motion pictures. We took the quickest and easiest way out. Everyone was so depressed after we had been there a month, we would say, 'Oh Christ, let's leave that scene out.'" This lack of control was something new for Zanuck. Previously, certainly during his best Hollywood days, he had been adamant about not going into production without a knowledge of possible shooting difficulties. No improvisations for emergencies for him, because there would be no emergencies. Zanuck always went into battle with his battle plans. But here in French Equatorial Africa he found himself beset for six months by all sorts of unforeseen artistic, economic, climatic, alcoholic, physical, psychological, and romantic problems. The answer, but no solution, was to escape. Says Zanuck, "We ended up doing most of the close-ups and some of the scenes in a studio outside of Paris."

4.

The Paris Years

An American businessman who made a fortune, and suddenly women came into his life. They show him how to live. It's Dodsworth. *He wanted to sit in cafes. He wanted to savor life. He fell in love with France, a very sensual attractive country. He wanted to change everything about himself. In that way he's as interesting as Gauguin. You could write a* Moon and Sixpence *about Darryl. You could also write a* Blue Angel.

—Peter Viertel

Bella Darvi was, as one friend of Zanuck says, "a fine mistress for a movie mogul to have in Europe, except for her mania for gambling which almost wrecked Zanuck." Juliette Greco was another matter entirely. When they met, Zanuck was far richer and more powerful, but in most other respects she was at least on his level. She was not a starlet by any standards but a star. She was Greco, and in France that was like Piaf or Chevalier. And she didn't *need* anybody.

Between Greco and Zanuck, there were striking differences. Both were born rustics, but she more quickly had acquired the sheen of the city, perhaps because Zanuck's formative years were spent in Hollywood, not truly a city in a cosmopolitan sense. He was a producer, an entrepreneur, an assembler of talent, a communicator. She was an artist. He was proudly American, she was defiantly French. "They were not," says Edward Leggewie, in understatement, "made for each other." Adds Marc Doelnitz, "It was a very strange love story."

For her he was a new thing: her first mogul. And more. A strong man whom she would not permit to lead her, but who could stimulate her. And she could stimulate him. She could liberate him. He also, obviously, could provide her an opportunity to fulfill herself as an actress. He introduced her to Hollywood movies; she introduced him to Paris. Her gift was more successful. Greco never made it in pictures, but Zanuck undertook a long, mutually satisfying affair with Paris. For many of his Paris years, he continued to live in hotels, although his last three years, he leased an elegant apartment on the Left Bank several blocks away from Juliette Greco's apartment. At the time they were going out, he lived at a series of hotels on the Right Bank, although, once, at the height of their affair, Zanuck was found in her apartment in what might be considered a compromising situation. Greco was being visited by the television show, "At Home With," the Paris version of "Person to Person," when in walked Zanuck. "I believe you know each other," said the announcer. Greco greeted Zanuck by kissing him on both cheeks. "Juliette is not my protégée," declared Zanuck in French to the television camera. "She's the protégée of Paris and of France."

With Greco, Zanuck broadened his cultural and gustatorial horizons. They were seen not only in the lavish tourist spots like Tour d'Argent and Maxim's, but also at out-of-the-way gourmet restaurants like Chez l'Ami Louis. He sat at sidewalk cafes and thoroughly enjoyed the Parisian ambience. He became an intimate of such Parisian characters as Moustache, whose Left Bank cafe was a headquarters for the celebrities of the moment. Oddly enough for all he learned about Paris, he never made any true Parisian friends. His friends were mostly employees like André Hakim and Edward Leggewie, visiting Americans like Irving Hoffman and Charles Feldman, and resident expatriates like William Saroyan, Orson Welles, Art Buchwald, and Anatole Litvak.

His relationship with Saroyan and Welles, for two, is very representative of his Paris years. He enjoyed their company tremendously, but he did not always profit by it. "Once I was awakened at three in the morning. It was Saroyan calling from a casino, 'They're holding me prisoner here.' I said, 'How much are you short?' 'They won't let me go if I don't produce a thousand dollars.' I got up and wrote a check for a thousand dollars. I made it out to the club so Saroyan couldn't cash it and buy more chips. The night manager took it over himself and he told them it was the last money I was sending over." For some time Zanuck had Saroyan under contract as a writer. One play he wrote, *Lily Dafon*, was optioned by Zanuck as a potential DFZ Production. Lily Dafon is a beautiful seventeen-year-old Parisian who comes from a long line of liberated ladies. She has a sexy mother, grandmother, and even great-grandmother, and she becomes involved with a multimillionaire septuagenarian American named Hannaberry who has abandoned his wife in Texas. The parallel to Zanuck's romantic adventures is clear, and in fact when the property was submitted, his underlings shuddered at what they thought would be his reaction. Finally Edward Leggewie daringly pointed out the parallel to him. He had been unknowing, but was now unfazed. He insists he finally rejected the play not because it was about him but because he didn't think it was a good property.

Zanuck had known Orson Welles since Welles's early Hollywood days. Says Zanuck, "I consider Orson probably one of the greatest pieces of talent I've ever known, in whatever he does—although sometimes he's wasted."

In France, Zanuck and Welles became great companions, Welles sometimes calling on their friendship to bail him out of a difficult situation. Several years before he moved to Europe, during one of his visits to the Hotel du Cap, Zanuck called down for breakfast and the manager told him, "Orson Welles is sleeping in the lobby. He arrived at four in the morning and said he had to see you on a desperate matter." The manager had convinced Welles to wait until morning; Welles had asked him to take care of his taxicab. As Zanuck recalls, "The fare was more than $420. He had taken a cab from Italy."

Zanuck went down to the lobby. Orson had gone to Zanuck's cabana. "He threw his arms around me. I said, 'What the hell are you doing here? I thought you were shooting a picture in Italy.' He said, 'Unless you help, I'm dead. I need $75,000 to finish the picture. We're two-thirds through. The actors are not being paid.' I said, 'Jesus, I don't have that kind of money.' But being at times soft where talent is concerned, I telephoned the home office and said that we had a chance to get 60 per cent interest in a picture by Orson. It was *Othello*, and I had a little trouble with them about *that*. An exchange of telegrams and finally they said the money would be delivered in cash to me by a representative of the Paris office. A man came down with a mail sack with locks on it. It was in cash and the highest bill was 100 francs. The auditor insisted that I be there when it was counted. It took three hours! And Orson was going in and out of the water." Zanuck gave him the money. Welles thanked him and left.

"Fadeout," says Zanuck. "Four days later I ran into Anatole Litvak. He said he had heard that I helped out Orson. How did he know? Orson told him. Litvak had just seen him *gambling* in the casino at Monte Carlo. I was so mad. The picture of him without a cent and the cast unpaid. I thought I would take a pistol, get into a cab, go to the casino, and kill him."

Slowly Zanuck calmed down. He did nothing. Later he discovered that Welles had stayed three or four days at the casino, and "apparently did pretty well. He went back to Venice, paid everyone, and finished the picture."

In the winter Zanuck skied, at Davos, St. Moritz, and especially at Klosters. Zanuck was not a top skier, but was apparently a daring one, undeterred by bad weather or the difficulty of a slope. Irwin Shaw remembers him once falling off a ski tow, while trying to light his cigar. On one foggy, windy day he was trailing Shaw (a top skier) down a particularly winding trail. Zanuck peered through the fog, trying to catch sight of Shaw up ahead. Snow started to fall. Zanuck skied faster, and then suddenly sailed off a curve right into the rocks. The crash knocked him out. Finally the ski patrol arrived and carried him down. "Jesus, I was in misery," remembers Zanuck. "I broke my shoulder and collarbone. I had a gash on my right hand. My hand was out for four months. Did you ever try to go to the bathroom and be forced to use your *left* hand?"

Greco has said, "I belong to Paris like a street lamp or a stone out of Notre Dame. I am French in style, temperament and expression. The French public and I have always had a strange love affair with each other. That's why they couldn't forgive me for Zanuck." It was not *Paris* that resented Zanuck, it was Greco's friends. They never accepted him, and in some cases actively discouraged the relationship. For one thing they felt she had sold out to him for the sake

of a movie career, and she in turn became increasingly
embittered for having done it and having failed as an actress.

One of Greco's most intimate friends was Françoise Sagan,
but she did like Zanuck. "He is very sentimental," she says,
"and I like sentimental people. I suppose he can be hard,
but I think he is looking for feeling. We are two poor
sentimental people. There is something lost, something of a
child, maybe a bad child, something afraid. He is the sort
of person caring about a dog, and crushing someone. I think
he's very alone. He has lived in a money world where money
is more important than anything, and it makes you sad after
such years. I think he would have been someone much happier if he had not been in such a business as cinema and
money. I think he's a good man, but his life made him sad.
The first time we met was in Cannes, with Juliette and Orson
Welles. A strange dinner. Orson Welles hit me on the back
and said, 'Don't speak to movie people.'" She concludes
about Zanuck, "I think I like him for his wickedness."

Through all the love and the disharmony, he continued his
obsessive, disastrous attempt to make Greco into a movie star.
In both *The Sun Also Rises* and *Roots of Heaven*, Greco was
scarcely noticed, which is strange considering that in both
cases her parts were larger than they would have been if
someone else had played them. She was not bad in either,
but she was not distinguished. And even though she had
often been praised for her unusual personality, whatever
magnetism she possessed singing in a club or on stage, she
lost in pictures. "I was uprooted," she said, "an object without a soul operated by remote control. I was making foreign
movies in a foreign language with foreign actors for foreign
audiences. I had to get out of this golden, asphyxiating,
absurd merry-go-round." It wasn't any merry-go-round that
killed Greco as an actress. It was her own lack of acting
talent—and the fact that, as Zanuck later put it: "She never
photographed as well as she looked in person or on stage.
I got her the best hairdresser, the top photographer, the top
guys. I had her nose fixed *twice* by Sir Archibald McIndoe
in London. She acted well enough, but she didn't project. The
camera is a monster and there's not a damn thing you can do
about it. Greco couldn't be photographed. She was dead right
there."

The final flop was *Crack in the Mirror*, a murky courtroom

melodrama in which Orson Welles, Bradford Dillman, and Juliette Greco each played two parts, as did Darryl Zanuck. He produced it, and under the old alias Mark Canfield wrote the screenplay. But during shooting, he sat alone in the background, seldom making suggestions and on several occasions not viewing the rushes. A good friend said, "It was as if DZ was attending his own funeral and knew it." (The only successful DFZ production during this period was *Compulsion*, which Dick Zanuck produced in Hollywood, and Darryl had nothing to do with.) After one private screening in Paris of *Crack in the Mirror*, friends came out of the theater to find Zanuck standing next to a tree by himself. It was a long way from those yes-men curbstone critiques after previews in Hollywood.

Greco's and Zanuck's names filled the columns, especially their public disagreements. "He likes to be with me," she said at the time, "and when he is there I am happy. We fight a lot. People who like each other do fight—no fight no fun." Two such disparate, equally volatile people could never subdue their temperaments. There were good times, and Greco likes to think she helped him—at least up to a point. "I don't think he was entirely free," says Greco—until she freed him. "For him, I meant *revolutionnaire*." And she describes how restricted he was in his previous life. "I think Darryl didn't realize what he wanted to realize, what he had been building up to. Twentieth Century-Fox, which isn't *la merde*, wasn't his cup of tea. But he worked night and day, like a dog. He was inside an ivory tower. Afterwards he became DFZ company and started to do what he wanted to. He wanted to make his own pictures, and when he was at the top of his power, he wanted to act like a very young man. He was never young before. After sweating his own blood for many many years, he happened to be free and then he became not an adult at all. Let him make some mistakes! Darryl is a child too. Not childish, but a child, a child with all the violence and wantings, and all the strengths, of a child. Out of the ivory tower! Then everyone was picking on him because suddenly he is a human being.

"I didn't know the tycoon. I'm sick and tired of people telling me he was a tycoon. They made him a tycoon. He is not inhuman. They made him inhuman. Everybody came to me and said, 'You don't know what you're doing. He's such a powerful man.' He didn't kill me. He made me happy. Sometimes. Not others. That's life." Did she make him happy? "I did my best." Did she hurt him? "Certainly. Yes. No more than any woman saying good-by to a man. That's the story of every man and woman." But he *was* Zanuck, and she *was* Greco, and everything they did seemed larger than life —and twice as horrible.

Finally Greco left him. In her absence his constant companion was a miniature schnauzer, a present from Greco, a dog with a name suitable to Zanuck's state—Iago de Roc-Fort. He was always with the dog. He had dinner with the dog at a table for two. "It was a friendly little dog," says Edward Leggewic, "but it's not a picture of Darryl F. Zanuck you imagine." The Plaza Athénée hotel claimed that Iago had ruined furniture in Zanuck's suite. In reprisal, Zanuck's friend, Art Buchwald, wrote a column about Iago's bill of complaints against the Plaza Athénée: the high prices ($5 a day for Iago without meals), snoopy housekeepers ("When Mr. Zanuck is out and Iago is trying to nap, she sneaks into the room and checks to see if he has done any damage to the rugs and the furniture"), discrimination against pedigreed dogs. "Iago takes at least one of his meals at the Relais Plaza, a grill room attached to the Plaza Athénée," wrote Buchwald. "He dines there with Mr. Zanuck, and claims he only barks at agents and screenwriters. This is no more than Mr. Zanuck does with the same people, and Iago doesn't understand why the management gets mad at him but not at Mr. Zanuck." But it was no joking matter. The Plaza Athénée demanded several thousand dollars payment for damages, and finally suggested that Zanuck and Iago remove themselves from the premises. Gradually Zanuck fell apart. He began drinking heavily. He would sit and watch television by himself for long hours. He refused to see old friends. Ridiculed, cuckolded, he was no longer the power, the tycoon, but just a small, lost man cracking up in Paris. He was, in the croquet phrase, "dead on three balls," situation hopeless—unless a miracle happened. His friends watched his collapse, but said nothing. Some were not concerned enough to take action. Most of them were simply afraid. How do you tell Darryl Zanuck he's destroying himself?

5.

Z-Day

I believe I have a tougher job than Ike had on D-Day—at least he had the equipment. I have to find it, rebuild it, and transport it to Normandy.

—Darryl Zanuck, in a letter to
Lord Louis Mountbatten, Earl of Burma

The Longest Day may well be the most important event in the life of Darryl Zanuck. It changed his life, *saved* his life, and saved the life of Twentieth Century-Fox as well, which is why he made it as if he were fighting for his life. For Zanuck it was not only a victory, but a comeback of Cinema-Scope proportions. Before *The Longest Day,* he was a washed-up, played-out producer. After *The Longest Day,* he was one of the most powerful men in the movies, even more powerful than when he had been previously ascendant, so powerful that he revived an almost defunct organization and established a dynasty. When he talks about it, it is with reverence, pride, and an enthusiasm unequaled in even this most enthusiastic man. When Zanuck sits back and tells about his favorite war experiences, sometimes he reminisces about his doughboy days in World War I, or about going on commando raids with Mountbatten's commandos in World War II, but most often he talks about his landing at Normandy on his D-Day —Z-Day!

For him, *The Longest Day* merits the highest accolades. The filming itself "is motion picture history" and the movie is a "classic," filmed against seemingly insurmountable odds. It was, he says, "such a daring, impossible undertaking. Had I known at the beginning what we were going to face, if I had even a hint of it, I would have thrown in the sponge."

His son, perhaps the person closest to him, begged him to stop before he started. "The only picture I really warned him against was *The Longest Day*," says Richard Zanuck who had watched his Paris decline from the distance of Hollywood. "What scared me was that we were getting into an eight or an eight and a half million dollar picture, which at that time was really fantastic. I thought, Jesus, this is liable to be really the end of the line. I asked him, 'Who cares about World War II?' Most of the theatergoing public wasn't even born at that time. He was setting out to duplicate the entire invasion without using any stock or 'library' footage. It was awesome."

Zanuck first read Cornelius Ryan's book in October 1960. "I went absolutely nuts about it," he recalls, decided to film it and sat down almost immediately, even before he obtained the rights to the book, feverishly blue-lined the passages he thought should be dramatized. From that, he wrote a continuity outline and step sheet, started mapping his war plans, and addressed a thinking-out-loud memo to himself:

"I am not interested in making a film that is only historically accurate. It just so happens that this one happens to be accurate. I am interested in following the brave, funny, bewildering, human and tragic events of that day. Five hundred different books have been written by all the generals on both sides on the subject of D-Day. The only one that achieved success was *The Longest Day*. This is not because it ignored history or accuracy, but because it gave the public a chance to see our own errors and our own successes, our own confusion and our own clear thinking. It also gave us a chance, for the first time, to see what happened to the Germans on this day, and to understand why they made so many blunders and errors . . .

"If we try to paint a rosy, star-spangled banner drawing of D-Day, we are certainly headed for disaster . . . The only thing that will make it an enormous box-office smash is that we tell audiences *what they do not know about what happened on that day*."

Cornelius Ryan, a tough, bluff, confident journalist—a "reporter," he likes to call himself, proudly, with a trace of an Irish brogue—was in Hawaii on assignment for *Reader's Digest. The Longest Day*, his sixth book, had been published the previous year, had won him the best notices of his career, and was slowly building into a best-seller. It would easily sell more than the other five combined (his first book had sold only 823 copies) but profits were slow to come in. He had worked on *The Longest Day* for ten years, seven part time, three full time. Not until 1958 had he signed with a publisher, Simon and Schuster, for an advance of $7500. By the time the book was published, as Ryan tells it, he was $60,000 in debt. Then in 1959 what seemed like a windfall came his way. French producer Raoul Levy bought the screen rights to *The Longest Day* for $100,000 and for an additional $35,000 hired Ryan to write the screenplay. But by 1960 Ryan had been paid only $25,000, and it was obvious that Levy had no intention of paying him any more or of making the movie. Disillusioned, Ryan shelved his script. Now, in Hawaii, the telephone rang. It was MCA calling from New York to say that Darryl F. Zanuck wanted to make a movie out of *The Longest Day*.

In December 1960, Ryan flew to New York to meet Zanuck. Ryan's first impression was a peculiar mixture of admiration and antagonism that was to set the tone of their future relationship. "He was a somewhat handsome man in his own way. A very dominant character. He first deprecated my work, then praised some of it. I was amazed when Zanuck pulled something out of a briefcase and said, 'I've written the treatment already.'"

In January, Ryan flew over to Paris. Zanuck had taken over Levy's obligations, including $35,000 for the incomplete adaptation. Fox rented Ryan a room at the Prince de Galles Hotel to use as an office. Almost immediately work began in earnest. In some ways it was like Hollywood again for Zanuck. He would pace the floor, concoct dialogue, act out scenes, prod his writers. Secretaries transcribed everything. The script (and this later was to prove an important factor in the war between Zanuck and Ryan) was almost always a group effort, but as Ryan pictured it, "We sat there like so many dummies, and then Darryl Eisenhower would dictate to us what happened on D-Day." The battle lines were drawn—between Zanuck and Ryan. Although Zanuck insists that at first impression, "I thought he was a man of tremendous quality," and Ryan insists, almost with tears in his eyes, that he would have liked nothing better than to be friends with Zanuck, the truth is that as collaborators they were more often enemies. If Zanuck played at being Eisenhower, Ryan too often seemed to be his Rommel. On one side stood Zanuck, who knew how to make movies. On the other stood Ryan, the jealous guardian of his sacred prose. He wanted everything, or at least as much as possible, from his book to be put in his movie. Ryan stood up to Zanuck, which in itself for a writer is admirable, except that often, according to eye witnesses, Ryan was wrong. As for Zanuck, he needed Ryan, at least for the first draft because of Ryan's expertise. Ryan was a walking encyclopedia on D-Day, and if he didn't have the information, he knew where to find it. This was a distinct asset, until Ryan's scrupulous attention to facts and figures and his compulsive possessiveness about his work began to run counter to Zanuck's film experience. Worst of all, for Ryan, before his very eyes, Cornelius Ryan's *The Longest Day* became Darryl Zanuck's *The Longest Day*.

Although the script was Ryan's sole function, Zanuck had many other obsessive concerns. He had to find troops and also equipment—ships, planes, tanks, weapons, uniforms. Very early he decided whenever possible to use the original site to re-create a scene, which was a disadvantage as well as an advantage. It certainly lent authenticity—but it was also seventeen years later. Sites had changed. Rebuilding would be necessary. He could not have expended more effort and organization were he supervising the real invasion. No wonder some people confused the two.

From the beginning Zanuck realized he would have to have the co-operation (and more, such as soldiers) of England, France, Germany, and the United States, and in January he began sending out letters. In the preparation of his book, Ryan had accumulated many sources, and assumed that for the movie he would tap them once again, but he had not counted on Zanuck's weight, prestige, and push. Although a few of Ryan's sources were friends—such as General James Gavin—many were only journalistic acquaintances. Zanuck's sources were personal friends. Lord Mountbatten, Earl of Burma, was "Dickie." General Mark Clark was "Wayne" and his wife was "Renie." The Eisenhowers were "Ike" and "Mamie." Lord Lovat, commander of British forces, soon became "Shimi." He wrote personal letters to Eisenhower. He also contacted Admiral Friedrich Ruge for Germany, Pierre

Mesmer, the French Minister of Defense, who assigned him
General Pierre Koenig. Then he flew to London to see Mountbatten who arranged a meeting for Zanuck with the chiefs o:
the various forces involved. "I found a slightly hostile feeling
based on the fact that they thought this was another of those
American movies which showed how the Americans won the
war. They wanted to be sure I wasn't interested in making i:
a one-man American show. I told them that realistically :
had to have their cooperation. They said that before I wen:
into production they would have to see my script." Zanuck
readily agreed, as he did with the other countries. Only Germany approved without seeing the script. The others wanted
to be sure of their share.

A week after he had been in Paris, Ryan suggested the
inclusion and dramatic expansion of several romantic inter-
ludes, love stories that actually occurred, in life and in his
book. Ryan particularly pressed for two, one between an
American soldier and a French girl in a farmhouse near the
landing beaches, the other between a resistance fighter Janine
Boitard and Leonard Gille, Normandy's deputy chief of
Resistance. In response Zanuck sent Ryan a note, "a blistering memo," says Ryan. "How dare I suggest there be a love
story in *The Longest Day,* even though it was in the book.
He thought that was beneath me. On no account, he said,
would he have it in the script."

"I do not want to badger you or cramp your style," wrote
Zanuck, "but when you bring up, as you did at luncheon
yesterday, an extraneous idea like love scenes between Gille
and his fiancee, I have to speak up. These are just the things
that we do not want and are the same things that .ave killed
off so many other war pictures where they have tried to
introduce a touch of sex."

Since the affair with Greco had ended, Zanuck had not attempted a sustained relationship with any girl. He turned his
attentions to his film project and not to a film protégée, something he hadn't done for several years. That is not to say that
he had lost interest in the ladies. Actually it was only a matter
of time before he took up with someone else, full time. After
almost six tempestuous, torrid years of Darvi and Greco, he
was obviously in need of a companion. A nice girl to love

him, to listen to him, to make appearances with him at parties and premieres, someone to look beautiful, satisfy his desires, yet at the same time not to pose a threat to his emotional stability—someone like Irina Demick. Her name Gallicized to Demich from Dziemiach, and later, in June 1965, Anglicized to Demick, Irina was the daughter of Russian émigrés to France, and a model, mostly in film commercials. With Zanuck, she had dinner at Moustache, Chez l'Ami Louis, Le Coq Hardi. They went dancing at Regine's. And she let him lead her, a refreshing change from his last two liaisons. Says Edward Leggewie, "Irina was happy to make him happy. She's a very simple person, not at all scheming." As she recalls, "He tells me, 'Take a pretty dress and go to the hairdresser,' and then he puts me always in front. If I go alone, even if I am pretty, no one takes my picture." When she was with Zanuck, everyone took her picture. Soon she became a semi-name by proximity, the lady in the photographs with Zanuck. "She was certainly no pushover," says Zanuck, and then—"I was beginning to fall in love again."

Somewhere along the line Janine Boitard's minor role in *The Longest Day* was expanded. She became the only woman with something of a sustained part. And named to play her was Irina Demick. "They wanted Brigitte Bardot," says Irina, "but the role was too small. Then they wanted Marina Vlady, but she was not free." Irina was available, inexpensive, inexperienced, and pliable and when the time came, after the movie was finished, she became something of its chief publicist—by default if nothing else. "In four months I went four times around the world to do publicity," says Irina. "I go to every place. If they would take a real actress, she never do this." Even during the filming, Irina became more and more attached to Zanuck, in fact, one might say, totally dependent. As she says about herself and other of his close friends: "If Darryl is not there, we are nothing. We are satellites around the sun. If the sun is not there, we die. Before him, I never tried to make movies. If he was not there when it began, I would never be Irina Demick. I cannot be Irina Demick without Darryl Zanuck. I am a cabbage."

While Zanuck and his staff were scouting equipment and locations, Ryan plugged away at the script. As Zanuck remembers, in about a month he returned to Paris to find Ryan and a fat script. Says Zanuck, "He had things completely out

of proportion—twenty-six pages for something that should
take three lines, three lines for something that should take
twenty-six pages." So the work began. "It was a painstaking
thing," says Zanuck. "Rewriting and rewriting and rewriting
and rewriting." On April 5, the first final script was finished
and Ryan for one breathed a great sigh of relief. By his own
admission the writing had not been easy for him. If the book
had been a labor of love, the script was largely a labor. For
Zanuck, Ryan's end was his beginning. First he sent copies
of the completed script to selected authors for comments
and possible revisions. He wanted one for each country
participating in D-Day: James Jones for the United States,
Romain Gary for France, Noel Coward for Great Britain,
and Erich Maria Remarque for Germany. Coward declined
on the ground that he was too busy working on a musical
comedy, and suggested Terence Rattigan. (Eventually Zanuck
hired David Pursall and Jack Seddon.) Remarque commented
briefly on the script and his agent followed it up with a bill
for $5000. Jones and Gary agreed to participate, without
compensation.

In Hollywood it has always been standard, if not always
ethical, practice to have several writers working on a script
at once—sometimes with one not knowing about the other—
and to reassign a script before a writer was notified. There is
no sanctity when it comes to a script, which is why the
Screen Writers' Guild is often called in to mediate. As
Cornelius Ryan saw it he was *The* Writer, or *The* Author.
Soon after he finished the *Longest Day* script, he picked up
a newspaper and read that Zanuck had signed a squad of
script consultants. Under the Writers' Guild rules, since
Zanuck had hired other writers and not notified Ryan, Ryan's
outrage was justified and subject to compensation. But the
most insulting thing to Ryan was not the sequence of Zanuck's
assignment, but the mere fact of it. As Ryan saw it, Jones's
and Gary's contributions were minimal. "Romain read that
he was a consultant before he got the script. He wrote a memo,
I thought it made a lot of sense, but it was more a directive
than a script. Jones wrote a ten-page memo, a scathing ap-
praisal of the entire script," and according to Ryan, "I didn't
see one piece of Jones in the final script."

Later, when the movie was finished and Zanuck tried to
assign credit, alphabetically, to Gary, Jones, Pursall and

Seddon (as a team), and Ryan, Ryan took the matter to the
Guild, and after producing considerable documentation, won
his case, and received sole credit. Ryan himself admitted that
Zanuck and Elmo Williams were entitled to co-credit. "I
couldn't have done it myself," he says. "I was trying to save
my identity. I wasn't trying to deny Darryl's and Elmo's
credit." But he was trying to deny Jones's and Gary's credit.
The truth is that Gary and Jones were hired by Zanuck,
paid by Zanuck, devoted much time and work to the script,
and contributed to it. Zanuck wanted Jones because "it occurred to me that Ryan's GI talk didn't sound like GI talk."
By the time the script was sent to the Motion Picture Association of America (the Johnston Office) for approval, many
of Jones's lines were obliterated. Geoffrey Shurlock, the production code administrator, objected, for instance, to the use
of "casual profanity" and vulgar bits of dialogue such as crap,
stuff it, muck it, motherlover, s.o.b., bastards, Jeez, damn,
puke, and several typical Jones lines, such as "they couldn't
sink this clucking can if they tried to," and "wipin' the blue-
bird dung off them fat white cliffs of Dover." Concluded
Shurlock, "We are concerned with what seems to us to be
an excessive amount of slaughter in this story. We realize
that it is impossible to tell the story of the invasion of
Normandy without indicating the staggering loss of human
life. We do urge you, in those scenes you stage, to minimize
the dramatization of personal killings. We think that such an
effort on your part would avoid the 'bloodbath' effect." Zanuck reacted to very few of the objections, ignored others, and
hoped he didn't get in trouble. Jones, on the other hand, was
enraged. He wrote Zanuck, "I was *morally shocked* at . . .
their 'concern' over the 'excessive slaughter' in the story.
What the fuck do they think war is? What did they think
Omaha was, if not a 'bloodbath'? Perhaps if we stop talking
about war altogether, we can make everybody much happier
about having to undergo a good clean unbloody nuclear
war . . .

"I find it incredible that these ostriches can go on like they
do, building fallout bombshelters with one hand, and not
allowing honesty in combat films with the other. And if they
tell me this is what American people *want,* I can only answer
that they're full of *bullshit.*"

As for Romain Gary—"I was also worried about the French

section," says Zanuck, "and, how, proportionately, to enlarge it, to show how the Resistance fought." In his original memo, Gary did praise the script, but said that it needed sharpening. Like Jones, Gary went to work on specific sections. Among other things, says Zanuck, "Gary uncovered one of Ryan's major errors." The Ouistreham casino, the scene in *The Longest Day* of one of the crucial skirmishes between the Germans and French, had actually been demolished two years before D-Day by the RAF. "There was a hotel still standing in Ouistreham," says Zanuck, "but no casino," as Ryan's book had described it. Since Zanuck's men had already started to reconstruct the casino, and "because it turned out to be a great sequence, I talked Romain into leaving it in."

One crucial difference between Zanuck and Ryan, it seems, is that Zanuck was usually aware when he was altering a truth for dramatic purposes, whereas Ryan could never admit to an error. Says Zanuck, "These inaccuracies are not major. They are close to the event that occurred. We did land. We did take the beach. We took dramatic license to make it effective. Anything changed was an asset to the film. There is nothing duller on screen than being accurate but not dramatic. There's no violation if you use basic fact, if you dramatize basic fact." Many of Zanuck's alterations were in order to equalize each country's contributions. Asked if there are any factual errors in the book, *The Longest Day,* Ryan ponders a moment, then asserts unabashedly, "None that I can think of." Zanuck says, "My most frequent recollection of Ryan on location is of his sitting on the set and constantly signing autographs on the fly page of his book. Apparently his French publisher knew our production itinerary. Whenever we arrived at a new town or locale, the book was prominently displayed in store windows, including restaurants, drug stores and at Ouistreham in a butcher shop."

England, France, and the United States supplied an estimated total of 23,000 troops for the ten months of shooting. Germany didn't have any to contribute, except in the important leading roles as actors. France sent 1000 commandos even though it was involved in the Algerian war. The U.S. kept cutting back on its share of the Zanuck forces. He had asked for 1500, was made to accept 750, finally settled for

250. In the end, Zanuck was forced to complement his American army with French substitutes in American uniforms. Assisted by his staff, Zanuck began scouting for the smaller equipment. "At the time I foolishly thought it was around," he says. Some of it was around, but it took considerable excavation and exhumation to find it. There were no Spitfires in Britain, but there were some in Belgium, no Messerschmitts in Germany, but there were two in France. The Spitfires couldn't fly and had to be fitted with new Rolls-Royce engines. The Messerschmitts were battle ready. There were no gliders anywhere, so Zanuck's men went to the same company that had built the original gliders for Britain during the war, and commissioned duplicates. Zanuck himself called a costume shop in London and demanded 2000 World War II helmets and uniforms.

In re-creating D-Day, Zanuck had to face the inevitable fact that some people might object to being portrayed on screen. "I took the stand that I was reproducing history. Half the leaders had written books about their experiences. It was in the public domain. I wasn't defaming anyone. Only two people sued and won on the grounds that we violated their privacy. One was a waiter, an Englishman, and the other German, and they were small settlements." Zanuck was free to portray Eisenhower, Gavin, Rommel, Lord Lovat, Commander Philippe Kieffer, and Private first class Arthur B. Schultz among others. In fact most of them were enthusiastic about being portrayed—some watched the shooting, contributing themselves as free technical advisers and occasionally producing appropriate uniforms and decorations. Commander Colin Maud, for example, supplied his uniforms and the gnarled shillelagh he carried with him on D-Day.

When it came to casting, Zanuck decided to go for names. "I wanted the audience to have a kick," he explains. "Every time a door opened, it would be a well-known personality." He also decided to use, when necessary, the personal approach. Dick Zanuck in Hollywood was put in charge of the major part of the casting, particularly the search for young actors to play enlisted men. Memos and cables flew back and forth. Said Darryl Zanuck about General Cota: "He is shorter but from the photographs he looks like John Wayne. Since Wayne has taken care of the Alamo and has never lost any historical battle that he has ever appeared in, there is no reason why he should not take care of Omaha Beach." Also suggested for Cota were James Cagney and Burt Lancaster— Robert Mitchum got the part. William Holden, Gregory Peck, Richard Widmark, and Cary Grant were all mentioned for the part of General Vandervoort—Wayne got it. James Stewart, Burgess Meredith, Glenn Ford, and Cagney for Brigadier General Theodore Roosevelt—Henry Fonda got that one. William Holden and Audie Murphy were mentioned to play General James Gavin, and just to irritate Cornelius Ryan, at one story conference, Zanuck announced that Mickey Rooney would play the part. Ryan spluttered his outrage. Actually Robert Ryan got the part.

For the younger enlisted men, from a list of pop stars, the Zanucks picked Tommy Sands, Paul Anka, Sal Mineo, and Fabian (whose first instruction on arriving in France was to "cease shaving from now, until you have an opportunity to discuss with Mr. Zanuck and Mr. [Andrew] Marton the state of beard they would think you should have for your role"). The most difficult part to cast was that of Eisenhower, and the suggestions came in from around the world. Miss S. Toriumi, a Japanese agent, offered an American actor in Yokohama. Columnist Leonard Lyons proposed Red Barber. William McCaffrey, Barber's agent, followed it up with pictures, and when Barber was rejected, proposed another of his clients, Art Carney. Zanuck's art director Ted Haworth had gotten Al Steele roles as Eisenhower in *The Sixth Man* and *Who Was That Lady?* and now tried him again for *The Longest Day*. Someone else suggested Relman (Pat) Morin, chief AP correspondent, but Morin himself felt he was too old to play the part. Finally Dick Zanuck discovered Henry Grace, an MGM art director, non-actor, and look-alike, and signed him. To a great extent, the casting was by improvisation. The question was not always who fit the part (Wayne's general was conceived as a bookkeeper type) but who was available and when. Many rejected roles because of conflicts, and for other reasons. One, William Holden, asked for too much money. Many others volunteered, including Roddy McDowall, who was bored sitting in Rome waiting to play Octavius in *Cleopatra*. To get an actor of primary rank, Zanuck might juggle a schedule, or offer a selection of parts (Fonda, for one, had three to choose from). Those in the secondary group were often interchangeable. For one British enlisted man, it was either Sean Connery, Patrick McGoohan, or John Gregson. Connery, Zanuck was informed, "likes the role very much and would like to do it. However, he has a commitment for a picture in Jamaica which starts on November 7." The relatively unknown actor managed to squeeze in *The Longest Day* bit while still honoring his commitment in Jamaica. That picture turned out to be *Dr. No,* the first James Bond, and the beginning of *the* Sean Connery.

While Zanuck began his battle on the western front, his studio was involved in a war of its own. Split by dissension and facing possible bankruptcy, its management produced Zanuck and *The Longest Day* as scapegoats. Frantically, Spyros Skouras called Zanuck in Paris, and demanded, "You've got to stop what you're doing and fly here." "I can't," said Zanuck, "I'm in the middle of a picture." Skouras finished, ". . . or they're going to stop your picture and take their loss up till now." Zanuck hurried to New York, and on May 24, 1961, faced the board. Recalls Zanuck, "I must say that Skouras was against stopping the picture, but he had lost *all* control. Milton Gould was violently opposed to it. He and John Loeb spearheaded the attack. Who wants this kind of picture? Let's take a three-million loss and get out." Outnumbered, outflanked, and seemingly defeated before he began, Zanuck got up and began fighting with his mouth, which in moments of peril has always been one of his best weapons. He talked about D-Day, about the world-wide interest in the subject and the limited knowledge that people had about it. This would be the final word on the subject. "He was boiling," recalls one Fox executive. "He talked for four hours, and then he said, 'At this point, the main titles start.' "

General James van Fleet (a member of the Fox board) came to Zanuck's rescue. "He lost his temper," says Zanuck. "He practically called them idiots. He had landed in the first wave on D-Day. Usually at board meetings, he never said anything, but now he said, 'This picture will make more than any other picture.' Then Robert Clarkson began to sway for me. Robert Lehman began to sway for me. They asked me to leave the meeting and wait outside. Then they called me in and said I could go ahead but if I spent more than eight million, they would take my cameras away. I think the vote was six to five in my favor." With this less than enthusiastic vote of confidence, Zanuck returned to battle.

Zanuck found he could borrow or build all sorts of equipment, but one thing he needed, and could not afford to construct was an invasion fleet. When he learned that for the last ten days in June the Sixth Fleet was conducting maneuvers off Corsica, he immediately decided to have these vessels stand in for their World War II predecessors. With permission of the government, he took Elmo Williams and his crew to Corsica—and the complications began. "We were going to shoot out to sea with the whole Sixth Fleet in the background." He suddenly realized, "They had a goddamn aircraft carrier in the fleet." There were no aircraft carriers on D-Day. Zanuck went right to the admiral of the fleet and asked, "Can't you hide it?" "No," came the answer, "if we did, how could we have exercises?" So Zanuck sat down with Elmo Williams and measured the fleet. "We figured out that if we could get the aircraft carrier to keep to the right 2000 yards, we could photograph the whole fleet." That solved, Zanuck faced the next problem. "About three days before we were ready to shoot, a lawyer arrived saying he was a representative of the people who owned the beach property. For something like $15,000 they would *let* us shoot on the beach. Otherwise they would take modern automobiles and ride them along the beach," the Plage de Salleches. Grudgingly Zanuck paid. "As it turned out there's no such thing as a private beach." So he sued them. "After eight years in trial, I won a complete, total judgment." Back on Corsica, there was one small hitch: except for the fact that there was a beach and water, Corsica looked nothing like Normandy. Zanuck's men had set up obstacles and barbed wire and faked explosives, but the Plage de Salleches was as bright as a resort beach whereas Normandy was dark and foreboding. So Zanuck's men sprayed it with water and burned tires to smoke up the sky. It was hot to begin with, but the burning rubber shot the temperature up in the high 100s. It was, to say the least, a sweaty landing. There was one last problem, as recounted by Richard Oulahan in *Life*: "Zanuck's personal intelligence operations warned him that a nudist colony, just two miles inland from the Corsican beach, posed a potential hazard. It was arranged, therefore, for local authorities to post signs warning the nudists not to go near the water during the landings. Fortunately, the Marine-actors never learned about the colony. 'If they had,' reflects Zanuck, 'they'd probably have kept right on advancing.' " Finally Zanuck set up his cameras, and screening out the aircraft carrier, shot the Sixth Fleet landing at Corsica. As Zanuck recalls, it was "only nine and a half minutes of actual photography," but he had his fleet, and on screen the twenty-two ships looked like an armada.

Zanuck moved his office from Paris to the front, set up field headquarters and during August and September 1961, filmed on location throughout Normandy, scooting from place to place in his Alouette helicopter. Ste. Mère-Eglise was the scene of a night parachute jump. Since his paratroopers were not used to dropping at night into a populated area, Zanuck cleared the town of obstacles. Traffic was stopped. Stores were closed. The power was cut off, so that the jumpers wouldn't hit telephone wires. But, blinded by the hot lights and distracted by the building the movie men were burning, the men landed all over town, only one or two in the town square. After many tries and an assortment of minor injuries (on the first night jump, one man broke both his legs) Zanuck decided to settle for verisimilitude. The men, wearing rigged parachutes, jumped off high cranes into the square.

In another scene just as the camera was about to finish filming, Peter Lawford and his men coming down the road to relieve Richard Todd at the Orne Bridge, the director of the "British exterior episodes" Ken Annakin, announced, "This is for king and country!" Zanuck, cigar clenched firmly in his mouth, came blustering over to Annakin and corrected him, "This is for Twentieth Century-Fox!" Retake. The explosions were about to go off. Lawford and his troops were coming down the path. Action! Suddenly, clank, clank, clank, clank, a tank came clumsily along the road and stopped in front of the camera. It was the tank that Zanuck had ordered months before from the French government, and now arrived suddenly and obtrusively on the scene. As Zanuck, Annakin, and the cameramen stared, stupefied, the top of the tank opened and a French mechanic in blue overalls climbed out and said, "Voilà!"

The breach between Zanuck and Ryan grew wider and wider. It was a clear collision of temperament, personality, wills, and egos, and Zanuck was obviously going to be the victor. He had the power, and also the rights to Ryan's book. What finally split Zanuck and Ryan completely? Zanuck thinks it was Ryan's annoyance at the absence of the fleet in the rushes of the Point du Hoc episode. Zanuck informed him that the ships would be superimposed in later, as they were. Ryan was skeptical. Then, too, there was the appearance of James Jones on location. It was instant dislike. In Ryan's version, his split with Zanuck was caused partly by their running argument over the ending of the picture. "Zanuck had a bad concept," says Ryan. "He wanted a GI at water's edge, throwing stones into the water and saying 'Did we succeed? Did we succeed?' " The scene, as it appeared for a time in the script had a GI staring at the surf "sobbing quietly, tears running down his cheeks." He "picks up a stone and tosses it into the water—then he picks up another and another and another." Dick Zanuck liked the scene so much that he suggested the movie begin with a similar one. "Absolute corn!" says Ryan. "Zanuck at his best. I dared suggest that we might use the ending in the book." Actually since July 15 Ryan had stopped being a "writer" on the picture and was a "sort of adviser." Now Zanuck informed him that his services were no longer needed. On September 6, Ryan left—gone but not yet forgotten, particularly when Zanuck read in a *Newsweek* story about *The Longest Day,* a comment attributed to Ryan: "You know," he said, "when we signed this deal I got a cable from Hemingway. It said 'Don't Don't Don't.' "

Zanuck shot off an angry cable to Ryan back in Connecticut: "We're shocked by the distorted *Newsweek* article and am making official protest to owners and publishers as everyone can prove they were misquoted particularly regarding alleged remarks about me and Hemingway incident." There followed an endless exchange of cables and letters between Zanuck and Ryan, blistering ones from Zanuck, conciliatory ones from Ryan. Especially Zanuck pursued "the Hemingway incident." Finally Ryan explained, "He didn't exactly misquote me on the Hemingway incident—he just mixed it up. I told him that when it was announced that I was going to do the screenplay of my own book a number of my friends begged me not to do it including my wartime friend Hemingway who said 'Don't Don't Don't.' Their argument was that a serious writer should stick with his books and not risk the frustrations of adapting one's own book to the screen."

Zanuck replied, "Hemingway happens to have been a very intimate friend of mine for many years in Sun Valley. In my opinion Hemingway did not and would not make the statement which you attributed to him." Then he added, "Picking on Hollywood producers has become the favorite indoor sport of snide journalists and columnists. I expect to get my share of it but I do not think it is fair that it should be inspired by those that are associated with me or working for me." At this point the Zanuck-Ryan communications ended.

Zanuck had been filming for most of the summer and the fall, but except for the preliminary work at Corsica, he still had not staged the full landing at Normandy. Suddenly he was confronted with a crucial decision, similar to one faced by Eisenhower in the real invasion: whether to call off D-Day because of the weather. "It was the dead of winter now and I had to make the decision. We were moving to location off La Rochelle, to Ile de Re, which we were using for Omaha Beach because Omaha Beach is now a resort. We were going there in the worst possible weather, probably unphotographable weather. The normal thing would have been to close down, and edit what we had, and to pick up again in May or June or July and finish. We had to build sets on location. We had all the actors signed. They could not promise to come back next summer. I called together my entire staff, all the camera staff—five cameramen and crews—all the department heads, my thirty key men for operations, in the ballroom of the Hotel Malherb in Caen. We had a debate, whether to go on or quit until summer. I explained the situation. I decided to ask openly all opinions, and to read the weather reports Bernard Farell had assembled. It was an overwhelming judgment *against* going on. I've never trusted weather reports. Quite out of curiosity, I asked Farell when was the worst storm in the history of Rochelle and Ile de Re? He said the greatest catastrophe was on July 4, 5, and 6 in 1936. There were waves nine feet high. The town was practically evacuated. Buildings were almost blown down. I said, 'What was that date? *July 4?* Verify it for me! If that date verifies we go!' " It verified. Says Zanuck, "That was, for me, the most dramatic moment in the making of the movie."

As it turned out, it was even more decisive than he anticipated. If he had stopped he might not have been able to start again, certainly not in Europe, because of the crisis back at Twentieth Century-Fox. Now, having decided, like Eisenhower, to "go," Zanuck mobilized for the invasion. He moved to La Rochelle, and flew to Ile de Re every day in his helicopter. The crew came by boat, the captain having been convinced to continue running it out of season. Every day Zanuck would wake up at five, peer out of the window of his hotel room to see if the weather was clear. They shot from October 21 to November 27, without one day lost because of inclemency. But there were unforeseen crises, such as the day the army got lost. Daily, 800 French soldiers had been shuttled from their base near La Rochelle to Ile de Re, and then one morning, they didn't show up. Someone called their base. The men had left on time. Where were they? No one knew. Not to waste the day, they shot around them, close-ups of Henry Fonda and actors landing. Finally at 5 P.M., the army arrived, with the excuse of having gotten lost. They turned around and were sent home, presumably, to be punished for dereliction of duty. What did Zanuck say about the missing troops? "We kept it from him," says one of his staff. He was probably too busy to notice.

The day of shooting the landing—"It was the only time outside of the big jump that we had casualties. I had thirty second assistant directors in uniforms as my squadron leaders. One of the thirty handled each group. They picked which ones would fall as casualties, or who would make the beach. We ran a tape from the edge of the shore to the cliff, alleys, so that they wouldn't bunch up. We covered the tape with light sand. We had planned 150 explosives to go off. But we never thought about smoke. The final take, I shot a pistol. That signaled the cameras on the ground and air. Bang! It starts, and it's the goddamnedest mess I've ever seen in my life. They couldn't see because of the smoke. They were bumping into each other. Jesus Christ, and we with the cameras couldn't see. Christ! People were sitting holding their faces in their hands. Some had facial cuts where they had run into explosives. In one scene, where guys blow up in the air, this was not staged. They were running blind. We stayed up all night working out nonsmoke, or white smoke. I got two takes that were good and decided we wouldn't do it again. We would have killed somebody."

Zanuck ended up, by his estimate, actually directing about

60 per cent of the picture himself, with Andrew Marton, Elmo Williams, Ken Annakin, and Bernhard Wicki at his side. In March, he screened the first rough cut, and decided he wanted additional scenes. The last two scenes filmed were both written and directed by Zanuck, and starred Richard Burton. Zanuck called him in Rome where he was involved with that other Fox movie, *Cleopatra*. "I've got a great scene for you," said Zanuck. "Can you come up?" On a free Sunday, April 8, Burton flew from Rome to Paris, and Zanuck opened the Boulogne studio for him. In the scene Burton and Richard Beymer sit crumpled on the ground next to a dead soldier. "You know something," says Beymer, "I haven't fired my gun all day." "It's funny," says Burton, pointing to a dead German, "he's dead. I'm crippled. And you're lost." "I wonder who won?" says Beymer. Then, a direct cut to the troops, and Mitchum climbing into a jeep and saying, "O.K., run me up the hill, son." Zanuck loved the penultimate scene so much he asked Burton to fly up for another scene the following Sunday, one set in Britain in a pub before the invasion, that would establish his character early in the movie. Burton recalls the two days' work: "A rare event! I thought he was dead-on, which is rarely what I think about directors."

On July 3 Zanuck added one final bit (at the request of the British technical director) to *The Longest Day,* an insert of a British flag going up a pole. Most of his staff having departed, he designed the set and shot the scene himself. After ten months of actual photography, twelve scripts, and an expense of eight million dollars, the Supreme Commander wrapped up *The Longest Day.* The cinematic battle was over, he had been revived by the adventure, but his real war had just begun.

6.

Restoration

Christ, I was a victim of Cleopatra. *The goddamned asp was biting me!*

—Darryl Zanuck

When Darryl Zanuck left Twentieth Century-Fox in 1956 to go into independent production, Hollywood itself was in a period of transition. CinemaScope had peaked, and the old studio system was creaking. But when Zanuck left, both he and Fox were alive, and at least for the moment, well. Away from the studio, Zanuck fell apart, and almost in direct parallel, with Zanuck away, the studio fell apart. The complete collapse took six years. *Cleopatra* delivered the death blow, but the self-destruction had been a long time coming.

Buddy Adler was Zanuck's hand-picked replacement as head of production—with Skouras' concurrence. After his success at Columbia with *From Here to Eternity,* Adler had moved to Fox, and was given a succession of major movies to produce—*Love Is a Many-Splendored Thing, Bus Stop, Anastasia.* Four years after becoming head of production he died of cancer. In retrospect doubt has been cast on his term. In a memo written long after the fact, Zanuck conjectured that success, and the favorable press, had turned Adler's head. "He was a damn good production man, but his personal desires consumed him." In fairness to Adler, and *his* successors, he did have Spyros Skouras to contend with. For years Skouras had been in Zanuck's shadow. He is always given credit for his knowledge of exhibition and distribution (which mostly stems from his early years as an exhibitor) and for his role in instituting CinemaScope, but Skouras was never a production man. In Adler's day, power was shared between him and Skouras, which was a mistake. It gave Skouras a taste of production, and when Adler died, he chose Bob Goldstein to head the studio. According to Zanuck, Goldstein was way over his head.

After Goldstein came Peter Levathes, a former ad man and Fox's head of television. Levathes had two things in common with Skouras. He was Greek, and he didn't know anything about making pictures. "I have had very little association with Peter Levathes," wrote Zanuck in June 1962. "I am sure that he is an excellent executive, and that he has showmanship instinct, but he is completely devoid of any sort of production experience . . . He has to start every conference with a quotation, like, 'I realize I am not a producer . . . nevertheless, I feel . . .' Your top people listen politely . . . and do as they see fit . . ."

Dick Zanuck, who was representing his father's company at the studio, was much closer to the scene, and as he saw it, from Skouras to Levathes, "It was green light, then red light," which often left some doubt as to which Greek was running the studio. Dick remembers one particular red light vividly. In July 1961, he had been just about to start filming *The Chapman Report,* his second production for his father's company (his first, *Compulsion*), when the order suddenly came through from Levathes: "Don't pay anybody on *The Chapman Report.*" The order was delivered just as the director of *Chapman,* George Cukor, and its star, Shelley Winters, were rehearsing. Dick ran to Levathes' office for an explanation.

"The picture's been canceled," said Levathes flatly.

"Thanks for telling me," said Dick Zanuck. "Why are you canceling it?"

"I don't like the script," he said, and questioned the marketability of the movie.

"I don't give a shit," Dick answered. "The book's a best seller here."

Dick Zanuck called his father in Paris and told him of the cancellation. As Dick remembers, "When I called him, I expected him to be shouting. I thought, Jesus Christ, he'll go absolutely berserk. But he was very calm. Absolutely ice cold. I've never heard him like that. He was so cold, not to me, but it was like he was saying, 'They'll never know what hit them.' I said to my wife, 'He's really dangerous. Someone is going to get it.' " Zanuck called his old friend Jack Warner, and the movie was moved to Warner's studio, filmed, and made a modest profit. It awakened both Zanucks to the fact that Fox's troubles might well become theirs. When Dick Zanuck came back from Warners he found Fox full of "political infighting, back-stabbing, whispering down the corridors."

It was, in all respects, Twentieth Century-Fox's lowest period. In the thirties Zanuck may not have always made good movies, but at least many of them made money. Before World War II, there were a few astoundingly good ones, and a few more astoundingly commercial ones. The late forties and early fifties were, in all respects, Zanuck's golden years. Even in Zanuck's last few years at the studio there were successes of one sort or another—*The Robe, The Man in the Gray Flannel Suit,* but in Zanuck's absence, creativity, at least at the top, stopped. Occasionally an individual like Nunnally Johnson brought forth a *Three Faces of Eve,* or a Jack Cardiff a *Sons and Lovers;* more frequently Fox was wasting Marilyn Monroe, pushing Jayne Mansfield, foisting Fabian, paying obeisance to Skouras' piety, and grinding out Elvis Presley and Gary Crosby movies. The year 1961 can stand for Fox at its worst. It released only one good movie, *The* tion and neither Skouras nor Levathes had anything to do *Hustler,* and oddly enough, it was probably the best Fox movie of the sixties. It was entirely a Robert Rossen produc- with it. At a press conference at the time, Skouras announced a new internationalization of Fox, a deal he had signed with Carlo Ponti to film Jean-Paul Sartre's play *The Condemned of Altona* and Giuseppe de Lampedusa's novel *The Leopard.* A release was distributed and Skouras was introduced. He did not even try to say de Lampedusa, but he did try to name the stars and they came out something like, "Bart Lancester, and . . . Cardinal." The other property he referred to several times as *The Lady from Altoona,* with no joke intended, and then announced its stars, "Max Schelling and"—a long pause as he searched his memory for what's-her-name— "Carlo's wife." He seemed to know nothing whatever about the two literary properties Fox was going to film or the people in them. The fact that both turned out to be terrible movies cannot entirely be blamed, of course, on Skouras. The directors and the producer merit the greater share. But the point is Skouras' artistic pretensions as well as his fondness for the banal (the depth of his banality was probably reached in two

1962 pictures, *It Happened in Athens* and *The 300 Spartans,* which were not so much released, as leaked) was what got him in trouble. "And then," as Zanuck said, "came the catastrophe of *Cleopatra.*"

What happened on *Cleopatra* is a book in itself. The film's misfortunes, before Zanuck took it over, are not really relevant to the story of Zanuck, except as they demonstrate and define the destitution of Twentieth Century-Fox between the regimes of Zanuck. To the press and the public at the time, Elizabeth Taylor and her romance with Richard Burton were the chief causes of the movie's ills and its costs, but as David Slavitt pointed out in his *Newsweek* magazine cover story on *Cleopatra,* ". . . to blame her for the cost of 'Cleopatra' is like blaming the French Revolution on a shortage of cake." The same story quoted Skouras in a moment of surprising humility. " 'The film cost at least $20 million more than it should have cost,' " said Skouras. " 'I was the president then. I take the blame.' " In May 1963, at Fox's annual stockholders' meeting, when asked to comment on *Cleopatra,* Zanuck referred to that Skouras quote, and said, "I do not absolve Mr. Skouras of his share of the blame." It certainly was cumulative guilt, shared by Skouras, Levathes, producer Walter Wanger, director Joseph Mankiewicz. Certainly Elizabeth Taylor's illness, and her romance, did not speed the production (but they created enormous public interest in the movie). But Skouras is right. The weight of the burden falls on his shoulders. He was the head of the company, and if his relationship with Levathes was indeed green light-red light, he should have flashed red. Levathes of course came off second worst, and it was no help to his position for him to confess about *Cleopatra* that from its birth as a small Joan Collins picture, "like Topsy, it just grew." Someone had to provide the atmosphere for it to grow in, and that atmosphere might be described as anarchy. Foolishly, Skouras insisted on constructing Egypt in England. The first director, Rouben Mamoulian, protested. Then Miss Taylor got sick. The weather turned terrible. In rain and sleet, Skouras' city floundered. In January 1961, Mamoulian quit and was replaced by Joseph Mankiewicz. The two met.

"You're a director and I'm a director," said Mankiewicz. "Now what do you really think of the picture?"

"Well, I resigned, didn't I?" said Mamoulian.

"Let me rephrase the question," said Mankiewicz. "What would you do if you were me?"

"I'd resign," said Mamoulian.

Up to this point the studio had spent what has been estimated at from $5 million to $7 million (in its 1961 annual report Fox listed a loss of $3,662,000 for the aborted London version of *Cleopatra*) for about ten minutes of unusable celluloid. The movie was moved to Rome. Script writers were hired and fired (including Lawrence Durrell twice). While Mankiewicz wrote his own version, the company plugged ahead with pre-production. As one of the crew remembered, "They built sets on speculation. No one quite knew what Mankiewicz would write into the movie, so they built a Roman Forum and the city of Alexandria, just in case."

A major part of the problem was Skouras' own increasing insecurity. Faced by a split board and a spiraling *Cleopatra*, he obviously wanted the movie over with, edited, and distributed, before it finished him and his company.

In the steadfastly commercial world of Hollywood, *Cleopatra* was an inexcusable blunder. But as *Cleopatra* was sinking and submerging Fox along with it, Zanuck was in France waging and winning a war of his own. In spring of 1962 he was still involved in *The Longest Day*. Then Richard Burton flew to Paris to film his scenes in *The Longest Day*, and told him some of what was going on in Rome. "I began worrying like hell about my family and my shares in the company," recalls Zanuck. "Burton suggested that I should just drop in on *Cleopatra* and pull my chair up on the set and I'd scare the bejesus out of them."

Added to Darryl Zanuck's burgeoning concerns was the serialization in April, prior to publication, of Juliette Greco's memoirs in both *Paris-Match* and *The People* in London. The book was less a memoir of Greco than an accusation of Zanuck. He was held up to considerable scorn and derision. She made fun of their romance, of his jealousies, of his habits. If Greco's memoirs had been published the previous year, during his down period, they might have devastated him. Now they merely enraged him, and he immediately set out to do something about it. He instituted a suit against Greco in Milan where under Italian law a verdict of guilt carried a criminal penalty. The suit asked $20,000 damages for false statements and invasion of privacy. Greco and her lawyers panicked, stopped publication of the book. *"Match* settled for two cover stories on *The Longest Day,* for a condensed version they had printed," says Zanuck. The book was withdrawn from sale by order of the court. But the damage had been done, to Zanuck but mostly to Greco. In a curious turn of fate, the memoirs rebounded against her. As she recalls, "Everyone in Paris was saying, 'She's a bitch. She's horrible.' Paris was thinking of me as mud and shit."

In Paris Darryl Zanuck pondered the future of Fox. For months Zanuck had been hearing rumors that Skouras would be asked to retire, and for as many months, he had been urged by many Fox executives to consider becoming Skouras' replacement. As a matter of pride and to protect his stock interest, Zanuck was beginning to think about it. "I saw it all going down the drain," he says. On June 6 he dictated what he labeled a "management and production formula for Twentieth Century-Fox."

"If and when Spyros decided that he wanted to step out of the presidency, I would present the following concrete recommendations based on the industry as it exists today. Whether or not I become the President is actually immaterial. I own with my family about 280,000 shares of stock, and the voting control of it all. I have a personal interest in the survival of the Corporation as well as a certain amount of pride in what was once described as 'the best operating Studio in the industry.' I also have selfish interests . . . I would close down the Studio and only complete the films that are either already in production or committed for . . . I would sell the Studio to the Fox Realty Company or a third party.

"During the transition period," he continued, "the President of Fox, who should also be in my opinion, the Chief Producer, would take four or even six months to not only complete and edit the films already in production, but to weed out the misfits and to study story properties and make future constructive production plans . . . I firmly do not believe that our world grosses will suffer radically even if we do not start another picture in the next six or eight months . . .

"My record since my first independent production, *Island in the Sun,* which was a profitable venture, has not been good. I cannot defend my position nor can I blame it on bad luck. The figures speak for themselves, and while most of my films received better than average critical acclaim, they did not live up to expectations and two of them were out-and-out flops. I believe that I have now profited by errors in judgment, and I am no longer confronted with private or personal problems which obsessed me prior to commencing *The Longest Day.* I will continue to make mistakes in this highly speculative business, but the 'know-how' I have acquired as a result of my failures and the lessons that I have learned have been of enormous value . . ."

On June 7 Levathes fired Marilyn Monroe from *Something's Got to Give,* and several days later suspended filming indefinitely. The action meant that *Something's Got to Give* would not become another *Cleopatra,* but it also meant taking an immediate loss of two million dollars. About the same time Walter Wanger was fired from *Cleopatra.* Whose head was next? It looked like Skouras'.

Zanuck's attorney, Arnold Grant, called Zanuck in Paris and told him that Skouras was going to be retired as president at the next board meeting. Judge Samuel Rosenman, chairman of Fox's board, was going to replace him temporarily until an official successor could be found. On June 11, Zanuck met in New York with Robert Lehman, an influential member of the board, and Judge Rosenman, in Lehman's office. It surprised and embarrassed Zanuck when they asked him whom he would suggest as Skouras' replacement. Then they suggested James Aubrey, Mike Frankovich (who had once briefly been Richard Zanuck's bodyguard and was then an executive at Columbia Pictures), Otto Preminger, Max Youngstein, William Perlberg, among others. When Zanuck heard the list, he said later, "I frankly wanted to vomit. With the exception of Aubrey, these men are good personal friends of mine. They worked for me and with me for many years. I know their capabilities and I know their limitations. I know they are utterly idiotic recommendations for the presidency." Zanuck's name was mentioned neither as a candidate for president nor as a candidate for the Board of Directors.

Subsequently Zanuck met with Rosenman, Grant, and Otto Koegel to discuss distribution of *The Longest Day.* Zanuck wanted his own people, specifically Seymour Poe and David Raphel, to handle it, at a cost of about $50,000, a sum which Zanuck was prepared to pay himself. Rosenman not only didn't want Zanuck's people involved in distribution, but he also wanted to scrap the idea of releasing *The Longest Day* as a reserved-seat road show production. Fox, in need of quick cash, was planning to exploit Zanuck's masterpiece as a saturation picture, invading neighborhood houses at a sweep, which would sink future grosses, and be an aesthetic knock of the movie itself. Rosenman said, "As a matter of fact, I wish we didn't have the picture."

Zanuck said, "This has got to be a road show picture or I'll buy it back at cost."

Grant added, "Are you ready to take a check for eight million dollars and give us the picture?"

"If it was up to me," said Rosenman, "I would love to do it, but the company owns it."

If Rosenman took their offer, they planned to try to sell it to Jack Warner as a road show. But the discussion ended right there. Rosenman put on his coat, said, "I'm late for lunch," and started to leave.

Grant tried to stop him. "How can you have Mr. Zanuck fly all the way here from Paris and not let him say what he has to say?"

But by then Zanuck himself was in no mood to prolong the meeting. Later that day, he telephoned Grant and said, "All my life, I've never been so mistreated. They treated me like a school kid."

As Zanuck flew back to Paris, he thought about his meeting with the board and realized clearly that Fox's predicament was his predicament. Not only was his family's stock at stake but also his movie, which he considered his masterwork. Insulted, injured, and worried, he began to write his challenge. On June 28, some days after he returned to Paris, he sent a cable to the board. "It is unjust to blame Mr. Skouras alone for the decline of Twentieth Century-Fox," he wrote. "The Board of Directors and the Executive Committee approved all major decisions in production and administration during the last several years and particularly during the last fifteen months. A Special Management Committee was appointed by the Board of Directors with the power and authority to alter or nullify any decisions made by the President or any officer of the Corporation. This Committee . . . must share responsibility for what occurred . . .

"I have been inaudible for entirely too long. Now, as the largest individual stockholder, I intend to make my position clear on all major matters. I am not selling Twentieth Century-Fox short. As a matter of fact, I am optimistic. It is difficult to do worse than we have been doing since the formation of the Committee . . .

"I have not been offered the Presidency of Twentieth Century-Fox. Whether or not I would accept it if it were offered depends on certain vital circumstances. The chief executive officer must have the unqualified and unanimous support of a unified Board of Directors . . . to function properly . . . he cannot be placed in a position where he is 'second-guessed' by inexperienced 'committees . . .' "

Originally Zanuck had begun the cable, "I do not seek the presidency of Twentieth Century-Fox . . ." and sent it to Arnold Grant for comment. "It's a helluva telegram," replied Grant. "Only one thing: take out the first line. I don't believe in firing a gun unless you're going to war. You started the company. You left it healthy. You've been the father of a child and it's sick in its middle age. Twenty to twenty-five million were lost this year, forty million last year." Grant wanted Zanuck to challenge the board, even if it meant a proxy fight. Grant was sure of winning. "Lehmans and Loebs don't get licked," he explained. "When they know they may be licked, they walk away." By sending the revised cable, Zanuck, in effect, had tossed his own hat into the ring.

On Saturday the cable was published in the newspapers. On Monday Skouras and his lawyer met with Grant. Skouras controlled, or thought he controlled, four or five board votes —as well as a sizable chunk of stock—and tried to barter them, but Grant cut him off. "You can help us or you can fight us. We don't care. Win, lose, or draw, we're going to make you chairman of the board. You'll have no powers whatsoever. One vote." Then Grant called Louis Nizer and invited him to join in representing Zanuck's cause. He wanted Nizer not only for his estimable talents and prestige, but because he thought Skouras would try to enlist him, which he did—too late. Grant also had a meeting with Ed Weisl who represented Robert Lehman. Then he called Zanuck in Paris, brought him up to date on his meetings and they agreed that Zanuck would send a cable asking for a proxy fight, knowing that the board would do anything to keep it from reaching that point. Zanuck flew back to New York and began marshaling his supporters. He hired three Wall Street firms to collect proxies for him. He met with Lehman and Weisl and it seemed as if Weisl was bringing Lehman around to his side, but one point Lehman was adamant about: he was afraid of nepotism and wanted Zanuck to agree not to hire his son.

The next day Zanuck was interviewed for the job of president by a Fox selection committee. The interrogation soon became an inquisition. Zanuck found himself not so much a candidate as a target. His chief adversary was Milton Gould, a corporation lawyer who had been dubbed Jack the Giant Killer by the press. For Gould, it became a personal vendetta against Zanuck. He had been quoted as saying, "Zanuck will be president over my dead body." Now, everything was dredged up: Zanuck's attempts to make stars out of his girl friends, his drinking. He was heaped with abuse, personally attacked, accused of everything including using company money to pay his personal expenses, of having squandered fortunes at the gaming tables. The tone was one of moral outrage. Is this man fit to be president? The prime facts were Zanuck's dismal record as an independent producer. But precisely this point, Zanuck at his most vulnerable, was made to work in his favor. Grant summarized Zanuck's long record at Fox, and said that he should not be judged on his recent flops, but on his over-all career. But speaking about flops, what about Fox's record? How many millions had they lost in the last few years? In the last few weeks? Gould kept up the attack. Finally a seemingly bored Rosenman said, "I would like Mr. Zanuck to say what he would do for the company." Zanuck had prepared a speech, but after a long, tense hesitation, he said: "I've got nothing to say. If you want me, fine. If not, get somebody else." And he and his attorneys walked out.

For days, all was quiet. Then Zanuck was asked to appear before the Board of Directors on July 25. As the board meeting approached, it appeared that in addition to his own shares, Zanuck could count on Skouras, theater owner Harry Brandt, and others, all of which was considerably in excess of Gould and Loeb's 300,000. It also looked as if he had Lehman's vote. Was it enough to win the presidency without a proxy fight? Zanuck had asked to appear at 4 P.M., and exactly at that hour he and Grant showed up at the company headquarters at 444 West 56th Street and were asked to wait outside the board room while the board met. For three hours they waited, Zanuck chain-smoking cigars and pacing the floor. Finally at 7, Skouras came out, walked right past them on the way to the men's room. Grant stopped him and said, "We're tired of waiting. We're leaving." "What the hell's happening in there?" demanded Zanuck. "We've had a long agenda," answered Skouras calmly, "and we haven't even talked about you yet." Then Judge Rosenman passed by during the brief recess. He beckoned Zanuck aside and calmly said: "If you are elected, I understand you intend to keep Skouras on as chairman?" Zanuck replied in the affirmative: "For past services and face saving." The judge nodded, then casually said: "If you should change your mind, I think I might be useful." "At that moment," says Zanuck, "I *knew* we had won." About fifteen minutes after the recess, they finally called Zanuck in and advised him he had been elected president. The vote, not revealed at the time, was apparently eight to three, with only Rosenman, Gould, and Loeb as anti-Zanuck holdouts. At Zanuck's suggestion the board was expanded to fifteen with the addition of Zanuck, Grant, and director William Wyler. Loeb immediately resigned. Gould waited until the next morning. That night Zanuck called his son in California and gave his first order as president: "Close the studio!" The Second Reign of Zanuck had begun.

IV | *The Last Tycoon*

1962-

1.

Twentieth Century-Fox Rides Again

Who do you think is the best guy to run the studio?
                                                —Darryl Zanuck

Me.

                                                —Richard Zanuck

When Darryl Zanuck took charge of Twentieth Century-Fox in 1935, he at least had Shirley Temple. Now in 1962 he had no stars, no profits, and few prospects except that of a *Cleopatra* headache. His only chance of a palliative appeared to be *The Longest Day*. Because of Robert Lehman's objection to a son in the business, Zanuck thought it wise not to give Dick Zanuck any official title—yet. As his father's production representative and secret agent, he assumed control of studio non-operations. In his father's name, and with the assistance of Stan Hough, he began stopping everything in sight, just as his father had done twenty-seven years before. "Everyone was patting us on the back," recalls Dick, "and the next day we fired 2000 employees. I would go to the department heads and say, 'Let everybody go,' including in many cases the department heads themselves." Some people clung like rust to the old studio, and there were unions to contend with. "We'd spent nights trying to get rid of one janitor. We leveled the police force, the fire department, every conceivable department, and then we moved the survivors into one building—which cut down on janitors. We had executives working in the generator shaft. We closed the cafe and had a lunch wagon for sandwiches and Cokes. Including the janitor, we were down to 100 people. We had to keep a gardener and a plumber." One of the victims of the mass firing was Charles Brackett, at the time a Fox contract producer. Brackett's former partner, director Billy Wilder, was so enraged at the "brutal and callous dismissal" that he wired Zanuck, "No self-respecting picture maker would ever want to work for Fox. The sooner the bulldozers raze the studio, the better it will be for the industry." Says Zanuck, "Reviewing Wilder's professional record since his statement, he obviously got in the way of his own bulldozers." The only thing still filming at the studio was the television series, "Dobie Gillis," and almost everybody remaining was put to work on it. "We had more Academy Award winners working on 'Dobie Gillis' than on any epic," says Dick Zanuck. "Rather than fire Jack Smith, the head of the art department, we made him the art director of 'Dobie Gillis.' The head of the show's set decoration, Walter Scott, had won four Academy Awards." They had to carry grips and lamps, but for all purposes other than "Dobie Gillis" and *Cleopatra,* Fox was closed, and almost everyone was convinced it would never open again.

With a trunk filled with scripts that Levathes had planned to film, Darryl Zanuck returned to Paris. He plowed through the inventory. There were three immediate problems—*Take Her, She's Mine, Promise at Dawn,* and *Ulysses,* all of which had starting dates, and none of which by Zanuck's estimate were ready to start—because of script or budget problems.

Take Her, She's Mine was postponed (and six months later broadened from a domestic comedy into one with an international setting, it was the first movie to go into production under the new Zanuck regime). Both *Promise at Dawn* and *Ulysses* were canceled. A few of the properties in the trunk he liked. A few more, he didn't like and approved anyway because they needed the product. "I made two or three catastrophes from that trunk," he later admitted. *The Enemy Within,* based on Robert Kennedy's book about James Hoffa, was in that trunk. Zanuck approved, then disapproved. It dawned on him, "For Christ sake, Hoffa hadn't been *convicted.* We'd all end up in jail. I took it to the Board of Directors. They said, 'God, no!' Before I formally rejected it, I met with Bobby Kennedy and Budd Schulberg [who had written the screenplay] and I explained why the movie couldn't be made at this time." According to Zanuck, Schulberg blew his top. "I know you're against me *now!*" said Zanuck. "But wait a few years."

Schulberg looks back on the episode with the same wry detachment he views Zanuck's abortive involvement in *On the Waterfront.* "He almost had an apologetic tone. If the company was in different shape, he might do it. He felt the way to restore the company was with bread and butter pictures." Schulberg allows himself a complaint: "Every ten years I have a film I love that Darryl has a need to reject." But Darryl wasn't the only one. As with *Waterfront,* Schulberg tried to peddle the property to other studios—and was turned down by all of them. "I don't blame Darryl personally for not doing it," he concludes, "because the industry was not noted for its fearlessness. It had become institutionalized. People would take fewer and fewer chances." Says Zanuck, "Although it was peddled everywhere, the Hoffa story, *The Enemy Within,* never saw the light of a studio reflector, not for fear of dramatic content, but because of the certainty of a law suit." Schulberg waited five years and gave Zanuck another chance to take a chance. In 1968 he and Kazan brought their idea for a movie about Puerto Ricans to Fox, and found the company "extremely cautiously receptive," which meant no deal. Concludes Schulberg about Zanuck, "He's a nice man to visit, but I wouldn't want to work there." Zanuck's reply: "He certainly tried hard enough. He gave me the first crack at his three projects."

One of the movies Zanuck decided to go ahead with was *The Sound of Music,* although at one point Fox could have easily let it get away. During the period of extreme cutback, Dick Zanuck ran into Irving Lazar who had originally sold the property to Fox for $1,125,000. Lazar, who thought Fox would never make the picture, said, "I've got a buyer who'll give you two million dollars' profit." The offer was tempting, but as a matter of pride as much as anything, Dick turned it down.

In September *The Longest Day* opened in Paris, and for that day Zanuck owned the city. The premiere, at the Palais de Chaillot, was officially sponsored by the French government. All members of De Gaulle's cabinet were instructed to attend. Zanuck's personal guest was General James Gavin, American ambassador to France. For the occasion Zanuck hired Paris' super-press agent Georges Cravenne, and the imaginative Cravenne outdid himself. He advertised *The Longest Day* in lights on the Eiffel Tower, the first such event in history. And from the tower came the amplified voice of Edith Piaf singing "La Marseillaise" to a city-wide audience estimated at one million. Then fireworks were blasted off, "the most extravagant display of fireworks that Paris had seen in our time," wrote Janet Flanner. Crack regiments from each of the allied powers paraded to the theater. The French not only supplied a group of mounted Zoave natives, but also fifty tanks. De Gaulle himself could not have made a more triumphant entrance, and he could not have climaxed it with a film of his greatest victory. Zanuck continued the procession back to New York. For the New York opening there were no Zoaves, tanks, or advertisements on the Empire State Building, but all Broadway was lit up, and the celebrities—political, military, and Hollywood—turned out by the hundreds. Zanuck himself rode in the lead car with Irina Demick, General Omar Bradley, and Cardinal Spellman.

The picture received mixed notices from the critics, but the public ignored them. One of the most favorable "reviews" came from, of all people, Cornelius Ryan. "It's probably the most accurate wartime movie ever made," concluded Ryan, "a brilliant example of probably the final work of the last of the angry moguls. A fine fine movie. It will go down as a classic. I think that Zanuck was probably the only man in the world who could have made that picture."

The movie got off to a resounding start at the box office, and income from it ($17 million in its first year of release) tided Fox over until the studio could resume production again. With the confidence of the Board of Directors, Zanuck decided to ask that his son be named officially head of production, the title he had held unofficially since the day his father was elected president of the company. In a wave of good will, the board backed him up, and on October 8 Dick Zanuck was hired at $1000 a week. When stockholders at the next annual meeting questioned the salary, Darryl got up and said, "It is very hard for a father to defend his son. I criticize him myself. At twenty-four, I was getting $5000 a week at Warner Brothers. He's not doing so well. But then I wasn't saddled with a notoriously successful father."

There was one lingering problem, *Cleopatra*. "It never occurred to me, after I became president," he said, "that I would have to do anything more than to walk in and see the picture. But when Mankiewicz brought me his first cut and I looked at the film I was shocked. I asked to see the sequences that had been cut and decided that some of them should be restored, but I found to my astonishment that no loops had been made for certain of the eliminated episodes . . . I was powerless . . . In other words, Mr. Mankiewicz obviously considered the picture finished when he brought it to me."

While Zanuck considered the possibilities open to him, Mankiewicz considered the inevitabilities facing him. Finally Mankiewicz demanded to know where *Cleopatra* and he stood. "I want the responsibility to finish the editing—either that, or to be told to get out." He was told to get out. Zanuck called a press conference and said, "In exchange for top compensation and a considerable expense account, Mr. Joseph Mankiewicz has for two years spent his time, talent and $35 million of Twentieth Century-Fox's shareholders' money to direct and complete the first cut of the film *Cleopatra*. He has earned a well-deserved rest." And he then added, "After you have directed Caesar, Cleopatra, and Marc Antony for a year and a half, some of the tinsel may brush off on you." On the one hand Mankiewicz was philosophical about his firing—"I've been a cotton picker too long not to know that old Marse can do with the cotton exactly what he wants. I made the first cut, but after that, it's the studio's property. They could cut it into banjo picks if they want." He was also outraged. He said that he planned "by every available means to regain the usurped right to finish my work, and, hopefully, to prevent *Cleopatra* from becoming *The Longest Night*." His stars leaped to his defense. "What has happened to Mr. Mankiewicz is disgraceful, degrading, particularly humiliating," said Elizabeth Taylor. "He certainly should have been given the chance to cut it." Richard Burton added, "What was done was vulgar . . . I think Mr. Mankiewicz might have made the first really good epic." Zanuck replies, "Obviously Richard Burton had forgotten that he originally urged me to go to Rome and sit on the set to get Mankiewicz moving and scare hell out of him."

The Zanuck-Mankiewicz feud was settled, at least publicly, in December, when they met in New York and Zanuck told him that he would work with him 'hand in hand and that I would reserve the right delegated to me by the corporation, but that I would bend over backwards artistically so that I wouldn't have to exercise that right unless it becomes absolutely essential." According to Zanuck, "Joe accepted that, took the scenes that I had blocked out crudely and roughly, went to work on them, wrote them. We then revised them together." As Mankiewicz remembers it, most of Zanuck's cuts were to make Marc Antony a stronger man. According to Mankiewicz, Zanuck said, "If any woman treated me like that, I would kick her in the balls."

Soon Zanuck and Mankiewicz found themselves in Almeria, Spain, filming a new sequence, at an additional cost of two million dollars, part of which paid for eighty-seven horses that were lost during the shooting. Almeria was the last circle of hell for *Cleopatra*. Finally released in June 1963, the movie was not the mouse that Judith Crist said it was, or the giant that Bosley Crowther liked to think it was, and it certainly was not "history's most expensive sleeper," that David Slavitt half-hoped it was. On all counts—as epic, as love story, as intellectual exercise, as power play—it was a failure. All that survived from it was the Taylor-Burton entente—and people went to see "them," rather than "it."

What Zanuck wanted was a nice little break-even, which is approximately what it eventually became. It was *The Longest Day* and *The Sound of Music* that revived the company. In spite of the mixed critical reception—better for *The Longest Day* than *The Sound of Music*—both became enormous commercial successes, the first, the highest-grossing black and white picture of all time, and the second one of the highest-grossing pictures of all time. In 1966, *The Sound of Music* turned in most of its profits. "That's our miracle picture," said Zanuck. And in corporate terms, it was.

The industry had changed completely several times since Darryl Zanuck began, but one thing remained constant: if you want to stay in business, you've got to keep producing miracles.

2.

DZ and Dick

It's almost tribal; this is the king and this is the prince.
　　　　　　　　　　　—Helen Gurley Brown

Richard Zanuck is the ideal son of a Hollywood father—enthusiastically in the family business, unabashedly in love with the movies—and not a ninny, like so many sons of Hollywood fathers who ascended to power by sheer order of birthright. Certainly Dick Zanuck would never have risen so fast at Fox if he had not been Darryl Zanuck's son. Irving Hoffman, in commenting on Dick's success, was reminded of a story about Ernie Byfield, Jr., the son of the hotel magnate. "Someone was interviewing Byfield, Jr., and asked, 'How is it that a man so remarkably young is running the Ambassador East, Ambassador West, and the Pump Room?' He answered, 'Well, I happened to run into my father in the lobby and he took a liking to me.'"

What is overlooked by the people who stress the nepotism of the relationship is that Dick literally grew up at Twentieth Century-Fox. The studio was his schoolroom, his father his teacher, and he himself an apt pupil. Probably his deepest impressions of his father are of him in charge at the studio, and among his most vivid memories of his childhood are of sitting in on story conferences. Even more than his father, with Dick, the movies became his whole world, which is both his strong point and his weak point. "To Dick," says David Brown, "the studio is a living organism." He lives, thinks, breathes movies, watches them all the time, is insatiable in his appetite for them. When *Planet of the Apes* opened in Beverly Hills and became a smash hit, at least once every evening he would drive by the theater where it was playing to check the length of the line, and to glow about it. "That line," he said, "is the biggest emotional and physical thrill, bigger than any I can think of: sex, winning a race."

On his own, he has won a reputation as one of the best, toughest, shrewdest studio heads in California. He is a master at wheeling and dealing, which is so much a part of the business today. In his day, Darryl had absolute autonomy, not just in dealing with his board and his president but in dealing with his employees. Darryl never talked to agents, except Charles Feldman, unless forced to; Dick spends most of his time with them. Darryl could flip a card-wheel and produce a cast and practically a picture. Dick has to make hundreds of calls, conduct hundreds of meetings, wheedle, cajole, promise, threaten, and sometimes, pay through the nose. He likes that. Added to this was Fox's anomalistic position among the studios. While most of them have gone the way of United Artists and become distributors and packagers, Fox still rolled its own. It was the last of the great producing studios, which meant that Dick Zanuck dealt more than anyone else. He did not, with few exceptions, buy the package, but dickered for each of the various ingredients.

Where Dick's total involvement in the movies hurts him is that unlike his father he has known no other world. Even before Darryl became a boy wonder in Hollywood, he had been shunted back and forth across America, had lived in at least two cultures: the open wild Nebraska and the restricted urban California. He had fought in the war, and found his way up in an alien (to him) industry. And although all of his adult life has been spent in the movie business, he has lived not only in Hollywood but in New York and France, and has interests far outside the industry: hunting, skiing, speaking French, knowing food. He has been decorated by many European governments, and has traveled in high social and political circles. His many years in France have given him the sheen of a cosmopolite, some of the tastes of a bon vivant. Dick travels where he has to, but he is happiest in Hollywood.

The relationship between the two Zanucks was mutually rewarding, mutually admiring. Neither is demonstrative, but they have genuine affection for, and great understanding of, one another. Although seldom in the same city at the same time (for most of the year, Dick is in Hollywood, Darryl in

New York), they communicated daily: hour-long phone calls
on their direct connection, acres of telexes, oceans of memos.
Each was aware, at least professionally, of exactly what the
other was doing at almost any given time. The relationship
was, first of all, professional, and they wanted to keep it that
way. Darryl almost always refers to his son as Dick Zanuck,
and to Dick, Darryl is "DZ."

Dick Zanuck is probably Darryl Zanuck's closest observer
—for an obvious reason: he wants to know how it's done.
When he talks about him, it is with unbounded Zanuck
enthusiasm, and sometimes it sounds as if Dick were describing not just Darryl but also himself.

"I don't think DZ is a power guy as Harry Cohn was,"
says Dick. "He didn't use power as much as personality.
Probably he had a Napoleonic complex, being a small guy,
a driving guy. He had endless energy, endless ambition. He
does not admit defeat easily. He rationalizes to a lot of different people, but inwardly he knows he made a mistake.
He's so full of enthusiasm. He blows himself out of proportion. One of his great characteristics is that he generates great
enthusiasm—and generates enthusiasm in others. He brings
people to a fever pitch. Producers, directors, writers—he
churns them up. He draws from people the best they can do.
He took more guys who have not done anything, and made
more heroes than anybody in the business. He made them
realize that what they were doing was the best in the world.
Some people felt his sting, but they would be back next year
making pictures for him. He keeps people off-balance, even
those closest to him. He has no patience for many things, but
when he wants to get something he can be unbearably patient,
ruthlessly patient."

Dick admires his father on all possible levels—as a maker
of movies, as a manipulator of men, as a lover of women,
as a tycoon, as a father. However, at a certain point, being
the son of Zanuck is something to overcome. Darryl is not
only someone for Dick to admire and envy but someone to
prove himself to. Dick wants to be Zanuck himself. But he
never can really be Zanuck any more than Napoleon's son
could be Napoleon. The best he can hope for is to become
Zanuck II.

The relationship, professionally, was that of a king and
crown prince, the king retaining the ultimate power but re-

linquishing the day-to-day responsibility. Between the two monarchs, at Fox, was a court adviser, a regent—David Brown, vice-president in charge of the story department. It was almost a triumvirate: DZ, RZ, and DB, but not quite—and perhaps could never be: Brown was close, but not that close. Senior vice-president Harry MacIntyre was also a respected member of the inner circle.

Darryl Zanuck "uncovered" Brown in 1952 when Brown was managing editor of *Cosmopolitan* and until Zanuck quit the company, Brown was his Hollywood story chief. When Zanuck returned to power, Brown became one of his most trusted lieutenants, and rose steadily in the company hierarchy. At the 1969 stockholders' meeting, he was added to the Board of Directors. Brown was considered the house intellectual, a title that was his partially by default and partially because of his dealings with publishers and authors. Brown is a friendly, somewhat pear-shaped man. In *The Studio,* John Gregory Dunne's book about Twentieth Century-Fox, a book that was greeted with amusement and dismay by the forces at Fox, Dunne describes Brown as "handsome." Darryl Zanuck (who was more philosophical about Dunne's criticisms than his cohorts) jokingly shot off a telegram to Brown asserting that the description of him was the only error in the book. Brown's role in the company was an interesting one, because he was something of a mediator. He was between Dick and Darryl, friendly with both, trusted by both, but necessarily having to ameliorate any possible differences they might have. David's first fidelity was to Darryl, who was his mentor, but he knew—or thought he knew—the inevitability of the ascension.

3.

A New Century

The Sound of Music did more damage to the industry than any other picture. Everyone tried to copy it. We were the biggest offenders.

—Richard Zanuck

During the first five years of the Second Reign of Zanuck, there was a steady rise in company net earnings. The prime reasons were *The Sound of Music* and *The Longest Day*, which more than offset the disappointments over *Cleopatra* and *The Bible*. There were several other hits, namely *Valley of the Dolls* and *Planet of the Apes*. As non-road shows they could not be expected to be in *The Sound of Music* class, but —in spite of negative notices—they were hits at the box office. Other Fox movies were disappointments, but as the road-show euphoria continued, no one seemed to notice, no one at least, except the critics.

The truth is that even during those five fat years at Fox, the company was not making very many good movies, no *Graduate, Bonnie and Clyde, In the Heat of the Night, Rachel, Rachel,* some of the more successful American productions. Fox had only a few good pictures, and one of them, *Pretty Poison,* although not typical, is somewhat revealing of the state of the studio that produced it. No one quite knew what to do with the movie, so it was dumped into the neighborhood theaters where it was discovered as a sleeper by critics, whose cries of outrage caused the distribution department to give it the art-house bookings it deserved. It still lost money. Along the way, Fox had a few minor disasters, such as *A Flea in Her Ear,* starring Rex Harrison. "A catastrophe!" says Zanuck. "An absolute bust everywhere."

239

What really got the Zanucks into trouble was their biggest hit, *The Sound of Music*. They, as well as other company heads, tried to duplicate it, not just its profits, but its substance. First Fox made *Dr. Dolittle,* and then *Star!*—and would like to forget about both.

Dr. Dolittle was a pitch, like *The Sound of Music,* directly at the family audience, but it was made without the ingredients that turned its predecessor into a huge popular success. For a fantasy, it was lacking in imagination. It was tedious for children, and outright boring for parents. For a live-action movie, it was surprisingly stolid and tame. One reason for its failure was that the animals simply could not be counted on to perform their various tricks. *Dolittle* bombed and all the razzle-dazzle promotion of producer Arthur Jacobs only made the movie's failure more obvious.

Fox's next big road show, *Star!,* had both the star, Julie Andrews, and the director, Robert Wise, of *The Sound of Music,* and little else. Ostensibly this was the life story, with music, of Gertrude Lawrence. But the script was stodgy, and at the same time downbeat—missing out on two audiences, those who would settle for a sentimental movie like *The Sound of Music,* and those who wanted something a little more serious. What infuriated Fox was not that the New York *Times* critic, Renata Adler, panned the movie but that the pan ran only two paragraphs. *Star!* lacked quality and also importance, in any sense, except that of its budget. For once the public seemed to agree with the critics. No one wanted to see the picture, and by the time it reached the neighborhood theaters, it was being billed as *Loves of a Star!* The ad copy tried to sell the picture as sexy, one of the many things it certainly was not. Finally it was withdrawn from circulation, and months later, re-released as *Those Were the Happy Days,* it flopped again.

With the double disaster, everyone began second-guessing. The truth is that Darryl Zanuck, for one, had serious doubts about *Dolittle* and minor doubts about *Star!* before they were made. On *Dolittle* he knew, from his years with Rin Tin Tin, that the animals would present a major financial and technical problem and he felt that the picture was "not a real road show, but a special audience show"—and you don't spend $15 million on a special audience show. On *Star!* while admitting that the star-director collaboration made it a very "hot piece of property," he had "hesitations" about the script and wrote to the director Robert Wise recommending cuts. Wise replied that Zanuck had also recommended cuts in *The Sound of Music,* that were never made. "I decided to accept the rebuff," says Zanuck, "rather than make an issue of it." About *Star!* he explains, "I felt the first half was sensational—when she was a cockney. From there on, she became, in my mind, an unpleasant bitch and a repulsive alcoholic. The last half of the story was dull and unpleasant. This girl, this talented idol had become a social 'tramp.' " Then he adds, "I knew Gertrude Lawrence personally and I didn't like her either."

However, both Dick Zanuck and David Brown were enthusiastic about *Dolittle* and *Star!* and Darryl decided not to go against them. "Sometimes where I'm nervous on a project and I know they're high on it I have the authority to say, 'No,' but it's difficult to men so valuable to the company . . . And after all they could be right. I decided it wasn't up to me to put on the brakes. They wish today I had." But, Zanuck says, at the time, "we were all punch drunk with the overwhelming success of *Sound of Music.*" Because of *Star!* and *Dolittle,* it was clearly a tragic year for Fox, and at the May 1969 stockholders' meeting, Darryl Zanuck was asked why the two road shows had flopped, and how much money they had lost. He hesitated for a long tense moment, then avoided answering, as was his prerogative.

Although in recent years, Fox movies—flops and hits—are more an indication of Dick Zanuck's than Darryl Zanuck's taste, the elder Zanuck bears at least equal responsibility for his company's fortunes, and in the case of certain individual pictures, the burden is clearly his. In contrast to *Dolittle* and *Star!* he had no hesitation about *Che!* In fact he was the one who first suggested it, wiring Dick Zanuck at the studio: "Put a writer on it." In charge of the production was Sy Bartlett, one of Zanuck's top writers and producers during the late forties (he wrote the novel *Twelve O'Clock High* and collaborated on the screenplay), and directing was Richard Fleischer, who in the sixties had assumed a position similar to Henry King's in the thirties and forties, as Zanuck's protean but indistinctive house director. The result was one of the worst movies ever made at Fox, made doubly worse because of the seriousness and potentiality of the subject. At the one critics' screening of *Che!* at Fox in New York, the room was filled with laughter. In the reviews the laughter turned to derision. Zanuck was unfazed. "I was proud of the movie," he said. "It was absolutely authentic in every goddamn detail. Because we told the facts, but did not glorify Che as another coming of Christ, the 'left-wingers' and the elegant 'avant-garde' who thought being a part of the intellectual majority was a badge of superiority, are today singing a different tune, or conveniently moving to the suburbs, where so far there are less 'explosive incidents' and fewer Che 'Bible carriers!' One day, when bombings and wanton disregard of life and respect for law and order have become unfashionable, we're going to reissue *Che!* Seen again by an enlightened majority, it may be recognized for what it was— an accurate portrait of a brilliant but misguided rebel." Zanuck seemed to be more stubborn about *Che!* than he was even, in the forties, about *Wilson*. About the reviews—"As far as I'm concerned, too many serious critics let their own personal political opinions dominate. What I got from Vincent Canby's review: it was vitriolic beyond the point of criticism, as if he was reviewing a bad sermon on an intimate personal friend." Zanuck believed "the reviewers would get smashed down by the public." Instead, *Che!* got smashed down—a relatively low-budget flop, but still a flop. "If you understand why Darryl Zanuck made *Che!* as he made *Che!*" says one of his former directors, "you'll understand the whole man: everything is 'entertainment.'" But *Che!* was inferior entertainment, and the same charge might be leveled at other Fox movies—1969 proved a banner year of failures for Fox, not only *Che!* but *Staircase, Justine, A Walk with Love and Death, Hard Contract, The Magus.*

With Fox approaching a perilous state, Zanuck performed the neat trick of, essentially, invoking a vote of confidence in himself and his son. Darryl Zanuck was boosted to chairman of the board and chief executive officer. In announcing that "Richard Zanuck is the logical choice to become president of this corporation," Darryl Zanuck made it quite clear, that the change was only in titles and not in command. But all the apparent optimism couldn't obscure the fact there was no quarterly dividend.

Complicating Zanuck's life was the fact that in 1969 he faced his first crucial corporate test—the threat of a raid by outsiders on the corporation and the rumors of a take-over. Fox was not only the last of the big studios, it was one of the few untouched by a conglomerate. Paramount was a subsidiary of Gulf and Western, United Artists of Trans-American, MGM of Seagram, Warner Brothers of Kinney. Zanuck tried to buttress the organization against the danger. He decided the standard Hollywood board of directors, with people from various company divisions, associated industries, and friends, was out of date. On his new board, only four out of thirteen were from Fox: the two Zanucks, David Brown, and Harry MacIntyre. The rest were important men from diverse fields: William Randolph Hearst, Jr.; Jerome Straka, former president and chairman of Chesebrough-Ponds; William Hughes Mulligan, dean of Fordham Law School; William T. Gossett, retired president of the American Bar Association; John P. Edmondson, former executive vice-president of Dutton; William C. Keefe, vice-chairman of Panhandle Eastern Pipeline; Dr. Kevin C. McCann, president emeritus, Defiance College; Paul Miller, chairman of the board and chief executive officer, Gannett Company; Frederick L. Ehrman, partner, Lehman Brothers. Says Zanuck, "If there's a raid all of the rich tycoons in the world can't save you. I would rather have men of national prestige and stature on the board. A company is respected by raiders according to the caliber of the Board of Directors. Secretary of State William Rogers was a member of our Board until President Nixon took him away from us." Zanuck also attempted to differentiate between raiders: some were friendly, some unfriendly. Even as rumors multiplied about takeovers by companies in and out of the movie business, Zanuck continued to be convinced he could fight from a position of strength. "We have one big weapon," he said, "one vital weapon, which they may not understand, or give a damn about. Without the combined talents of our production and distribution organization, what the hell is the company? Eight or ten aged stages —what are they worth? A lousy building at 444 West 56th Street? Many studios have twice the physical facilities we do. What would they buy? Talent! Without the two Zanucks, anybody would be out of their goddamn minds to want the company. While we don't do it all, we are the heads of the two major divisions. We are the cornerstones, and unless they have us in their corner what the hell have they got?"

Mostly Zanuck was trying to wait out the failure of 1969

until its one supposedly sure success came along—*Hello, Dolly!*
Twenty million was tied up in that blockbuster, and because of
the original contract with the play's Broadway producer, David
Merrick (who, oddly enough, was also a stockholder in
Twentieth Century-Fox), the movie could not be released
until he approved the date. Meanwhile bank interest accumulated. Word leaked out that Fox planned to open *Dolly*
in December 1969, but at Merrick's orders, that fact had to
be kept unpublicized until close to the last minute. But of its
own volition, and because of its star, Barbra Streisand, the
movie kept gathering publicity. By the time it opened on
December 16, it was the most publicized, most long-awaited
commercial movie of the year. The opening night at the
Rivoli Theatre (which once upon a time had housed *The
Sound of Music*) was an extravaganza, partially provided by
the star and her exuberant fans, who surrounded her limou-
sine and forced the delay of her entrance and the movie, and
partially because of the hoopla provided by Twentieth Century-Fox. After a half-hour delay and an altercation in the
aisle between a press photographer and Miss Streisand's
manager, Zanuck stood up in his seat and commanded, "Start
the picture!" It started. The premiere and the elegant party
after were lush, lavish affairs, but in many ways a wake for
a dying industry. Predictably, the movie got mixed reviews
(raves from less demanding critics, many pans, and a wryly
restrained review from the New York *Times*'s Vincent Canby,
who confessed that his criticism was extraneous anyway).
Dolly looked as though it might be the last big movie, the
last musical blockbuster. Zanuck was quick to acknowledge
that likelihood. Perhaps in about five years, it might be time
for a musical cycle again, he said, but for now, it seemed
probable that no studio would undertake a big-budget movie.
"When you're flush," he said, "you can afford to take chances.
That day has passed."

The truth was that many days had passed. The year 1969
proved a crucial one for the entire movie business. Almost
all studios were in upheaval. MGM, for one, had gone
through two sets of management. Theater business was down.
The majors were losing fortunes on their big movies. Yet
at the same time in one sense the business was booming.
To the astonishment of the industry, which had been predict-
ing its own death since the rise of television, there was an

enormous audience, a young audience. The Film Generation had been born. Youngsters were turned on by the medium, and instead of dreaming about writing novels, they wanted to make movies. And they wanted to go to them. In the same year that the multimillion-dollar blockbusters were bombing, the minibudgets were booming. *Midnight Cowboy, Easy Rider, Alice's Restaurant* were huge hits in 1969, and so were their stars, Dustin Hoffman, Jon Voight, Peter Fonda, Arlo Guthrie. As Dick Zanuck admitted, "We misjudged the public taste," and for one thing, "the audience can no longer be conned by big star names." It was in a way a justification of Darryl Zanuck's old philosophy that movies make stars and stars don't make movies—one of the several of his presentiments that he seemed to forget. As 1969 ended, Fox was still the last of the big studios but there was a huge question mark on its horizon: how much longer could it exist as a studio? When would it be forced to go the way of United Artists and solicit independent productions?

In late November, Zanuck said "that there has been a revolution in public taste, which has resulted in the rapid obsolescence of films and story properties, which, when originally initiated, represented sound business risks." He did not announce the names of any properties that had actually been canceled, although later he said that with any picture costing over four million dollars "you're sticking your chin out."

Going into 1970, Zanuck suddenly found himself faced with a possible proxy fight from, of all people, David Merrick. "I only met him once," said Zanuck about Merrick, "and found him quite pleasant—which is contrary to his reputation." In their first formal encounter, at the May 1970 stockholders' meeting, Zanuck vanquished Merrick, although Merrick vowed to fight again.

In 1969 Fox had several profitable pictures, including *The Prime of Miss Jean Brodie* and in Europe *The Sicilian Clan,* but only one major hit, *Butch Cassidy and the Sundance Kid.* There were pressing problems in that coming year's product. Fox had two road shows scheduled for 1970, both war movies with budgets so high that before he released them Zanuck said that were he to have the chance to begin them in 1970, he wouldn't. There was *Patton,* starring George C. Scott, to whom Zanuck was awarding the 1971 Academy

Award, even before the Academy did, and there was *Tora! Tora! Tora!* with what Zanuck generally referred to as its "monumental world-wide publicity." Both pictures seemed to get their impetus not from *Sound of Music,* but from Zanuck's own *The Longest Day. Tora* was in fact something like a sequel. This was the World War II spectacle about the Pearl Harbor attack. There had been trouble in its early production stages. "A publicity-hungry New York Congressman, John M. Murphy, began harassing me," says Zanuck. Representative Murphy had gotten inspiration for the assault from a CBS television show, "Sixty Minutes," in which Mike Wallace had questioned the propriety of the Department of Defense co-operation with the movie. "Congressman Murphy decided to ask for passage of an idiotic bill to prohibit in the future any co-operation between the Department of Defense and movie companies, irrespective of subject matter." Since *Tora* had finished principal photography, such a bill would not affect it, but Zanuck must have felt his patriotism was in question. He went on the attack, taking a full-page ad in the New York *Times* and the Washington *Post* and other papers, defending his position. When finished, *Tora* cost in excess of $20 million—for the second year in a row, a large sum was tied up and unreturnable, until late season release. A great deal less money, but an equal amount of Zanuck's energies, was tied up in *Hello—Goodbye,* starring Michael Crawford, Curt Jurgens, and Zanuck's companion, Genevieve Gilles.

Since Zanuck was closely involved in *Tora! Tora! Tora!* and *Hello—Goodbye,* this led skeptics to believe that he had not really changed very much, except that his war pictures had become bigger and more spectacular and his girl friends younger and more attractive.

4.

Genevieve

*The difference in our ages doesn't seem to exist—for either
of us.*

—Darryl Zanuck

When they first met, Genevieve Gilles (shortened from Gill-
aizeau) was nineteen. He was sixty-three. Genevieve was born
in Paris, lived most of her early life away from her home,
much of it at a Catholic school. By the age of seventeen she
was a fashion model. "I was pretty and I was tall and what
can I do?" she explains her entry into the modeling profession. "I was very ambitious. I don't know what for." She met
Zanuck at a dinner party at Maxim's, and within a year she
became his constant companion. Her fashion career continued. She appeared on magazine covers in the U.S. and in
Europe. Like Darvi, Greco, and Demick before her, she went
everywhere with Zanuck, although in her case the relationship was much more private. Zanuck had ignored the press
with this romance, and for some reason, the press had
practically ignored the romance. In articles and pictures,
Zanuck's companion was often unidentified. They acted with
great discretion, one might even say taste. Taste is in fact
her hallmark. "The first thing he recognized in me," she says,
"was that I was elegant." Genevieve is certainly the most
stylish of all Zanuck's girls and she knew it. "All the girls
about him—no class," she says. "Greco has a wonderful
voice but . . ." There was no need for Zanuck to suggest
certain wardrobes for Genevieve as he had for other friends.
In fact, during the relationship, Zanuck has himself suddenly
blossomed in sartorial splendor—well-shaped suits and blazers

247

—although as always when he wears a tie it is a black one. Why? No one knows.

Young, fresh, incredibly vibrant, and incredibly freckled, Genevieve speaks about her relationship with Zanuck. "He has everything, but I think he must be alone. He don't like to be alone. I don't think anybody knows him very well." The best and worst about him? "The best. *Amitié*. If you can get this from him, you can get everything. He'll give you his heart. He'll help you. When he likes somebody, he gives everything. You can ask the moon." The worst? "He's a kind of egoist. Jealous. Possessive. He don't like to lose something he try to keep." Then she concludes, "I am very happy with him. I like what he does. He's not too young, but he don't give me any problems. Dick looks like his father, but he is not like his father. His father is a character, a big personality. Very nice too. He looks mysterious, but he is not mysterious."

She began her movie career with a short, *The World of Fashion*, a mini-spectacular that called for many changes of costumes and sets. It was in effect a lavish, public screen test for Miss Gilles. "It cost $48,000," says Zanuck, "and it has grossed in excess of $500,000." He loved the movie, and her in it. Then he chose her first feature, a romantic comedy, *Hello—Goodbye.* "It's a perfect feature introduction for her," says her mentor, "and she doesn't have to be Sarah Bernhardt to play it." For one thing the role was a girl like Genevieve. "She's like me," she admitted. "It's about a girl who's married to a very rich man like Onassis who falls in love with a mechanic. It's very *moderne*." With Genevieve in front of the camera and Zanuck not far behind, Ronald Neame began directing. Within weeks Neame was out, and Zanuck's old croquet comrade Jean Negulesco was rushed into action. The movie continued without incident or delay, Zanuck in the background, nurturing it toward completion. She insisted that she did not want to be a movie star, but that movies were just something she wanted to try. "I work and I try," she said. "If I am a success, I didn't steal anything." If she were a success, might she then leave Zanuck? She said, no. "If I become a star, and leave him, he looks like a jerk. That would make too many people happy."

Most of the time they are in New York. Almost every Sunday they have dinner at Trader Vic's. Often friends, such as Salvador Dali and his wife, join them. "He and Dali," re-

called Genevieve, "all they talked about was *maisons de
tolérance*. Always sex, between Dali and him. It's boring
when you talk about sex during dinner." Almost every night
she and Zanuck see movies privately screened at Twentieth
Century-Fox. Sometimes there are just the two of them in the
screening room, sometimes a few other guests. They see Fox
pictures and pictures from other companies, sitting in the
back in large leather chairs, like kids at a Saturday matinee
—except for all the fun, Zanuck is always working. According
to Genevieve, they see "many times bad pictures. I see more
pictures twice and some of them five times." They often
disagree. He says, "I study pictures that make or lose money
and try to understand why."

The occasionally go to the theater, but only for particular
reasons—to see *Plaza Suite,* because George C. Scott was
going to play *Patton,* to see *The Great White Hope,* because
Fox was going to film it, to see *Hair,* said Genevieve, "because there were naked girls in it." Out of curiosity sometimes
he likes to go odd places, such as a certain Lesbian club in
Paris. She doesn't like to go there—for one thing, she's afraid
people will think she's "one of them"—but she lets him believe she likes to go. "He is so intelligent, but he is like a
child. He is in his car with a chauffeur and we'll pass a girl
and he will say—'Look at that!' Onassis is like that, too.
Darryl has a book with all the girls' names in it, and if he
likes one, he puts stars next to her name. Four stars! Five
stars!" How many stars does she have? She laughed and said
"the moon."

As the girl with Zanuck, she is the centerpiece of his
personal life, his principal companion and confidante, the
consort to the king, but with a prestige of her own. Anything
she wants is hers: clothes, jewelry, furs. "It's a pretty heady
experience," says Helen Gurley Brown, a close observer of the
scene. "He is totally devoted to her and she is A Princess."
Wherever he goes, she goes, although in a curious return to
old-fashioned morality, they studiously keep separate res-
idences. Each likes it that way; it gives her a certain inde-
pendence. "He loves me, and says I am good for him. If
tomorrow I want to marry someone, I don't know how to
leave him. And I don't want to ever hurt him . . ."

The fidelity seems deep. "When I first knew Darryl," says
Genevieve, "he drank a lot, not only whiskey, but mostly a

Greek wine. Since he lives in his apartment at the Plaza in New York or at the George V in Paris and I live in my own East Side apartment in New York or my small apartment in Paris, I didn't realize the real extent of his drinking." She explains that he hid his alcoholic problem from his executives in New York and at the studio: "He was very clever, very subtle. When he knew he had an important business or conference or something like that, he would never touch a drop, but he carried a flask and would take one drink just before his conference began and one after. Maybe some knew, but said nothing . . . Then on one of our trips to Hollywood on his studio business, we had adjoining bungalows. The icebox was in my bungalow. He would sneak in at night and empty a full bottle. I decided to tell his doctor, Lee Siegel. Siegel saw him alone on several occasions. Darryl suddenly told me that he would never touch a drop of any sort of alcohol again—and he didn't. At first it was terrible for him. He lost weight and could not eat. When we left for New York he could hardly walk. The TWA man had to almost carry him on the plane. When we arrived in New York he had to be almost carried off the plane and Henry, his chauffeur, helped me get him to his car. He never spoke a word. I temporarily abandoned my apartment and took a room at the Plaza on the same floor as his. I checked the bottles in his bar and had a key to his room, so I could examine the bar when he was out. Gradually he began to eat and walk normally. He now drinks only non-alcoholic near beer or Coca-Cola.

"When Dr. Siegel came to New York six months later, he gave Darryl a complete examination. He was perfect. I claim no pride for my part in his recovery—but I would never go through it again for any man, even if he was a combination of Dustin Hoffman, Prince Philip, and the Pope."

5.

Amitié

*If I had gotten a divorce instead of a legal separation, I
would have been married three times since. I would have
had three more divorces. I would have had a lot less money
and a lot more misery.*

—Darryl Zanuck

Zanuck's marriage to Virginia Fox and his romances with
Greco and Darvi had ended with much bitterness on both
sides. His affair with Irina Demick had ended amicably.
"There is no before and there is no after," in her relationship
with Zanuck, Irina says, then adds with much conviction but not
too much clarity of thought, "except that now I am married
and I have changed my way of life. He is a very good friend
and now he is a very good friend of my husband. People
are astonished at the *amitié* between Darryl and me." Amaz-
ingly, not only Genevieve and Irina feel *amitié* for Darryl;
so, in different ways, do Bella, Juliette, and Virginia.

In the spring of 1968 Bella took an overdose of barbi-
turates, one of her many attempts at suicide. She was rescued,
and after spending some time in a clinic, in Provence, she
moved in with an American lady friend in Roquebrunne-Cap
Martin, in a villa suitably named Bel' Horizon. Battered,
bruised, splotchy, puffy, one side of her face bandaged, she
certainly did not look like the face that launched a mogul,
that broke up a marriage, that turned a movie studio upside
down. She looked like an international playgirl very much out
of luck. "I'm nowhere. I'm out," she confessed. Did she
regret anything in her life? Suppressing tears, she answered,
softly, "I regret I regret I regret."

Zanuck had a friend ransom her clothes from the Hotel

de Paris in Monaco where she had been staying at the time of the last suicide attempt—and paid her overdue hotel bill. Eight months later, Bella was on her feet, and literally back in the chips. She had found someone new to befriend her, and was in the casino again—gambling away her life—until her next suicide attempt. On September 17, 1971, in Monte Carlo, she turned on the gas in her stove and died.

Greco, on the other hand, seemed to prosper without Zanuck. She married and in recent years has had an enormous professional comeback on records. In reordering the tangle of her previous life, she has created An Official Position in regards to *l'affaire Zanuck*. She says that she didn't personally write her memoirs about Darryl. "Things written down in my name I never wrote. At that time I was dictating and at the last moment some pages were put in my manuscript." And then, "I love Darryl very deeply. My husband, he loves him. What a marvelous man . . ." Does she regret her life with Zanuck? "I don't regret it," she said. "Today I don't regret anything I have been doing with my life."

Virginia Zanuck has also reconstructed her past to suit her present. She is still Mrs. Zanuck, the only Mrs. Zanuck, and she could not be more devoted to her husband's memory if she were his widow. She visits their home in Palm Springs and the tall floodlights tower like totems on the unused croquet lawn. She walks inside the cavernous guesthouse, cold and bare like a mausoleum, and says, "This house was alive with voices and laughter." The main house she shared with her husband is inhabited only by an elderly caretaker and is otherwise locked against memories. Mostly Mrs. Zanuck waits in their beach house in Santa Monica, still decorated as it was when Darryl lived there. Hidden in a wall, like a safe, behind a picture, is his cigar humidor, opened by triggering a secret button—and in the humidor is a box of his special brand of cigars. In 1968, eleven years after their separation, Darryl sent Virginia a bust of himself, and it is on prominent display. Darryl Zanuck is a man greatly respected in her house.

6.

Action

> *One time I saw Darryl Zanuck in Pamplona watching a bullfight. It started to rain. Everyone left the arena except Zanuck. He sat there and his cigar did not go out. God does not rain on Darryl Zanuck.*
>
> —Kenneth Tynan

Zanuck shows no signs of slowing down. He works long, seven-day weeks, five days in his office at Twentieth Century-Fox in New York, weekends in his suite at the Plaza Hotel. While Zanuck puffs and paces, his two secretaries take turns at dictation. As always, he never honors a holiday, nor takes a non-work vacation.

He is neither mired in the past nor anticipatory about the future. "I wouldn't have my fortune told," he says. "Never. I'm a Virgo but I've never asked what Virgo means. I have an absolute horror of that. I don't want to know what tomorrow holds for me—or today. If it would be bad, I would be disappointed, and if it would be good, I might be just as disappointed. I would become addicted to it. You have to live your own life and take' what comes. I suppose I'm in the minority, but I think you've got to settle your own problems." And you settle problems as they arise. "I make business plans far in advance, but my daily life is not plotted out at all." Hardly anyone knows where he is going or when. His name is never listed in the comings-and-goings section of *Variety*. "*I* know," he asserts, and that is enough. He has simplified his going into a routine. He always carries the same luggage: one suitcase for suits, one for shirts and underwear, one for medicine, and a leather sack for his cigars (he sends cases of near beer ahead of him). On planes he always travels first class, sitting in the last row, so he can push his chair as far back as he wants to—and read a script, or sleep.

As a continuing reaction against the confinement of his Hollywood years, he refuses to be tied down by anything, especially possessions. He splits his year between the George V in Paris and the Plaza in New York, and except for a few paintings and stacks of books, and, in New York, a huge piece of pre-Columbian sculpture willed to him by Charles Feldman, and a gold Marini statue of the birth of Adam, a gift from Dino de Laurentiis, the suites are impersonal and unostentatious. He has not owned a home since he left Hollywood. "Elsa Maxwell spelled it out for me. She said, 'I don't own anything because when you start possessing things, they end possessing you.' If you have a château in Klosters, you feel compelled to go to Switzerland. If you have a home in Jamaica, you feel compelled to go there. There are servants there, waiting. The place possesses you. All my rich and titled English friends don't really want to go to the country for the goddamn weekend, but they have the place so they start weeks ahead inviting guests. That's why I like hotels. I damn near bought a country place just before I became president, forty-five minutes from Paris. Then suddenly I said, "There I go, another possession!' when I would rather be in Paris, where I could go to Chez l'Ami Louis, Relais Bisson, or Lipp's, or wherever. The same thing with a boat. When Howard Hughes used to give me his boat, and I would go to Mexico, after three or four times, oh, Jesus, I'm sick of being stuck for days on this thing. I want to go *when* I have to *where* I want to."

His style has become indelible. He is the man with sunglasses and the big cigar. He always wears the glasses—dark, black glasses with sides to them so they enshroud his eyes—indoors and outdoors, accepting awards, making speeches, appearing on television, and, always, while watching movies. Some friends suggest that the glasses are the key to the man, that they are his Rosebud. After a lifetime of watching movies, he should have worn his eyes out—but he still watches, and as Edward Leggewie says, "He has eagle eyes. He can see a little hair on the screen." Vanity is a possible explanation: to hide nearsightedness he wears dark glasses—but personal vanity, except of a sexual nature, is not charac-

teristic of the man. He is not hiding—like a movie star behind
The Shades. They are a trademark, not a disguise. More likely
it is a withdrawal of a certain kind. The wraparound lenses
enclose him. When he sees a movie, he is the camera, and
his glasses the movie screen. And outside the screening room,
as he watches, life becomes the movies.

He now smokes a special cigar, but it looks like the real
thing: huge, enormous. A phallic symbol? Sex is an important
theme in his personal life, and also of his professional life—
of his cutting peak to peak, of his always feeling a need to
prove himself, again and again, even in the areas of his own
mistakes.

He wastes little time on introspection, although occasionally he reveals something of himself. "I am basically hard and
firm and tough," he says. "I can't tolerate laziness whether
from waiters or script writers. If they're getting tipped, then
you're deserving of service." Is he sentimental? "I know I've
a sentimental streak. I can get outrageous about things then
have sleepless nights about perhaps going too far. By the
same token, I can say, I didn't get tough enough." The
sentimentality is usually kept private—but not always. In
1968, Fox's foreign sales convention took place in Cannes
shortly after Robert Kennedy was assassinated. After his
prepared speech to his assembled European salesmen, Zanuck
added a few words, "What I say, I feel I have to say to you
as an American . . . I was in California when a tragic event
recently occurred—an assassination of a friend of mine . . ."
His voice broke, and quavered. He began to sob. "There are
200 million Americans, but only one man killed Bob Kennedy . . . not an American. It's not an American crime. Try
and . . ." He increased his sobbing, choked, and managed to
finish, ". . . spread that word. Thank you." And still crying,
he turned from the podium.

Outside of Irving Berlin, Orson Welles, John Huston, and
Aristotle Onassis, he has few friends, and most of those who
were very close, such as Irving Hoffman, Gregory Ratoff, and
Charles Feldman, are dead. "He has never fundamentally
been in need of friends," says Michael Romanoff. "His work
and his play and his children are his friends." But John
Huston remembers the time, a recent birthday party for
Huston, when Zanuck addressed the guests, and said that he
didn't envy Huston for his talent, or success, but for his

friends. "I haven't got such friends," he said. "I don't know why. Perhaps because I'm a boss . . . and can't afford to have friends . . . or I'm afraid to have friends." Says Huston, "It was so quietly, composedly spoken. It came out like poetry. I couldn't respond to it. It was so moving half of us were in tears."

What makes Darryl run? Money? While all around him independent producers are making fortunes in percentages, he is salaried. "By my own design," he says, "I'm by far the lowest-paid president in the industry. I'm not fabulously rich, a multimillionaire, by any manner of means. I've invested my money so that I can continue to live as I do now without my salary—unless the cost of living goes sky-high." He laughs. "We have an incentive plan for people we wish to have stay with us. I excluded myself from the plan." One reason is the matter of image. "If the plan came up at the stockholders' meeting and the fact that Mr. Zanuck was not in it, it would have a very salutary effect: Mr. Zanuck didn't cut himself into some future melon." But the truth is, he doesn't need it; he lives very well, but not lavishly.

Is it power? "I don't know. The power thing doesn't come into it so much. There is a certain satisfaction from being the chief executive officer of a corporation. What pleases me is when I can make a contribution to a script. I get enormous satisfaction out of that, more than from okaying a good bank loan." But what about the power of influencing people through movies? "I had that too goddamn long. I get no glory out of that."

A British journalist once asked him what made him decide to take over Fox again, and he answered, "Pride, pride, pride. It's the answer to everything. You want to make good, show you're still there. You want to prove you can still cut the mustard." Pride is certainly a part of what motivates Zanuck, but an even larger part is simply the doing. He hates to be bored. He hates to be doing nothing. Nothing about him is passive.

"Beyond even my three Oscars and my three Thalberg awards," he says, "I cherish most my honorary membership in the Motion Picture Directors Guild. During my career my bloodiest battles have been with directors for cutting or 'destroying their masterpieces.' Now I have the distinction of being one of them." Zanuck flew from Europe to accept the

membership personally. "George Stevens made a deeply moving address," he remembers. "The inscribed director's chair
was presented to me by Joe Mankiewicz. I couldn't resist
ending my acceptance speech, 'Of course you all know I have
probably butchered more films in the cutting room than all
the producers in the entire industry put together.' " The chair
resides, on permament display, in his New York office.

The year 1970 was a disastrous one in Hollywood. The old
studio system, long disintegrating, was finally dying. Power
was fragmented—and in the hands of actors, independent
producers, and agents. The industry was in a state of panic.
Fox's 1969 loss of $36.8 million (before a credit of $11.6
million) was more than doubled in 1970—the company lost
$77.3 million. *Patton* and *M*A*S*H* had been enormous hits,
and *Patton* made even more money in 1971 after it won seven
Academy Awards including Best Picture and Best Actor. But
Tora! Tora! Tora! was a disappointment, *Hello, Dolly!* a failure, and *Myra Breckinridge,* a catastrophe. Suddenly there
was great concern over the future of Fox. Budgets were
rigidly tightened, productions were cancelled, foreign offices
were closed, and the New York staff was cut back. The Board
of Directors named an independent committee to study
restructuring of the company, and by the end of the year the
committee recommended that Richard Zanuck and David
Brown leave the company. As with a losing baseball team, in
time of crisis movie companies ask for the "resignation" of
the field manager, in this case Richard Zanuck, and of the
coach, David Brown. As president and head of production,
Dick Zanuck had primary working responsibility for the
movies that came out of the studio, which means that he was
"blamed" for his failures such as *Star!, Dr. Dolittle,* and *Myra
Breckinridge,* while his successes, such as *M*A*S*H,* were
ignored.

The board formally requested the resignations and on
December 29, 1970, Dick Zanuck and Brown resigned. At
the same time it was announced that Darryl Zanuck would
retain his post as chairman and chief executive officer of the
company with the same duties and responsibilities that he
exercised in the past. Elmo Williams, the producer of *Tora!
Tora! Tora!,* was designated as the executive head of production.

Because of Dick Zanuck's dismissal and Darryl Zanuck's survival, many people speculated that Darryl had fired his son. He denied the accusation, saying it was entirely the board's decision. But he apparently had neither the will nor the power to prevent the firing. Clearly if it was a choice of his own position or that of his son, DFZ came first. For all the closeness of the father-son relationship—and at least before the split they were extremely close—there was always a bond of rivalry. Now one endured even at the other's expense, although in cinematic terms it would be a much more exciting story if both had galloped out of Fox and made movies together. But Zanuck has always been an independent, even a solitary, figure. And the truth is that Dick could also look out for himself. After all he was trained on the Zanuck survival course. Looking around, he weighed his options, then switched from Fox to Warner Brothers, taking David Brown with him. In a very short time he had moved a step ahead of John Calley, the production head, and was—right next to Ted Ashley—in command of Warners, just as his father had been so many years before. It was one full revolution of the Zanuck cycle.

Darryl Zanuck had weathered the first purge, but his days at Fox seemed numbered. Hoping for a prosperous future, Fox had to forget completely about the past. William T. Gossett, as chairman of the executive committee, was able to name Dennis C. Stanfill as Dick Zanuck's successor as President. Together, Gossett and Stanfill were becoming increasingly powerful at Fox. With some haste they began bastioning the vulnerable company against a proxy fight waged by a group of insurgent stockholders. Proxy fights had been rumored or threatened in the recent past, but had not materialized. This one was definitely in earnest—and aimed at the May 18, 1971 annual stockholders' meeting. Each side began jockeying for votes. Management won the support of David Merrick, formerly a dissident major stockholder, but now for all purposes—except voting—staying out of the dispute. The insurgents won the support of both Richard Zanuck and Virginia Zanuck (who after the Darryl-Richard split regained control of their share of the family stock). There were even blandishments made to Darryl to join the rebels, but he remained allied with management. Management and insurgents conducted an expensive war of advertisements, each accusing the other of foul deeds, each making a claim for having only the stockholders' interest at heart. Gossett-Stanfill, representing the incumbents, dubbed themselves a "New Management Team," and even managed to include Zanuck. At the same time rumors increased about Zanuck's imminent departure from the company.

On April 7 Zanuck resigned as chief executive, retaining his post as chairman. It was the first in a series of removals of mantles of office. On June 17, the night before the annual meeting in Wilmington, Delaware, Zanuck announced that he was retiring as chairman and would return to independent film production. The timing of the announcement seemed particularly to the advantage of the "New Management Team." To many of the stockholders Zanuck was the symbol of the company. If Zanuck had resigned earlier presumably Fox would have lost some pro-Zanuck votes.

The final battle, the stockholders' meeting, was as one stockholder remarked, "a lot more interesting" than many recent Fox movies. What was pre-sold as a collision of faceless money-men became in effect the last hurrah for the last tycoon. Fittingly, a meeting that began with anger ended in a chorus of eulogies from all sides—management, insurgents, stockholders—for Darryl F. Zanuck. The forces at Fox proved that, like the movie industry itself, they are at the same time bitterly competitive and rampantly sentimental.

The scene of the meeting was the Playhouse Theater in Wilmington's Hotel Dupont. The inconvenience of the location —previous meetings had been held in New York and Los Angeles—made doubly difficult by a railroad strike, severely reduced attendance. The audience was sparse, although there were many members of the press.

On stage were Gossett, Stanfill, Zanuck, and selected officers. Stage right in a box sat other board members, and stage left in a box sat The Opposition, like a parliamentary bloc. One of the leaders of the proxy-warriors, the dapper Charles M. Lewis, a partner in the brokerage firm of Treves and Company, stood like a sentry during most of the proceedings.

The battle when it began was not from the boxes but from the rabble. Two professional stockholders and meeting-goers, Evelyn Y. Davis and Lewis Gilbert, as if liberated by the dissension within the company, exceeded even their own record for back-talk. At times they screamed simultaneously into microphones, demanding recognition from the moderator, a Delaware attorney, excoriating both management and dissenters. Malcolm Kahn, a disgruntled Fox employee and spokesman for the opposition, was finally given the floor and he spoke ruefully about the problems he had seen at Fox.

The meeting became a babble of antagonism with no one liking what anyone else was saying or doing—with one definite exception. Everyone, including Mr. Kahn, was united on one thing—admiration for Zanuck. Through it all, the diatribes against the company, the criticism of the insurgents, and the encomiums for him, Zanuck sat quietly and impassively, with his emotions masked behind his wraparound sunglasses and his long cigar. Zanuck, who had presided at many meetings in the past, handling the obstructionists with deftness and even wit, now had the look of someone who had been through all this before—perhaps too many times.

Finally a question from the audience was addressed directly to him. Before the question was finished, the photographers swarmed magnetically to his side of the stage. Would he serve his full twelve months as a member of the board? Softly he said yes. Who would lead the company in creative matters in the absence of Zanuck? There was an undertone of desperation in the question. Gossett spoke. He promised that the company would continue to receive "advice and guidance from the greatest of them all, Mr. Zanuck." Then he added that "the committee passes on the recommendation of the head of production."

The committee. The word was like a death knell. In the old days, the thirties and forties when Zanuck ruled supreme at Fox (and Harry Cohn, Louis B. Mayer, and Jack Warner at their studios), it was the individual, the president or the studio boss who determined the product. Zanuck chose the movies, stars, directors, writers; fired at will; edited scripts; supervised shooting; watched all the rushes; helped cut the print; had the final word on every single picture that came out of his studio. Actual one-man rule had been dead for many years in Hollywood, except in the symbolic personage of Zanuck. One by one, the other moguls had died, retired, or been deposed. Decisions were being made by new young men, such as David Picker at United Artists, and many of their bosses, such as Kirk Kerkorian and James Aubrey at

M-G-M, were transplants from other industries. Any of them could be toppled. Hollywood was faceless and headless. Of all the studio heads and producers who founded and shaped the industry, Zanuck was the sole active survivor, the last tycoon. And now he, like his friend Jack Warner, was retiring from management and returning to independent production.

A stockholder asked him directly how active he would be in company policy. Zanuck stood up and spoke slowly. "I will continue to be very active," he said. "I've been devoted for many years in the only industry I know." Briefly he reminisced about his days writing Rin Tin Tin movies, the institution of CinemaScope, his contribution to the script of *Patton*. He added that now as a producer, "I may be lucky enough to come up with another *Longest Day*. Then he said in a barely audible voice, "This has been a long day too."

Gossett praised Zanuck as a "giant among film-makers," and asked him to assume the new post of chairman emeritus. All factions applauded. The meeting was adjourned, to be reconvened in New York June 8 at which time the result of the proxy balloting would be announced. Kahn, the dissident, leaped on stage to shake Zanuck's hand. He was followed by a clamoring horde of reporters, photographers, and television cameramen who crowded around Zanuck as if around the winner after a championship prize-fight. They ignored Stanfill and the opposition. As one aged lady stockholder observed, it was Zanuck who was the "star of the day."

Facing the crowd, he said, "I've tried to keep alive. I have kept alive. I couldn't be happy doing anything else. This is my life. This is the life I continue to want to live."

He rose and began walking across the stage toward the lobby of the hotel. The press pursued him. One reporter asked him, "Does your retirement mean the end of an era?" "I don't imagine so," he answered, but then was unable to name any active mogul.

On June 8 the result of the proxy fight was announced. Management had won with 3,900,087 votes to the insurgents' 2,428,139. As expected, the insurgents immediately contested the ballots. Even without another proxy fight, the future of Fox was still in doubt, and very much dependent on the success or failure of its next films—which would presumably, in time, include pictures personally produced by Zanuck.

As the months passed, details were still being worked out for Zanuck's independent company—the location of his headquarters, the size of his budgets, the actual movies he would make—but the future of Zanuck was clear. He was out of executive harness. The last tycoon was at least for now a post-tycoon. "I'm flirting with two or three ideas for movies," he said, then added enthusiastically, "I can't wait until I get back into something that gives me personal satisfaction—not headaches!" His story and his role in films were far from finished.

Even before his retirement as a Fox executive, he talked about his dream of returning to more personal production. "If some subject came along that struck me as being another *Longest Day* or *Patton* or *Tora! Tora! Tora!* something that I would want to devote a couple of years to, I would do it." Would it necessarily be a war picture? "Hell no! How could I? I've already made them all—unless a new one comes along . . . I might make a drama with historic overtones." Might it be a subject of contemporary interest, such as poverty, student unrest, racism, areas that might have interested the Zanuck of the forties? He shook his head, paused, and made his announcement. "I'm hooked on Indians now. I'm flirting very much with Buffalo Bill. I think it is the kind of subject . . . if I can handle it myself, that might be an Epic. I made pictures about all of them. Belle Starr, Wyatt Earp, Jesse James. I even made a picture called *Buffalo Bill*, I think maybe with Joel McCrea [with McCrea, directed by William Wellman, in 1944]. But if I did it today it would be far different, a panorama of the West. Up to now it's always been cowboys and Indians. There is a great tragedy in Buffalo Bill. He ends up in a Wild West show to keep alive. I got this bug on, a colorful, honest panorama, not a glamorization, a *Grapes of Wrath* Indian picture. There was a *great* friendship between Cody and Sitting Bull. The pathetic end of Bill Cody and his Wild West Show. He had one bad eye, you know. If he tried to shoot with a bullet, he couldn't hit the side of a barn. He had a revolver with buckshot in it, with a big spread so he couldn't miss. Buffalo Bill's Wild West Show!" He savored every word. "Buffalo Bill's Wild West Show. I remember seeing him when I was a kid in Omaha. He had shoulder-length white hair. He charged into the arena on his white horse, his six-shooter at the ready. An Indian girl rode ahead of him and threw up white balls. He aimed his gun . . ." and suddenly it was not Buffalo Bill but the Wahoo Kid pointing his gun, and pulling the trigger, "Boom! Boom! Boom!"

FILMOGRAPHY

Before the thirties, producers were "supervisors," and not credited. The movies at Warners that I have credited to Zanuck as producer are among the many either made with him as supervisor or under his specific direction as production chief. All the films at Twentieth Century were produced by Zanuck. I have listed all the films at Twentieth Century-Fox that were labeled "produced by Darryl F. Zanuck," and a selection of others produced at Twentieth Century-Fox by his associates for which he still bore a great share of the responsibility. As a writer, Zanuck used his own name and three pseudonyms, Gregory Rogers, Mark Canfield, and Melville Crossman.

WARNER BROTHERS

1924

Find Your Man. From a story by Darryl F. Zanuck, directed by Mal St. Clair, starring Rin Tin Tin.

Lighthouse by the Sea. Adapted by Zanuck from a melodrama by Owen Davis, directed by Mal St. Clair, starring Rin Tin Tin.

1925

On Thin Ice. Adapted by Zanuck from *The Dear Pretender,* directed by Mal St. Clair, starring Tom Moore and William Russell.

The Limited Mail. Adaptation and scenario by Zanuck, directed by George Hill, starring Monte Blue.

Red Hot Tires. Adapted from a story by Gregory Rogers, directed by Erle C. Kenton, starring Monte Blue and Patsy Ruth Miller.

Hogan's Alley. Written by Gregory Rogers, directed by Roy del Ruth, starring Monte Blue, Louise Fazenda, and Ben Turpin.

1926

The Little Irish Girl. Adapted by Zanuck from a story by C. D. Lancaster, directed by Roy del Ruth, starring Dolores Costello.

The Social Highwayman. Adapted from a story by Zanuck, directed by William Beaudine, staring Montague Love.

Footloose Widows. Screenplay by Zanuck, directed by Roy del Ruth, starring Louise Fazenda and Jacqueline Logan.

Across the Pacific. Adapted by Zanuck, directed by Roy del Ruth, starring Myrna Loy and Monte Blue.

The Better 'Ole. Screenplay by Zanuck, directed by Charles Reisner, starring Sydney Chaplin.

Oh! What a Nurse! Scenario by Zanuck, story by Robert E. Sherwood and Bertram Block, directed by Charles Reisner, starring Sydney Chaplin.

1927

Tracked by the Police. Based on a story by Gregory Rogers, directed by Ray Enright, starring Rin Tin Tin and Jason Robards.

The Missing Link. Based on a story by Charles Reisner and Zanuck, directed by Reisner, starring Sydney Chaplin.

Irish Hearts. Story by Melville Crossman, screenplay by Bess Meredyth and Graham Baker, directed by Byron Haskin, starring May McAvoy and Jason Robards.

Old San Francisco. Based on a story by Zanuck, directed by Alan Crosland, starring Dolores Costello and Warner Oland.

The First Auto. Adapted from a story by Zanuck, directed by Roy del Ruth, starring Barney Oldfield and Russell Simpson.

The Black Diamond Express. Story by Zanuck, directed by Howard Bretherton, starring Monte Blue.

The Desired Woman. Based on a story by Mark Canfield, directed by Michael Curtiz, starring Irene Rich and William Russell.

State Street Sadie. Story by Melville Crossman, directed by Archie Mayo, starring Myrna Loy and Conrad Nagel.

The Jazz Singer. Directed by Alan Crosland, starring Al Jolson.

1928

Tenderloin. Written by Melville Crossman, directed by Michael Curtiz, starring Dolores Costello and Conrad Nagel.

The Midnight Taxi. Written by Gregory Rogers, directed by John Adolfi, starring Antonio Moreno and Helene Costello.

My Man. Written by Mark Canfield, directed by Archie Mayo, starring Fannie Brice.

1929

Noah's Ark. Based on a scenario by Zanuck, directed by Michael Curtiz, starring Dolores Costello and George O'Brien.

Say It with Songs. Adapted from a story by Zanuck, directed by Lloyd Bacon, starring Al Jolson.

Disraeli. Scenario by Julian Josephson, based on Louis N. Parker's play, directed by Alfred Green, starring George Arliss.

Madonna of Avenue A. Story by Mark Canfield, directed by Michael Curtiz, starring Dolores Costello, Grant Withers, and Louise Dresser.

1930

The Life of the Party. Adapted from a story by Melville Crossman, directed by Roy del Ruth, starring Winnie Lightner and Charles Butterworth.

The Office Wife. Based on a story by Faith Baldwin, directed by Lloyd Bacon, starring Lewis Stone.

The Doorway to Hell. Story by Rowland Brown, directed by Archie Mayo, starring Lew Ayres.

1931

Little Caesar. From the novel by W. R. Burnett, directed by Mervyn LeRoy, starring Edward G. Robinson.

Illicit. Based on a play by Edith Fitzgerald and Robert Riskin, directed by Archie Mayo, starring Barbara Stanwyck.

The Public Enemy. Based on a story by Kubec Glassmon and John Bright, directed by William Wellman, starring James Cagney, Jean Harlow, and Mae Clark.

Smart Money. Story by Kubec Glassmon and John Bright, directed by Alfred E. Green, starring Edward G. Robinson and James Cagney.

Five Star Final. Adapted from a play by Louis Weitzenkorn, directed by Mervyn LeRoy, starring Edward G. Robinson. A First National Picture.

1932

The Crowd Roars. Written and directed by Howard Hawks, starring James Cagney and Joan Blondell.

The Mouthpiece. Based on a play by Frank J. Collins, directed by James Flood and Elliott Nugent, starring Warren William.

The Dark Horse. Story by Zanuck, directed by Alfred E. Green, starring Warren William and Bette Davis. A First National Picture.

I Am a Fugitive from a Chain Gang. Based on the book by Robert E. Burns, directed by Mervyn LeRoy, starring Paul Muni.

1933

Forty-second Street. Based on the novel by Bradford Ropes, directed by Lloyd Bacon, starring Warner Baxter and Ruby Keeler.

Baby Face. Adapted by Gene Markey and Kathryn Scola from a story by Mark Canfield, directed by Alfred E. Green, starring Barbara Stanwyck and George Brent.

TWENTIETH CENTURY. All films produced by Zanuck and released by United Artists.

1933

The Bowery. Directed by Raoul Walsh, starring Wallace Beery and George Raft.

Broadway Thru a Keyhole. Based on a story by Walter Winchell, directed by Lowell Sherman, starring Paul Kelly and Constance Cummings.

Blood Money. Directed by Rowland Brown, starring George Bancroft.

Advice to the Lovelorn. Suggested by Nathaniel West's novel *Miss Lonelyhearts,* directed by Alfred Werker, starring Lee Tracy.

1934

Gallant Lady. Based on a story by Gilbert Emery and Douglas Doty, directed by Gregory La Cava, starring Ann Harding.

Moulin Rouge. Based on a story by Nunnally Johnson, directed by Sidney Lanfield, starring Constance Bennett and Franchot Tone.

The House of Rothschild. Based on an unproduced play by George Hembert Westly, directed by Alfred Werker, starring George Arliss.

Looking for Trouble. Based on a story by J. R. Bren, directed by William Wellman, starring Lee Tracy and Constance Cummings.

Born to Be Bad. From a story by Ralph Graves, directed by Lowell Sherman, starring Cary Grant and Loretta Young.

Bulldog Drummond Strikes Back. Based on the novel by H. C. McNeile, directed by Roy del Ruth, starring Ronald Colman.

The Affairs of Cellini. Adapted from Edwin Justin Mayer's *The Firebrand,* directed by Gregory La Cava, starring Fredric March.

The Last Gentleman. Based on a story by Katherine Clugston, directed by Sidney Lanfield, starring George Arliss.

The Mighty Barnum. Written by Gene Fowler and Bess Meredyth, directed by Walter Lang, starring Wallace Beery.

1935

Clive of India. Written and adapted by W. P. Lipscomb and R. J. Minney from their London play, directed by Richard Boleslawski, starring Ronald Colman and Loretta Young.

Folies Bergere. Screenplay by Bess Meredyth and Hal Long, directed by Roy del Ruth, starring Maurice Chevalier.

Cardinal Richelieu. Directed by Rowland V. Lee, starring George Arliss.

Les Miserables. An adaptation of Victor Hugo's novel, screenplay by W. P. Lipscomb, directed by Richard Boleslawski, starring Fredric March and Charles Laughton.

Call of the Wild. From the novel by Jack London, screenplay by Gene Fowler and Leonard Braskins, directed by William Wellman, starring Clark Gable and Loretta Young.

WARNER BROTHERS

1935

G Men. Based on a story by Gregory Rogers, screenplay by Seton I. Miller, directed by William Keighley, starring James Cagney.

TWENTIETH CENTURY-FOX

1935

Metropolitan. Based on a story by Bess Meredyth, screenplay by Bess Meredyth and George Marion, Jr., directed by Richard Boleslawski, produced by Zanuck, starring Lawrence Tibbett.

Thanks a Million. From a story by Melville Crossman, screenplay by Nunnally Johnson, directed by Roy del Ruth, produced by Zanuck, starring Dick Powell, Ann Dvorak, and Fred Allen.

The Man Who Broke the Bank at Monte Carlo. Screenplay by Howard Ellis Smith and Nunnally Johnson, directed by Stephen Roberts, produced by Zanuck, starring Ronald Colman and Joan Bennett.

Show Them No Mercy. Based on a story and screenplay by Kubec Glassmon, adaptation by Henry Lehrman, directed by George Marshall, produced by Zanuck, starring Bruce Cabot and Cesar Romero.

1936

King of Burlesque. Screenplay by Gene Markey and Harry Tugend, directed by Sidney Lanfield, produced by Zanuck, starring Warner Baxter, Alice Faye, and Jack Oakie.

Professional Soldier. Based on a story by Damon Runyon, screenplay by Gene Fowler and Howard Ellis Smith, directed by Tay Garnett, produced by Zanuck, starring Victor McLaglen.

The Prisoner of Shark Island. Screenplay by Nunnally Johnson, directed by John Ford, produced by Zanuck, starring Warner Baxter.

It Had to Happen. Based on a story by Rupert Hughes, directed by Roy del Ruth, produced by Zanuck, starring George Raft.

The Country Doctor. Screenplay by Sonya Levien, directed by Henry King, produced by Zanuck, starring Jean Hersholt and the Dionne Quintuplets.

A Message to Garcia. Suggested by Elbert Hubbard's essay and the book by Lieutenant Andrew S. Rowan, screenplay by W. P. Lipscomb and Gene Fowler, directed by George Marshall, produced by Zanuck, starring John Boles, Wallace Beery, and Barbara Stanwyck.

Captain January. Screenplay by Sam Hellman, Gladys Lehman, and Harry Tugend, directed by David Butler, produced by Zanuck, starring Shirley Temple.

Under Two Flags. Screenplay by W. P. Lipscomb and Walter Ferris, directed by Frank Lloyd, produced by Zanuck, starring Claudette Colbert and Ronald Colman.

Half Angel. Screenplay by Gene Fowler and Bess Meredyth, directed by Sidney Lanfield, produced by Zanuck, starring Brian Donlevy.

Sins of Man. Screenplay by Samuel G. Engel, directed by Otto Brower and Gregory Ratoff, produced by Zanuck, starring Jean Hersholt and Don Ameche.

White Fang. From a Jack London story. Screenplay by Gene Fowler, Hal Long, and S. G. Duncan, directed by Daniel Butler, produced by Zanuck, starring Slim Summerville, Charles Winninger, and Lightning.

The Road to Glory. From a story and screenplay by Joel Sayre and William Faulkner, directed by Howard Hawks, produced by Zanuck, starring Fredric March, Warner Baxter, and Lionel Barrymore.

Sing, Baby, Sing. Screenplay by Milton Sperling, Jack Yellen, Harry Tugend, directed by Sidney Canfield, produced by Zanuck, starring Adolph Menjou, Gregory Ratoff, and the Ritz Brothers.

Pigskin Parade. Screenplay by Harry Tugend, Jack Yellen, William Conselman, directed by David Butler, produced by Zanuck, starring Stuart Erwin, Jack Haley, the Yacht Club Boys, Bette Davis, Judy Garland, and Anthony Martin.

Lloyds of London. Screenplay by Ernest Pascal and Walter Ferris, directed by Henry King, starring Tyrone Power and Madeleine Carroll.

1937

One in a Million. Story and screenplay by Leonard Praskin, directed by Sidney Lanfield, produced by Zanuck, starring Sonja Henie.

On the Avenue. Screenplay by Gene Fowler and William Conselman, music and lyrics by Irving Berlin, directed by Roy del Ruth, produced by Zanuck, starring Dick Powell, Madeleine Carroll, and Alice Faye.

Seventh Heaven. Screenplay by Melville Baker, directed by Henry King, produced by Zanuck, starring James Stewart and Simone Simone.

Wake Up and Live. Screenplay by Harry Tugend and Jack Yellen, directed by Sidney Lanfield, produced by Zanuck, starring Walter Winchell and Ben Bernie.

Lancer Spy. Screenplay by Philip Dunne, directed by Gregory Ratoff, produced by Zanuck, starring George Sanders and Peter Lorre.

Wee Willie Winkie. Directed by John Ford, associate producer Gene Markey, starring Shirley Temple.

1938

In Old Chicago. Screenplay by Lamar Trotti and Sonya Levien, directed by Henry King, produced by Zanuck, starring Tyrone Power, Alice Faye, and Don Ameche.

Happy Landing. Screenplay by Milton Sperling and Boris

Ingster, directed by Roy del Ruth, produced by Zanuck, starring Sonja Henie.

Kidnapped. Directed by Alfred Werker, produced by Zanuck, starring Freddie Bartholomew.

Josette. Directed by Allan Dwan, produced by Zanuck, starring Simone Simone, Don Ameche, and Bert Lahr.

Three Blind Mice. Directed by William A. Seiter, produced by Zanuck and Raymond Griffith, starring Loretta Young and Joel McCrea.

I'll Give a Million. Based on a story by Cesare Zavattini and Giaci Mondaini, directed by Walter Lang, produced by Zanuck, starring Peter Lorre and John Carradine.

Little Miss Broadway. Directed by Irving Cummings, produced by Zanuck, starring Shirley Temple and George Murphy.

Alexander's Ragtime Band. Music and lyrics by Irving Berlin, directed by Henry King, produced by Zanuck, starring Tyrone Power, Alice Faye, and Don Ameche.

Hold That Coed. Directed by George Marshall, produced by Zanuck, starring John Barrymore and George Murphy.

Straight, Place and Show. Directed by David Butler, produced by Zanuck, starring the Ritz Brothers.

Suez. Directed by Allan Dwan, produced by Zanuck, starring Tyrone Power and Loretta Young.

Submarine Patrol. Directed by John Ford, produced by Zanuck, starring Preston Foster.

Just Around the Corner. Directed by Irving Cummings, produced by Zanuck, starring Shirley Temple.

Thanks for Everything. Directed by William Seiter, produced by Zanuck, starring Jack Haley and Adolph Menjou.

Kentucky. Directed by David Butler, produced by Zanuck, starring Loretta Young and Walter Brennan.

1939

Jesse James. Directed by Henry King, produced by Zanuck, starring Tyrone Power and Henry Fonda.

Tail Spin. Directed by Roy del Ruth, produced by Zanuck, starring Alice Faye, Constance Bennett, and Nancy Kelly.

The Little Princess. Directed by Walter Lang, produced by Zanuck, starring Shirley Temple.

The Story of Alexander Graham Bell. Directed by Irving Cummings, produced by Zanuck, starring Don Ameche.

The Return of the Cisco Kid. Directed by Herbert I. Leeds, produced by Zanuck, starring Warner Baxter and Lynn Bari.

The Gorilla. Directed by Allan Dwan, produced by Zanuck, starring the Ritz Brothers.

Young Mr. Lincoln. Directed by John Ford, produced by Zanuck, starring Henry Fonda.

Susannah of the Mounties. Directed by William A. Seiter, produced by Zanuck, starring Shirley Temple.

Second Fiddle. Directed by Sidney Lanfield, produced by Zanuck, starring Sonja Henie and Tyrone Power.

Stanley and Livingstone. Directed by Henry King, produced by Zanuck, starring Spencer Tracy.

Hotel for Women. Directed by Gregory Ratoff, produced by Zanuck, starring Linda Darnell and Elsa Maxwell.

Hollywood Cavalcade. Directed by Irving Cummings, produced by Zanuck, starring Alice Faye and Don Ameche.

Drums Along the Mohawk. Directed by John Ford, produced by Zanuck, starring Henry Fonda.

The Rains Came. Directed by Clarence Brown, produced by Zanuck, starring Tyrone Power and Myrna Loy.

Daytime Wife. Directed by Gregory Ratoff, produced by Zanuck, starring Tyrone Power and Linda Darnell.

Swanee River. Directed by Sidney Lanfield, produced by Zanuck, starring Don Ameche.

1940

The Blue Bird. Directed by Walter Lang, produced by Zanuck, starring Shirley Temple.

He Married His Wife. Directed by Roy del Ruth, produced by Zanuck, starring Joel McCrea and Nancy Kelly.

The Grapes of Wrath. Screenplay by Nunnally Johnson based on the novel by John Steinbeck, directed by John Ford, produced by Zanuck, starring Henry Fonda.

Little Old New York. Directed by Henry King, produced by Zanuck, starring Alice Faye.

Johnny Apollo. Directed by Henry Hathaway, produced by Zanuck, starring Tyrone Power.

Star Dust. Directed by Walter Lang, produced by Zanuck, starring Linda Darnell and John Payne.

Lillian Russell. Directed by Irving Cummings, produced by Zanuck, starring Alice Faye, Don Ameche, and Henry Fonda.

I Was an Adventuress. Directed by Gregory Ratoff, produced by Zanuck, starring Zorina.

Four Sons. Directed by Archie Mayo, produced by Zanuck, starring Don Ameche.

Maryland. Directed by Henry King, produced by Zanuck, starring John Payne and Walter Brennan.

The Man I Married. Directed by Irving Pichel, produced by Zanuck, starring Joan Bennett and Francis Lederer.

The Return of Frank James. Directed by Fritz Lang, produced by Zanuck, starring Henry Fonda and Gene Tierney.

Public Deb. No. 1. Directed by Gregory Ratoff, produced by Zanuck, starring Brenda Joyce and Elsa Maxwell.

Brigham Young—Frontiersman. Directed by Henry Hathaway, produced by Zanuck, starring Tyrone Power and Dean Jagger.

Down Argentine Way. Directed by Irving Cummings, produced by Zanuck, starring Don Ameche, Betty Grable, and Carmen Miranda.

The Great Profile. Directed by Walter Lang, produced by Zanuck, starring John Barrymore.

1941

Tobacco Road. Screenplay by Nunnally Johnson, directed by John Ford, produced by Zanuck, starring Charley Grapewin and Gene Tierney.

Blood and Sand. Directed by Rouben Mamoulian, produced by Zanuck, starring Tyrone Power, Linda Darnell, and Rita Hayworth.

A Yank in the R.A.F. Based on a story by Melville Crossman, screenplay by Darrell Ware and Karl Tunberg, directed by Henry King, produced by Zanuck, starring Tyrone Power and Betty Grable.

How Green Was My Valley. Screenplay by Philip Dunne, directed by John Ford, produced by Zanuck, starring Walter Pidgeon, Maureen O'Hara, and Roddy McDowall.

1942

Son of Fury. Directed by John Cromwell, produced by Zanuck, starring Tyrone Power and Gene Tierney.

To the Shores of Tripoli. Directed by Bruce Humberstone, produced by Zanuck, starring John Payne.

This Above All. Directed by Anatole Litvak, produced by Zanuck, starring Tyrone Power and Joan Fontaine.

Thunderbirds. Screenplay by Lamar Trotti, from an original story by Melville Crossman, directed by William Wellman, produced by Trotti, starring Preston Foster and Gene Tierney.

1943

China Girl. Produced and written by Ben Hecht, based on a story by Melville Crossman, directed by Henry Hathaway, starring George Montgomery and Gene Tierney.

At the Front. Filmed by the Army Signal Corps, Colonel Darryl Zanuck in charge of production.

1944

Lifeboat. Directed by Alfred Hitchcock, produced by Kenneth MacGowan, starring Tallulah Bankhead and William Bendix.

The Song of Bernadette. Directed by Henry King, produced by William Perlberg, starring Jennifer Jones.

The Purple Heart. Written by Jerome Cady from a story by Melville Crossman, directed by Lewis Milestone, produced by Zanuck, starring Dana Andrews.

Wilson. Screenplay by Lamar Trotti, directed by Henry King, produced by Zanuck, starring Alexander Knox.

Laura. Produced and directed by Otto Preminger, starring Gene Tierney and Clifton Webb.

Winged Victory. Stage and screenplay by Moss Hart, directed by George Cukor, produced by Zanuck.

1945

A Tree Grows in Brooklyn. Directed by Elia Kazan, produced by Louis Lighton, starring James Dunne.

The House on 92nd Street. Directed by Henry Hathaway, produced by Louis de Rochemont, starring William Eythe.

1946

Dragonwyck. Written and directed by Joseph Mankiewicz, produced by Zanuck, starring Gene Tierney and Vincent Price.

The Razor's Edge. Screenplay by Lamar Trotti, directed by Edmund Goulding, produced by Zanuck, starring Tyrone Power, Gene Tierney, and Herbert Marshall.

My Darling Clementine. Directed by John Ford, produced by Samuel G. Engel, starring Henry Fonda and Victor Mature.

1947

13 Rue Madeleine. Directed by Henry Hathaway, produced by Louis de Rochemont, starring James Cagney.

Boomerang. Directed by Elia Kazan, produced by Louis de Rochemont, starring Dana Andrews.

Miracle on 34th Street. Written and directed by George Seaton, produced by William Perlberg, starring Edmund Gwenn.

Kiss of Death. Directed by Henry Hathaway, produced by Fred Kohlmar, starring Richard Widmark and Victor Mature.

Gentleman's Agreement. Screenplay by Moss Hart, directed by Elia Kazan, produced by Zanuck, starring Gregory Peck and Dorothy McGuire.

1948

Call Northside 777. Directed by Henry Hathaway, produced by Otto Lang, starring James Stewart.

Sitting Pretty. Directed by Walter Lang, produced by Samuel G. Engel, starring Clifton Webb.

The Snake Pit. Screenplay by Frank Partos and Millen Brand, directed by Anatole Litvak, produced by Litvak and Robert Bassler, starring Olivia de Havilland.

Unfaithfully Yours. Written, produced, and directed by Preston Sturges, starring Rex Harrison.

1949

A Letter to Three Wives. Written and directed by Joseph Mankiewicz, produced by Sol C. Siegel, starring Linda Darnell.

Yellow Sky. Directed by William Wellman, written and produced by Lamar Trotti, starring Gregory Peck.

Pinky. Screenplay by Philip Dunne and Dudley Nichols, based on the novel *Quality* by Cid Ricketts Sumner, directed by Elia Kazan, produced by Zanuck, starring Jeanne Crain and Ethel Waters.

1950

Twelve O'Clock High. Screenplay by Sy Bartlett and Beirne Lay, Jr., based on their novel, directed by Henry King, produced by Zanuck, starring Gregory Peck.

The Gunfighter. Directed by Henry King, produced by Nunnally Johnson, starring Gregory Peck.

Panic in the Streets. Directed by Elia Kazan, produced by Sol G. Siegel, starring Richard Widmark.

No Way Out. Screenplay by Joseph Mankiewicz and Lesser Samuels, directed by Mankiewicz, produced by Zanuck, starring Richard Widmark and Sidney Poitier.

Mister 880. Directed by Edmund Goulding, produced by Julien Blaustein, starring Edmund Gwenn.

All About Eve. Written and directed by Joseph Mankiewicz, produced by Zanuck, starring Bette Davis, Anne Baxter, and George Sanders.

1951

David and Bathsheba. Written by Philip Dunne, directed by Henry King, produced by Zanuck, starring Gregory Peck and Susan Hayward.

People Will Talk. Written and directed by Joseph Mankiewicz, produced by Zanuck, starring Gary Grant and Hume Cronyn.

1952

Viva Zapata! Written by John Steinbeck, directed by Elia Kazan, produced by Zanuck, starring Marlon Brando.

Five Fingers. Directed by Joseph Mankiewicz, produced by Otto Lang.

The Snows of Kilimanjaro. Screenplay by Casey Robinson, directed by Henry King, produced by Zanuck, starring Gregory Peck, Ava Gardner, and Susan Hayward.

1953

The Robe. Directed by Henry Koster, produced by Frank Ross, starring Richard Burton and Victor Mature.

1954

The Egyptian. Screenplay by Philip Dunne and Casey Robinson, directed by Michael Curtiz, produced by Zanuck, starring Edmund Purdom, Jean Simmons, Gene Tierney, and Bella Darvi.

1956

The Man in the Gray Flannel Suit. Written and directed by Nunnally Johnson, produced by Zanuck, starring Gregory Peck and Jennifer Jones.

1957

Island in the Sun. Screenplay by Alfred Hayes, directed by Robert Rossen, produced by Zanuck, starring James Mason, Joan Fontaine, and Harry Belafonte.

The Sun Also Rises. Screenplay by Peter Viertel, directed by Henry King, produced by Zanuck, starring Tyrone Power, Ava Gardner, Errol Flynn, Mel Ferrer, and Juliette Greco.

1958

The Roots of Heaven. Screenplay by Romain Gary and Patrick Leigh Fermor, directed by John Huston, produced by Zanuck, starring Trevor Howard, Errol Flynn, and Juliette Greco.

1960

Crack in the Mirror. Screenplay by Mark Canfield, directed by Richard Fleischer, produced by Zanuck, starring Juliette Greco, Orson Welles, and Bradford Dillman.

1961

The Big Gamble. Screenplay by Irwin Shaw, directed by Richard Fleischer, produced by Zanuck, starring Juliette Greco and Stephen Boyd.

1962

The Longest Day. Screenplay by Cornelius Ryan, directed by Ken Annakin, Bernhard Wicki, Andrew Marton, produced by Zanuck.
Hello—Goodbye. Directed by Jean Negulesco, produced by Andre Hakim, starring Genevieve Gilles, Curt Jurgens, and Michael Crawford.
Tora! Tora! Tora! Screenplay by Larry Forrester, Hideo Oguni, and Ryuzo Kikushima, directed by Richard Fleischer, produced by Elmo Williams.

Index

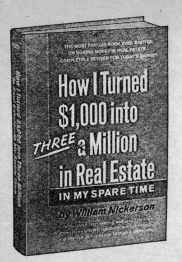

THE MOST FAMOUS BOOK EVER WRITTEN
ON MAKING MONEY IN REAL ESTATE
COMPLETELY REVISED FOR TODAY'S MARKET

How I Turned
$1,000 into
THREE a Million
in Real Estate
IN MY SPARE TIME
by William Nickerson

"Is it still possible today to make a million by my formula?"

People are always asking me this question. And in spite of tight money and high taxes, I answer "Yes—more than ever!" The new updated edition of my book (*How I Turned $1000 Into Three Million*) shows you how   by William Nickerson

In my book I reveal—and tell how to use—these 4 basic principles of traveling the surest road to great fortune still open to the average person:

1. How to harness the secret force of free enterprise—the pyramiding power of borrowed money.

2. How to choose income-producing multiple dwellings in which to invest your own (and your borrowed) capital.

3. How to make your equity grow.

4. How to virtually eliminate the "tax bite" on your capital growth.

▼   AT YOUR BOOKSTORE OR MAIL THIS COUPON NOW FOR FREE 14-DAY TRIAL   ▼

For everyone who just misses making big money in the market.

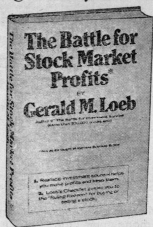

In this entirely new book,
THE BATTLE FOR STOCK MARKET PROFITS,
Gerald M. Loeb,

the celebrated "Dean of Wall Street," draws on his fifty years of experience to prepare you for the stock market of the seventies.